CYNTHIA J. GIACHINO

AN AUTOBIOGRAPHICAL NOVEL

QUIET.
FEAR.

ReadersMagnet, LLC

Quiet. Fear.
Copyright © 2023 by Cynthia J Giachino

Published in the United States of America
ISBN   Paperback: 978-1-960629-29-6
ISBN   eBook: 978-1-960629-30-2

All rights reserved. No part of this publication may be reproduced, stored in a retrieval system or transmitted in any way by any means, electronic, mechanical, photocopy, recording or otherwise without the prior permission of the author except as provided by USA copyright law.

The opinions expressed by the author are not necessarily those of ReadersMagnet, LLC.

ReadersMagnet, LLC
10620 Treena Street, Suite 230 | San Diego, California, 92131 USA
1.619. 354. 2643 | www.readersmagnet.com

Book design copyright © 2023 by ReadersMagnet, LLC. All rights reserved.

Cover design by Kent Gabutin
Interior design by Dorothy Lee

TABLE OF CONTENTS

1986 – Session One – Breakdown 13

CHILDHOOD 1952–1965

The Dawn Of Lilly – 1952 21
The Purest Color 26
Trusting Times 31
The Breathing Furnace 44
1986 – Session Two – Open Eyes 57
Deception 63
Enter The Devil 69
Wild Boars 78
1986 – Session Three – Schemes And Lies 85
A Lie Is A Sin 89
Payback Time 93
The Pirate's Cove 100
1986 – Session Four – Snow Drifts 110
The Canons Of Church 114
The Milkman 120
1986 – Session Five – Red Light, Green Light 126
Blackout 130

TEEN YEARS 1966–1972

Times Of Confusion 138
What No One Sees.. 143
1986 – Session Six – Serious Confrontations............................. 148
No Fairy Godmother... 154
One Look, One Touch 159
In The Moment... 169
Sneaking Around 172
Can't Lose What You Don't Have... 179
1986 – Session Seven – A Shocking Awareness 185
Under The Skin.. 190
No Safety Lock 197
In Dying Misery 202
Ambushed... 209
1986 – Session Eight – Storage Com Partments 221
The Raging Monster... 226
Discarded 237
Into Nothingness 245
1986 – Session Nine – Never Too Late..................................... 252
The Golden Ale.. 257
This Is Happy 266
1986 – Session Ten – Crutches 272

YOUNG ADULT 1972–1976

After Hours... 278
California Dreaming 285
Three Isn't A Crowd 291
Keep Your Hands Off... 298
Flying Cows And Musical Notes... 304
A Barrel Of Monkeys 310

1986 – Session Eleven – Sorrowful Acceptance 321
Hesitantly Suspicious 327
An Unknown Soldier 340
In The Real World 350
1986 – Session Twelve – Then And Now 353
Hallelujah 360
Forever In My Heart 364

ADULTHOOD 1976–1986

Completely Unexpected 369
Candlelight 375
Code Blue 380
1986 – Session Thirteen – Enduring 387
No More Hiding 392
Easy Pickings 398
Waves Of Destruction 404
The Raw Reality 413
1986 – Session Fourteen – Safe Behind Locked Doors 421
A Fortress Of Forgiveness 426
Epilogue 435

Dear Readers,

When I chose to free my secrets to the world, after facing long time fears, I had also hoped to open conversation and understanding amongst readers about children and adults who have fallen victim to the suffering of long-time injuries from sexual, emotional and / or physical abuse. It is a life goal to bring awareness to the reality of the sacrifices and bravery that a child/adult of such trauma needs to bring forth to heal. And that some healing may never take place, but one can learn how to cope with what can't be changed.

We should never have to walk alone in quiet fear. It is a true crime of all societies. Females and males of all ages.

Thank you for reading this healing journey and please open the door of conversation with another.

Always,
Cynthia J Giachino

Dedication and Acknowledgement

It is a rare occasion to accomplish a task such as this alone. I want to thank the following groups of people for their support and assistance in this six-year writing project. (It did take a small village to be able to get to the point of healing that I am at.) Much gratitude to my editor and mentor. Family members. Friends – Janette, Lynne, Sara, and Carol. Psychologists, psychiatrists, doctors, counselors, and therapists who have worked with me throughout my adult life. My loving dog of seventeen years, Autee, who is always close by. And to you, my readers, you are the purpose of this story.

Dedication

I dedicate this book to my grandchildren, who showed me how a childhood filled with love and safety can be. Thank you, my dears, for opening that door. Love you forever and to the moon and back.

1986 – SESSION ONE – BREAKDOWN

"Damn, I should have canceled this appointment!" Lilly grumbled as she set a fast pace toward the large glass entry doors, catching a glance of her reflection.

What was I thinking when I put this outfit on? How did I forget to finish my makeup? This is why I am here. I cannot go anywhere without panicking and muddling up my head with too many thoughts!

She ducked into the bathroom, headed directly to the sinks and mirror, dampened a paper towel with cold water, and laid it on her sweaty face, feeling an instant calm.

Minutes later, she slid it off and observed her reflection. "Oh my," she said disapprovingly, looking at the puffy bags under her eyes. "Thank you, Mother! You could have spared me from this one genetic trait!"

Digging deep into her oversized tote, she shifted through grocery receipts, gum wrappers, and old Kleenex, in search of makeup. Amid the debris, she found an old powder case and a berry-colored lipstick.

Balling up some toilet paper, she blotted the powder over her face and under her eyes, applied the lipstick and then rubbed a dab on her cheeks for blush.

Standing back from the mirror, she observed her clothing: blue jeans with ripped out knees, a pink hoodie she threw on when she got out of bed to get her son ready for school, and blue clog morning slippers. "Well, it is what it is!" she hopelessly muttered to herself.

Pulling her hair into a ponytail, she tied it off using an old black twisty and then straightened her posture. She was as ready as she could be. Cautiously, she stepped out into the waiting room, paused, and visually swept her surroundings for exits, windows, and the placement of people. A learned habit from the past.

A wave of doubt fell upon her. *Nothing is keeping me from turning around and leaving. No one is making me go to this appointment. There is still time to make an exit!*

The deep voice of the receptionist at the front desk interrupted her thoughts. "How may I help you?" There she was, the gatekeeper, looking up over her glasses with a hypnotic glare.

Lilly cleared her throat, "Um, I'm Lilly. I have an appointment with Dr. Bricks."

"Sign in here." The gatekeeper pointed to a clipboard. "I need to make a copy of your insurance card and your driver's license. Have a seat. There's coffee or water over there." She pointed to a small table in a corner of the room.

Lilly chose to sit far away from the other patients and near a stand filled with magazines that gossiped about the rich and famous.

She picked one up and quickly became lost in its stories. They took her mind far away from her reality until she heard a voice calling her name.

Nervously she shuffled the magazine back into its correct place, smoothed her hoodie, and walked toward the door. *My heart is beating like a jackhammer. I can feel it in my throat.* Uncertainty returned, *why did I do this?* Her eyes fell upon the open door and the waiting doctor.

He was surprisingly handsome: tall, pleasantly thin, in his mid-thirties, with thick wavy black hair. He combed it back, leaving a barren forehead and moved her vision down to his thick-framed glasses and clear blue eyes.

Not what I expected, she thought, thinking that most psychiatrists looked like an old version of Santa Claus.

He offered his hand.

I don't do hands with strangers, she reflected.

Immediately, he read her body language, put his hand down and introduced himself. "Hello, I'm Dr. Bricks." His voice was steady with an ideal volume; not threatening but not feeble either. Lilly picked up a comforting sense of order and security in his character.

"My office is this way." He turned to the left and moved down a narrow hallway.

She attempted to follow him, but her uncooperative feet ignored the message from her brain, and she remained frozen to the carpet.

Can it be any more obvious that I do not want to be here? Fear of the unknown had her dazed and cemented. "I'm a little nervous about this appointment," she explained.

"I understand. Our office is new to you. Take your time to feel familiar and safe with it," he offered with genuine concern. "Is there something I can do to help you feel more comfortable?"

"No...I'm fine. This is a little unnerving, that's all." She felt a strong need to lie, in order to keep a grip on her emotions. Dr. Bricks continued to walk slowly toward his office as she rigidly followed behind.

Where are the exit doors? She scoped the environment for the red and white exit sign. *If I must escape, I need to know where to run.* This was how her brain worked in unfamiliar places. She counted the number of doors that would lead her back to the waiting room's main exit. Finally, at the end of the hall and around its corner, she spotted the well-lit sign. A sigh of relief overcame her. She mentally noted *two doors down from his office!* He gestured for her to enter. She allowed him to go first.

As she followed, a whiff of fresh air wrapped its welcoming arms around her nervous and tense body. She faced the direction of the breeze and saw a wall of windows overlooking a rock garden and water feature. The familiar link to Mother Nature soothed her.

"Please, sit down." His voice remained calm as he gestured his hand toward an overstuffed chair.

Lilly looked past it, to a sofa further away, and then toward two contemporary sling-backs by the windows.

She chose a sling-back. If necessary, it would be easy to escape her thoughts by gazing out at the pond. Her mind could swim there for hours as she attempted to find answers to her complicated life.

Dr. Bricks quietly sat down on the chair next to her.

The room was overly quiet. She could hear every noise, including a tiny hum in the heating ducts. She turned her focus on what she could see. *He must like modern art,* she assessed as she observed several unique vases on the shelves, all showcasing unusual twists, textures, and colors.

"You enjoy art," he commented.

"Yes, I took a few classes in college and actually thought of it as a profession at one time." She could talk about art for hours, and that is exactly what she wanted to do. Get control of the conversation. An hour of art talk would be better than an hour of talking about her problems and secrets.

He walked to a shelf and picked up a vase. "I spent some time in Africa and Spain before I began my practice here in the States. That's where most of the pieces come from."

That's right, she thought. *He's a rich, spoiled brat who will have no idea how to relate to someone like me. Sure, he studied at the best schools and traveled the world, but he didn't experience it. Maybe he isn't as wise as he appears.*

He continued, "When I was in Africa I worked with women and children who had been physically and emotionally affected by rape. It was there that I began to develop an interest in helping victims of trauma."

Lilly re-thought. *Okay, rich but not spoiled rotten. I jumped to a conclusion. And did I hear him mention trauma? He's obviously read my records.* She veered away from the subject. "What brought you back to the States?"

"My wife wanted to begin a family, and it was safer to do so back here."

That's a good sign. It shows that he cares and is protective of those he loves. Lilly listened more intently. "Do you have a family now?" she asked.

"I do!" He smiled proudly. "I have two little girls, ages four and seven."

Lilly perked up. "My son Owen is three. Being a mother is still new to me, and sometimes I get some odd conflicting feelings. Is it right or is it wrong? What is normal and what's not? I don't know why I doubt myself. I'm fine. I have a career, a husband, and a child. I have friends and the past is the past." Quickly Lilly shut her mouth, realizing she had opened the kingdom of heaven for him to begin therapy.

"Raising a child can bring back memories of one's own childhood— the good and the bad." He informed her.

Lilly sat up straighter, giving the comment serious thought. "You're telling me that it's not uncommon to have the past come back after becoming a mother?"

"Yes, that's true."

"So, I'm not crazy reliving my childhood as I watch Owen grow up in his."

"That's absolutely correct, but your childhood is in the past and Owen's is in the present. That's important to keep in perspective."

"But how do I do that? For example, Owen likes me to rock and cuddle him, especially at night or late afternoon. I love that time together. I know he is safe in my arms, and nothing will harm him. Then out of nowhere, I get these feelings that cuddling is a bad touch." *I am spilling out way more information than I intended to!* She closed her eyes to slow her mind down.

"How is cuddling 'bad'?" he asked.

"You know…am I touching him too much? Are they wrong touches?" Lilly flushed with embarrassment.

"There is nothing abnormal about cuddling with your son." Dr. Bricks's face was soft and believable as he spoke directly to her. "In fact, it's healthy. It provides security and safety, which is vital in child development."

"A child needs to know they are safe and protected," Lilly repeated. "You're right! I've been needlessly worrying. I'm too concerned about doing everything perfect, even parenting."

He took off his glasses and set them down on his pad of paper. "It's difficult, being perfect."

"I don't know any other way. It's how I was raised." Lilly fidgeted in her chair, crossing her legs, and swinging the one that was free. "To be perfect was the way to my parents' hearts and happiness. And I think it's the way to make Owen and Mick happy too."

"That's an awful lot of pressure: being responsible for everyone's happiness and in doing so, being perfect at the same time."

"You have no idea!" Lilly snipped.

"Understand your standards of happiness aren't always going to be the same as everyone else's." The doctor stated.

"True." She sat back, having never given this much thought before. "Of course, what makes me happy isn't always going to make others happy. But how do I change?"

"We will work on thinking realistically. It takes time. For now, whenever you begin to doubt or push to perfection, stop and look around your environment. That will help you stay grounded and view the situation with a greater sense of what you truly need to focus on, which is the present, Lilly."

"That sounds so simple." She paused. "How did I get this messed up? Am I mentally weak or ill for being here and talking to you?" she asked with sarcasm.

The room grew uncomfortably quiet. In Lilly's head, she heard her parents' remark: *Take care of your own problems or keep them in the family. People who talk about their life's imperfections, to a doctor, are mentally ill.*

CHILDHOOD

1952-1965

THE DAWN OF LILLY - 1952

The angry winter sky opened, blasting the sharp crystalized snow against Vincent's face.

"Driving forty miles to the nearest hospital in this blizzard is going to be a challenge," he muttered to himself as he threw shovel after shovel of snow, with a portion of each, blowing right back into his face.

Gwen kept watch from inside the house. Of *all weeks for a blizzard, why tonight?* She thought.

Chilled by the wind, she moved away from the window and settled into the rocking chair. The radio and television had lost reception. *It's only a matter of time before the phone line goes down and contact with the outside world will be impossible.* She reminisced of past storms. The clicks of the grandfather clock's pendulum and the howling winds filled the deadened silence.

She wrapped a crocheted shawl over her shoulders and smoothed her hands over her swollen belly. "Not tonight," she pleaded softly, closing her eyes in prayer.

The spasms grew more uncomfortable. She stood up and paced between the living room and kitchen window, continuing to check on Vincent's safety. His silhouette was diminishing in the whiteout as he worked tirelessly to clear the long narrow driveway.

"You've been my little stinker," she told her unborn child. "At first you were pure joy, but then came the inescapable morning sickness, which was worse than my other pregnancies. Then in the fourth month, I almost lost you, but your strong will and determination made everything good again. I know how badly you want to make an entrance into this world, just not tonight. No human or animal should be out in this blizzard!"

She pulled the shawl tighter around her shoulders and waited for Vincent. Until he was safe and back in the house, there would be no sleep.

In the early morning hours, Gwen shot out of bed like a launched missile heading for its target. Hers was the bathroom. Vincent threw back the covers and quickly followed.

"My water broke." Gwen was ghostly pale. "My third child, Vincent, labor could be quick, and the blizzard hasn't stopped. I can still hear the wind rattling the windows."

"We're ready. Don't worry. Let me do that for you. I'll go and pick up the neighbors to watch the kids." He rushed out to the garage, thankful that he had shoveled and packed the car earlier.

Gwen went into the bedroom to get dressed and saw two sets of eyes at her door. One set belonged to her oldest, Joan, who was nearing eight, the other to her son, Anthony, who was three.

"The garage door woke us up," yawned Joan.

Gwen paused, taking in the innocence of their sleepy faces. "It's time to have this baby! Daddy went to pick up Mr. and Mrs. Hammond. They will stay with you. Now go back to sleep. We'll call you from the hospital."

❋

The country road that led to the highway had become a world of white on white. Vincent narrowed his thoughts to the beam of light before him and the gripping sound of chains on the snow-packed pavement.

Gwen sat in silence, looking straight ahead into the blinding snow while concentrating on her breathing. "Once I reach the highway, the roads will be somewhat plowed, and we'll be halfway there," he reassured her.

In the rearview mirror he caught the blurred flashing lights of a police car. He veered only a bit to the right and stopped the car just short of a snowbank. The officer pulled up behind. Vincent watched a silhouette of a man approach his door.

He handed Gwen a heavy wool blanket and then rolled down the window. "Good evening, officer," he said, squinting from the icy flakes that were blowing in his face.

"What are you doing out in this storm, Vincent? Didn't you hear the highway is closed?" The officer had to shout through the pelting winds.

"No, sir, I didn't hear that. We lost the television, the radio, and the phone. Gwen is in labor. We've been driving an hour, and we're only halfway to the hospital."

The officer shined his light onto the passenger side, revealing an exasperated look on Gwen's face. "Hello, Gwen. I'm going to help you get to town." He turned to Vincent. "Follow behind my squad car. I'll take the lead."

"Thank you!" Vincent felt blessed. "Honey, did you hear that? We're going to be fine. Our little girl is getting a police escort to the hospital!"

"You said 'girl.'" Gwen smiled.

"I did, and we'll call her Lilly."

"Your favorite flowers," Gwen looked lovingly at her husband.

"Look at all this white snow! Feel the freezing cold winds! And miraculously our white lilies come up every spring."

"They're a strong plant. Lilly will be a good name for a girl, that is, *if* we don't have a boy."

Thirteen hours later Gwen and Vincent held Lillian. And four days later they brought her home to their family and country life.

"Look at my face! It shows how exhausted I am! Four days at the hospital was not enough rest. That was the most difficult labor and I thought it would be the easiest with her being number three. We had no way of knowing she was going to be a breech baby!" Gwen spoke to her reflection, taking in a deep breath and slowly letting it go.

From the corner of her eye, she caught a glance of their wedding photo and began to reminisce. *I fell in love with him in eighth grade and that love has grown through the test of time. The Depression was tough for both of our families, but especially his, since they lost their farm and then came the war. Now here we are, with three lovely healthy children and a big home to raise them in. I don't feel any different about him than I did the night of our wedding; except, maybe I love him more.*

Joan's loud call for her mother interrupted Gwen's daydreaming.

"I'm in the bedroom," a frustrated Gwen replied, opening the door to the annoyed look on her daughter's face.

"Lilly is fussing!" Joan complained.

"If I warm up the bottle, do you mind feeding her? I need to get a load of laundry going."

"I'll warm the bottle myself! There's nothing else to do around here!"

Gwen watched Joan stomp off to the kitchen.

After supper and the evening news came the bedtime routine. Vincent helped with baths and brushing teeth. Then Gwen took over with bedtime stories and prayers. When all was quiet, she and Vincent tiptoed to the nursery to peek in at Lillian.

"She has your almond-shaped eyes." Gwen smiled.

"And your mouth and chin. I think she's a good mix of both of us," replied Vincent, smiling down at their sleeping baby.

"Do you think Joan and Anthony will eventually accept her? Both seemed bothered today."

"Of course, they will," Vincent reassured her. "Be patient."

Gwen leaned over and kissed him on the cheek. "I love you," she said, looking up into his brilliant green eyes.

"I love you more," he said, after a passionate kiss.

THE PUREST COLOR

"When do you think we should have Lilly's baptism?" Gwen asked Vincent as she poured him a cup of coffee.

"Sometime in late spring would be good. The weather is more dependable for safe travel," he replied.

"That would be perfect timing," Gwen smiled with the thought of spring.

"Who did you ask to be her godparents?"

Gwen replied thoughtfully. "At first it was easy—my brother David and his wife Dee. They would always be close, only seven miles away. Then Millie called and was so upset with my choice that she hung up. Now I don't know what to do."

"Your sister has a knack for getting under your skin."

"But she carried on and on about how this could be our last child and she would never have another opportunity to be a godmother and have a goddaughter. She was so upset and now I feel guilty. Then Joan heard us talking and *she* got upset."

"Why would Joan care who Lilly's godparents are?"

"That's what I thought, but she does. She said Millie and Frank are always included in our special celebrations, and it would be fun to have only nearby family. Who we can get together more often. Maybe she was tired."

"Possibly, she stays up late reading her books!" Vincent released a long sigh and continued to address Gwen.

"Joan's right. Millie does want to be a part of everything we do. She should have never married on the rebound and moved away with Frank.

This is home to her, and it always will be, but she had to leave for the city to prove she was better than the rest of us. I think you should stay with your first choice - David and Dee."

"You make Millie sound bitter and mean." Gwen frowned at Vincent.

"I'm only saying what you already know. Millie didn't listen to your mother about marrying Frank. She begged Millie to wait. Millie could have had any man, with her Hollywood starlet look, but she thought Frank's charm of big dreams and adventurous talk was a ticket out of the woods. Now she's weaving her life back through our children."

"What am I to do? Becoming a godmother would give Millie something positive to think about, being so far from us and childless. On the other hand, it would be nice to have a quiet, simple ceremony with David and Dee."

Vincent held her hand in his. "Frank isn't a Catholic and that's a concern. He's never been a man of faith."

"I realize that, so I asked Millie if *she* would be Lilly's godmother and David could be the godfather."

"Good thinking! What was her answer?"

"She grew angrier. If she couldn't be a godparent along with Frank, then she didn't want to be one at all." Gwen threw her head back and closed her eyes. "You know the relationship between Millie and me runs deep. After Dad died, the two of us took care of each other and the house while our other siblings helped Mom with the business."

"It sounds like your mind is made up. The only glitch is that Frank will have to convert—will there be enough time for him to do that?"

"Millie said he's already taking classes through their church. He attends weekly Mass and is learning the prayers. He's baptized too, so that will help shorten the process."

"Well, I'll be damned. He did not believe in religion and wouldn't marry Millie in a church, but now he wants to change all that to be a godfather. Hmm, life sure is full of surprises. Well, it's settled. Give her a call tomorrow and see which weekend will work for them."

✺

Millie reassured Gwen, "Don't worry. Frank will be a Catholic in time for the baptism. He is so excited. I wish you could see his enthusiasm. He took two weeks off work. He bought a gold ring with a cross on it to symbolize his new faith. Our mother is going to be happy to have all her children and their spouses going to one church and being one faith. Don't you think so?"

"She will be, and Father Johan is doing the baptism. You know he married Vincent and me. He also baptized Anthony and Joan; it's as if he's part of our family."

"I know—I hear about him whenever I talk to Mom. I think she wanted me to marry him, or anyone, other than Frank."

"You're being silly! Mom doesn't feel that way," Gwen replied, thankful that Millie couldn't see her face, because she had just blatantly lied.

"She doesn't like him, and she makes that known. I feel bad for Frank when we visit. That's why we stay with you. We feel more comfortable at your home."

"You are both welcome anytime. So, the plans are set?"

"Yes, thank you so much for letting us have this opportunity. Lilly is going to be our special goddaughter. We're thrilled!"

✺

Two months later, the family gathered at the church for the baptism.

"Good morning, everyone," Father Johan addressed them after Sunday mass. "I want to invite all of you to gather around the baptismal fountain."

Vincent and Gwen to my left and the godparents to the right. All others can stand behind."

Gwen handed Lilly to her sister, while Frank stood behind, laying his hand on the baby's shoulder. The godparents made an oath to guide Lilly in her faith, renouncing Satan, and believing in the teachings of the church.

Father Johan made the sign of the cross on Lilly's forehead and chest, banishing all darkness from her heart and cleansing her from original sin. He followed with the pouring of the blessed water and anointed Lilly with holy oil.

"Millie and Frank, I give you a lit candle as a symbol of faith, lived by love. May Lillian walk in the light of Christ and his peace be with her always."

When the ceremony ended, the entire family gathered on the altar's steps for photographs.

"I'll take the pictures," offered Frank. "I have this new camera, and I'd like to practice using it." He held up the camera, attached to a long neck strap that held it firmly in place with his muscular neck.

Vincent was impressed. "That's quite the camera! A big improvement from my old black box."

"It's a professional camera," Frank boasted. "I've been learning about photography in my spare time."

Millie was all smiles as she watched her husband. *He seems a different man, more confident and direct since he took interest in photography,* she assessed. *Maybe it will turn into a business, and he can get out of that dirty steel mill. Just think of a building with our name on it!*

She paused from her daydream to look in the direction of her mother. Their eyes met. Gwen noticed and approached Millie. "Is everything all right?"

"Look at Mom. She's staying as far away from Frank as she can and whenever he holds Lilly, she grabs her out of his arms. Can't she see how he has changed and how much he enjoys children? She'll never trust him, no matter what he does to win her over."

"Give her time. She doesn't see the two of you often." Gwen patted her sister on the back and flitted off into the gathering of people. Millie joined Frank. "Did you like the way your camera worked?"

"It's great. I can't wait to get the pictures developed!"

"I saw you playing with Lilly, dangling the car keys and having her reach out for them. You looked so happy."

Frank put his arms around his beautiful red-haired, green-eyed beauty. "I was. She's a cutie, but she doesn't make me as happy as you do." He leaned over and gave her a kiss.

Millie pushed him back. "Frank! We're on the altar!"

"That makes it more exciting!" he flirted.

She flashed him a devious look. "Be careful! My mother has many eyes."

TRUSTING TIMES

"I don't want to wear it!" protested three-year-old Lilly, tossing her orange life jacket to the ground.

"I can swim, and Mom still makes me wear one! If you want to fish, you must wear it." Anthony tried to explain, but Lilly did not want to hear it.

"It makes me hot!" Her protest turned into whining.

She's testing my patience and trying to get her own way! Anthony mused. "A rule is a rule, Lilly." He confirmed his decision as he pulled the two white center straps tightly around her middle.

"That's too tight."

He loosened them. "Listen, Lilly, no more whining or the fish will swim away." He handed her a baited hook and tossed the bamboo pole's line out into the water.

"See the red bobber?" He pointed to it.

"Yes, it's moving! I have a fish!" she squealed.

"No Lilly, the waves are making it move. The bobber needs to go under and pop up somewhere else. Then you *might* have a fish." He shook his head, feeling hopeless with his teaching. Then he picked up his pole, threw the line out, and settled down next to her.

They talked about the water and the woods. He told her stories about the Native American Indians who once lived there. Lilly listened intently without losing sight of her bobber.

Over an hour later, Anthony grew hot and impatient. "Guess the fish are somewhere else this morning. I'm melting! How about we take these life jackets off, and go play in the sandbox?" Anthony noticed her inattentiveness. "Lilly, are you listening to me?"

"I want to catch a fish." She sat focused on the bobber.

"Look, you're sweating and it's roasting outside. The sandbox is shady and cooler. I promise to take you fishing tomorrow!"

Soaked with sweat, Lilly agreed that tomorrow would be better. She handed her pole to Anthony, who quickly pulled in the fishing line, wrapped it around the bamboo, and tucked the hook under. "Here, you carry one and I'll carry one."

"It's too big. You can carry them."

"No, Lilly, Dad said we have to learn to put our poles back on the hooks by the chicken coop. Remember?"

Lilly took hold of the long pole and stumbled behind Anthony toward the coop. After they placed the poles on the correct pegs, they raced to the sandbox.

"Here's a popsicle stick. Watch how I make a road with it." Anthony demonstrated how to move the sand and make the proper sound effects of a grader. Then he handed her the stick and showed her where to plow. Lilly, bored with the job of making roads, grabbed a few of Anthony's army men. She lined them up and pretended they were marching.

"Those are mine, leave them alone!" Anthony ordered.

"No! I want to play with them too."

He swept them out of her reach.

Within a few minutes Joan heard the frustrating cries of Lilly fighting back. She went to the kitchen window and shouted, "Anthony, what have you done to your sister?"

"Nothing!" he snapped back.

"Right!" Joan turned off the stove's burner and went outside to check. Lilly was sitting in the middle of the sandbox, crying and rubbing sand all over her wet face. Joan picked her up.

"What's the problem, Lilly?" she asked.

"Anthony took my army men away," she sobbed.

"You don't need those ugly army men." Joan sat her down and took her hand. "Come, I'll clean you up before lunch." Hand in hand they walked back to the kitchen. Joan turned around one last time and shouted to Anthony, "Wait until Dad comes home. You're going to get it!"

Anthony shrugged the words off.

"I'm hungry," pleaded Lilly.

"No begging me. I do not cave into you like Mom. Here's a cracker and then you wait." Lilly took the cracker.

Gwen returned while the children were eating. She thanked Joan for babysitting and joined them at the table.

※

"Since we're all together, I would like to talk about our summer trip. Dad and I were thinking that we would go to the city and stay with Aunt Millie and Uncle Frank for a week. We could visit the museums and the zoo. Joan, you and I and Aunt Millie could shop at one of the malls for school clothes."

Joan lightened up. Since she was the oldest, she enjoyed *some* special treatment.

"Do I get to do anything special?" inquired Anthony.

"Yes, you get to go to the aquarium with Uncle Frank and your father."

"What's special about an aquarium?" he asked, scrunching up his face.

"This one is huge. It is as big as a football field! It has sharks swimming around and scuba divers taking pictures of them."

"Really?" Anthony was in awe.

"You'll see more fish than you ever imagined!"

Anthony glared at Joan and coyly smiled. He was getting his way too. Lilly's tiny voice came last. "I want to see fish. I want to go with Anthony."

Anthony rolled his eyes. Maybe he had created a monster. Whatever he did, she had to do too. Gwen leaned over and gave Lilly a kiss on the forehead. "You, young lady, can sit in the front seat with Mommy and Daddy all the way to the city."

That was enough to satisfy Lilly. Seldom did they allow her to sit between them, and it tickled her fancy.

※

July came in hot and humid, with a larger-than-normal mosquito population. The family was excited to take a break from the backwoods. In less than forty-eight hours they would have the car packed and ready for a week of shopping, museums, and sightseeing.

Gwen laid out seven complete outfits for Lilly and Anthony and began packing them neatly in a suitcase when she heard the phone ring.

She dropped the folded sweater into the suitcase and moved quickly to the kitchen, picking up the receiver.

"Hello?"

"Hi, Gwen, it's me, Millie. How are you?"

Leaning against the kitchen wall, Gwen took a cleansing breath and began conversation. "I was packing the suitcases."

"Anthony, Joan, and Vincent can pack their own," her sister taunted.

Gwen shot a dagger look at the phone. Millie knew everything and did everything better than anyone else in the family. It was always a competition with her. "I don't mind. It reassures me that nothing will be missing and every outfit matches. You know kids. They'll wear plaids with flowers if allowed to!" Gwen answered.

Millie laughed at the thought…and then continued, "We can't wait for you to come! Frank will have to work during the day, but he has the evenings and weekend free."

"That's not a problem. We have the museums to visit, shopping to do, and maybe we can take the children to a pool before supper."

"Yes, there is a large pool for the neighborhood just a few blocks away. Frank swims there regularly."

"He always was a swimmer, even back in his childhood days."

"Wish I shared his feelings toward water, but I don't. It destroys my hair and makeup. However, I do like to sunbathe."

"That sounds relaxing." Gwen sighed, thinking how long it had been since she had done that.

"I'm going to spoil you rotten. You could use a break too," Millie said in a comforting tone and then added, "There's something I want to talk about with you. Frank came up with an idea regarding the sleeping arrangements."

"What about them?" inquired Gwen.

"Last summer everyone slept in the attic. Lilly coughed all night in the heat and dirty air. That's why Frank suggested that this summer Lilly sleep downstairs in our bedroom. The air is cooler, and she may not cough as much. Everyone will get a better night's sleep. Don't you agree?"

"Oh, Millie, there's no need to fuss. The coughing wasn't that serious." Gwen found herself being untruthful to her sister, keeping how she really felt inside. Sleeping arrangements last year *were* awful and as much as Millie tried to make the attic feel like home, with area rugs and bedroom sets, it was insanely hot. There was only one tiny window, which housed a small fan, offering little to no relief. "I don't know, Millie. You know Anthony has asthma and one night we had to take him into the emergency room. Now we are watching Lilly more carefully. Let's not change anything."

Millie stayed on course. "I would be right there, next to her."

"I appreciate the thought, but I will feel better if Lilly is close to us."

"But I've already changed the beds around for your comfort! And I'm tickled pink thinking that Lilly, our goddaughter, and I will be able to have a slumber party! Please, Gwen," she pleaded, not willing to quit until she got her way.

Gwen knew there was no other recourse. "Just this once, and promise me that you will sleep with one eye open, waking me up if there is any concern at all," Gwen commanded, ignoring the fact that her gut didn't like the idea.

Millie's gleeful voice came back, "Of course, I assure you that nothing will happen to our little girl. I made an oath to protect her!"

Gwen hung up, feeling a bag of mixed emotions. Millie's authority had tugged at her since they were teens. However, now that Millie and Frank were Lilly's godparents, Millie constantly called with advice on how to raise their goddaughter.

She reheated a cup of morning coffee and picked away at a slice of banana bread. It wasn't long before Joan and Anthony ran into the kitchen, with Lilly tagging behind. "Mom, are we going to keep packing?"

"Yes, I am going to finish my coffee first. Since you are all here, sit down. We need to talk."

"About what, Mom?" asked Joan as she pulled out a chair.

"You both know that Aunt Millie has no children."

"She has Lilly," interrupted Anthony.

"No! Lilly is our family, not Millie and Frank's." Gwen was firm, and Anthony sat back, knowing he had upset his mother. "Millie's house is spotlessly clean. She has knick knacks in a glass hutch. Those doors stay closed, Anthony. Do you understand?"

With his head lowered, he agreed.

"Her carpeting is nearly white, which means no shoes in the house. Take them off at the door and the plastic on her couch—don't say anything about it being sticky or hot. Just be happy you have something to sit on when you watch television."

"Can't I sit on the floor?" Anthony asked, unhappy about all the instructions.

"No, she doesn't allow sitting on the carpet or eating in the living room."

"Aunt Millie has more rules than you!" protested Anthony.

"She likes to keep her house orderly, and I like visiting her because of that," Joan said, smiling.

"You would!" Anthony scoffed.

"One last thing: I always expect proper manners and politeness, and especially at the table. There will be no talking back to your parents or your aunt and uncle. Do I make myself clear?"

"Yes," they droned in unison.

"Mom does Lilly understand the rules?" inquired Anthony.

"Lilly, do you understand what being a good girl means?" asked Gwen.

"Yes, I can be a good girl. It makes you and Daddy happy. It makes Uncle Frank and Aunt Millie happy."

"Oh brother!" Anthony slapped his forehead. "Can I be excused?"

"I nearly forgot!" exclaimed Gwen. "We are going to sleep in the attic again, but Lilly is going to sleep downstairs with Millie and Frank in their bedroom. Millie thinks downstairs would be better for Lilly's cough."

"Don't you remember when *I* had to sleep on their couch in the living room for a few nights? It was not fun. I would rather sleep in the attic with the family," Joan stated emphatically.

"Why is that, Joan? I was hoping you would sleep on the couch again to be near your sister."

"Nope, never again, that couch is impossible to sleep on with the plastic cover. It was miserable, and Aunt Millie and Uncle Frank argued all night."

Just as Gwen was about to question Joan about her comment, Lilly began to tear up.

"Lilly, what's wrong?" asked Gwen, still mulling over Joan's remark.

"I want to sleep with you and Daddy."

Gwen picked her up and held her on her lap. "Mommy and Daddy will be in the same house, only upstairs. You and Aunt Millie are going to have a slumber party!"

"A party?" Lilly's disposition changed.

"Yes, a party!"

"Can I have a party too?" piped in Anthony.

Gwen was ready to pull her hair out of her head. Once again, her coffee was ice cold. She sent the children out to play while she finished the packing, by herself.

❊

"Is this the street, Dad?" Anthony was standing in the back seat behind his father, anxious to get out of the car.

"We will be on the ground in five minutes," answered Vincent. "Prepare for landing!" He parked the car on the street. "Me first!" said Anthony as he opened his door and jumped out.

Frank and Millie were waiting on the sidewalk.

"Let me help you with the suitcases," Frank offered as Millie and Gwen linked arms and walked up the steps of the front porch. "How was the traffic?" inquired Frank as he pulled a suitcase out of the trunk.

"The traffic was light, but the heat was miserable!" Vincent felt wilted in his damp white T-shirt and cuffed blue jeans. "I sure could use a cold beer. Do you have one in the fridge?"

"Sure do! I stocked it for us. It's going to stay miserably hot throughout the week."

Vincent sighed. "Well, we'll be indoors most of the time!" He followed Frank to the kitchen. Frank stopped and turned around. "We could take the kids to the pool after lunch."

"That sounds refreshing!" Vincent answered, wiping his forehead.

Chewing on the stub of his cigar and clanking the coins in his front trouser pocket, Frank continued, "Wait until you see what the city girls are wearing at the pool! Two-piece swimsuits, they call them bikinis. Some are scantier than others."

"I saw one in a magazine at work. It's no big deal, when you have wives as beautiful as ours!" Vincent winked.

"Yeah, guess you're right!" Frank pulled his hand out of his pocket.

※

Vincent waved off the bottle of beer Frank offered, "No more for me. I am exhausted. What do you say Gwen; time for bed?"

"Yes, my eyes are starting to roll. I'm going to check on Lilly and then join you. Millie, I put a bottle in the fridge just in case Lilly wakes up. I know she's a little too old for that and when we get back home, she's going to have to give it up. But not on vacation!"

"Don't worry! Lilly's in good hands; I will watch her like a mama bear and if there are any problems, I will wake you. Now go and get a good night's sleep." Millie shooed her along.

※

With the house quiet and everyone asleep, Frank paced like a caged wolf. Night was when his city awakened with a party-like atmosphere. This was his time of the day. The dark of the night camouflaged right from wrong. It was a time of lawlessness that gave him the security he needed for his second job, the one of money and friends who shared his interests. He was ready to go to work.

"Millie, I want to take Lilly out to see the city lights. Just a short drive, say, maybe thirty minutes or so."

"That's crazy, Frank. She's sleeping," Millie shot back at him. "Didn't Gwen say that she might wake up for her bottle?"

"Yes, but that doesn't mean you can take her out on the town for a ride! For crying out loud, Frank. What's wrong with you?"

Frank's nightly outings grated on her, especially now that he wanted to include Lilly, but never has he included her.

"Well, we could say she woke up and was fussy after her bottle, so I drove her around until she fell asleep."

Millie vigorously scrubbed the stovetop, afraid to look Frank in the eyes. When night came, he changed into a beast. "I want to show her the lights. Wake her up and get her ready. I'll warm the bottle." He didn't ask; he commanded.

"What do I say to Gwen if she comes down to check on Lilly?" Millie asked.

"Just what I told you: she couldn't sleep, was fussy, so I took her for a ride. They did that in the country with Anthony. Remember?" Frank grew annoyed with her silly questions.

"That's different. They are the parents. We cannot do whatever we want. They have rules and routines we need to follow."

"Too many if you ask me. I love riding around in the car at night, and I know this city like the back of my hand." He was angry with Millie but needed her help. He walked up behind her as she forcefully scrubbed the sinks and rubbed his body against hers.

"I'll be home soon. You can take a shower." He began to lick her neck and nibble at her ears. "I never get to be alone with Lilly when she comes to visit. She'll love the city lights. It'll look like Christmas!"

Millie threw her hands in the air. She was tired and didn't have the strength to get into an argument, besides, his advancements enticed her. "All right, but you promise me that you'll be back in twenty minutes."

He pulled her in front of him and gave her a long, wet kiss. "That's my girl. Promise: twenty minutes." He opened the fridge and took out the bottle. After he warmed it, he joined Millie in the bedroom.

"Look at her, Frank! How can you take her out like this? She's still asleep."

"Don't worry. Once when my little girl sees all the lights she'll wake up!"

"You better watch her like a hawk!"

He left too quickly to hear her warning.

Millie sat trembling. *What if Gwen wakes up and comes downstairs to find her baby missing? Vincent would go wild. He might call the police. We would never be trusted with our godchild again!*

Why do I always cave into Frank's insistence? Why do I fear him? He is the only person in my life I cannot manipulate. She paced and paced, watching the clock. Twenty minutes went by, then thirty, and still no Frank and Lilly. She sat on the sofa, praying and wondering, *where could he have taken her at midnight?*

Her prayers stopped when she heard the backdoor of the kitchen open. Frank was carrying a sleeping Lilly. He handed her off to Millie like an old rag doll and walked toward the bathroom for his nightly shower.

"Frank," she whispered in a gritted maddening tone. "Where have you been? You've been gone for over an hour."

"You don't say! It didn't seem that long!" He acted aloof, as Millie stared at him in disapproval. "We looked at lights and played a color game, and then she fell asleep with her bottle. I drove over to the smoke shop for some cigars. Then we came home."

"Are you crazy? You left her alone in the car while you went to buy some stupid cigars?"

"I carried her in with me and showed her off to my friend. She was knocked out cold—never woke up once."

"Did you ever think about what we're going to say tomorrow morning when she tells her mom and dad that she went for a ride with Uncle Frank? Do you realize what kind of trouble we could be in?"

"Yes, I thought about that. She won't say anything. She won't remember. It'll be like a dream, and that's how we'll approach it!"

Millie could see he was agitated, and his quick harsh temper was coming through under questioning.

"I hope you're right, Frank, because if they find out, they will never trust us with her again."

"Go to bed. Stop worrying. I'm taking a shower."

Millie paused, looking around the room. "Where's her bottle?"

"It's in the car. I'll wash it after."

Millie hugged Lilly tightly and carried her to the bedroom.

※

Lilly slept deeply for the rest of the night. She dreamt of bright lights and a room whose walls were painted red and decorated with gold. A queen took her out of Frank's arms and sent him out the big, tall doors.

Then she laid her on a large bed with a soft red bedspread. It felt like the fabric of a Christmas dress, soft and smooth. The queen had a nice smile, as she combed Lilly's hair. Then she played the piggy-toe game as she removed Lilly's shoes. The queen liked her and told her to stay awake because they were going to have fun, but first she had to meet the brave handsome king.

The king carried a small crown of diamonds. He placed the crown on Lilly's head and told her she made a beautiful princess, and they were happy to have her in their castle. He showed her a camera and pointed to the bright lights shining on the bed. They were going to take family pictures and all she had to do was listen to him. Lilly smiled at the big shining moons that made the room glow.

THE BREATHING FURNACE

"Anthony, I hear our old school bell ringing." Lilly tugged on her brother's shirttails.

Anthony stopped and listened...one, two, three, four...that was Gwen's signal for lunch. "We better head back. I wish Dad had never come up with the idea of hanging that bell on our front porch. Now we can hear Mom calling us no matter where we are, deep in the woods, or out on the river."

"I like the bell. It makes me feel close to home."

"You would! You're five years old! Come on! Dad warned us that we need to hightail it home, or we won't be able to play in the woods for a week; maybe longer!"

They walked out to the road where they had hidden their bikes in the ditch, picked them up, and feverishly pedaled toward home. "Bet you can't catch me!" Anthony shouted.

"Just you wait and see." Lilly stood up and began pumping her pedals with every ounce of muscle she owned, as Anthony continued to extend his distance. "Anthony! Slow down!" she yelled.

He applied his brakes and waited alongside the road, watching Lilly's legs nearly spin out of control. She was huffing to catch her breath and stopped alongside Anthony. "Sometimes you're plain old mean," she scolded.

"You always want to beat me!"

"That's not true!" Lilly yelled, but she knew he was right. She was younger than Anthony, but that wasn't going to keep her from doing everything he did.

She loved her brother, and they had fun together making up spy games and searching for Indian burial grounds. However, once they were in the house it was another story. He teased her, and she tattled on him, which usually ended in some form of punishment. Lilly learned quickly that when one got in trouble, so did the other. Therefore, it was better not to tell, especially with the Christmas months coming soon.

�֎

"Anthony, you've been watching out that window for an hour!" scolded Gwen.

"I know, Mom. But as soon as Uncle Frank and Aunt Millie come, it's officially Christmas!"

Gwen warmly smiled at her son. "It would be strange not to have them. They haven't missed the holiday since Lilly's baptism," she said, bending down to Anthony's level.

"And they always bring me a present!" he said with excitement.

"Let me know when they're here," she said, tousling up his hair and returning to the kitchen.

Less than an hour later, Anthony caught a glimpse of the big, black car coming down the hill of their driveway and yelled, "They're here! They're here!"

Gwen called out from the kitchen, "Everyone, they're here!"

Anthony watched as the car pulled up and Frank stepped out in fashion, wearing a long wool overcoat, hat, leather gloves, and shiny new shoes. To Anthony, he looked like a gangster right out of the movies, chewing his fat stubby cigar. He casually walked to the passenger's side and opened Millie's door. Anthony's eyes grew as big as half-dollars. He ran down the steps to the kitchen, yelling,

"Mom, Mom! Aunt Millie is wearing a big mink coat, like the ones on television!"

"Settle down right this moment, Anthony Michael, and go get Lilly."

"Where is she?" He danced in anticipation.

"Downstairs in the playroom; now hurry along!" Anthony sped off.

Gwen glanced at her reflection in the window's glass. Using her fingers, she fluffed her hair. "A mink coat," she mumbled. "They can't be as poor as Millie claims." She untied her apron, smoothed out her dress, and hurried to the door.

Frank shook Vincent's hand and gave him a solid *good to see you* pat on the back, acting as if they were old war buddies, which irritated Vincent.

Frank had dodged the war on a farmer's waiver but liked to act as if he had worn the uniform while Vincent had joined the Army Air Force and spent years overseas.

Gwen chimed in, "Millie, you look like a movie star! The coat is beautiful, and I love your hair pinned up in a French twist."

"Thank you. Frank bought me the coat just a month ago for the winter. You can try it on later if you would like. And I had my hair done at the beauty parlor."

"That must be nice." Gwen meant sarcasm, but it came out like a teenager buttering up the most popular girl in the class. Millie had a way to own the spotlight.

"Let's get inside where it's warm. The guys will take care of the luggage." Gwen opened the door to the foyer. "If you don't mind, Joan will take your coat and lay it on your bed."

"That's so kind of you, Joan, thank you." Millie gracefully folded the coat in half and handed it off. "Where did my Lilly disappear to?" Millie inquired as she looked around.

"She most likely went back downstairs to the playroom with Anthony. I'll call her." Gwen walked to the basement stairwell and shouted, "Lilly, come and visit with Aunt Millie." Gwen smiled at Millie. "She'll be up in a few seconds."

They waited, but no Lilly appeared. Gwen called again. This time they heard the plodding of her little feet taking one step at a time to the kitchen.

Lilly peeked around the corner and then ran directly to Gwen, hugging her around the waist and showing no interest in her godmother. Impatiently, Millie scolded, "Why, Lilly! You act like a baby, hiding behind your mother's skirt. Shame on you!"

Gwen grew edgy. "Lilly is not a baby, and she's right here, *listening*." She gave Millie a disapproving look. "And she is far from spoiled. Maybe she's tired. The children were up early today, waiting for *you*."

"All I see is a scared, spoiled little child peeking out from behind her mother. No wonder she had to wait until she was six to go to school." Millie rubbed the aggravating words into her sister.

Gwen glared at Millie and then instructed Lilly, "Sweetie, how about getting your new coloring books and coloring a picture for Aunt Millie."

As soon as Lilly was out of hearing range, Gwen approached her sister. "Do not talk like that in front of her. You should know better! She was ready for school at five, but her birthdate missed the cutoff date for the district, by one day! She was heartbroken!"

"She would be in first grade this year if you didn't live this desolate backward country life."

"Are you saying that if Lilly lived with you in the city, she would receive a better education than what we can provide her?"

Millie sat up in interest, "Would you really let us do that? Take Lilly home with us?" Her eyes jumped with excitement.

"Oh, I cannot believe you. Of course I wouldn't. She's my baby. What's wrong with you today?" Gwen returned to the stove while Millie returned to mixing a batter.

Within thirty minutes Lilly was back with a picture of the Nativity scene, colored exactly as it appeared in books and neatly outlined. "Here, Aunt Millie, I colored this for you."

"Thank you, Lilly. Can I take it home and put it on our refrigerator?"

Lilly nodded and again grasped onto her mother's apron strings. Gwen thought that something *could* be wrong. Lilly was normally cheerful and inquisitive. That wasn't the case today, as she only wanted her mother.

She checked to see if Lilly had a fever. She was pleasantly cool. Was she hungry? Did she want to play with Anthony? To each question Lilly shyly shook her head no. Gwen thought, *If only Millie would stop her constant chatter, then the entire kitchen would be less stressful and Lilly wouldn't feel so anxious.*

After another fifteen minutes of Millie talking under her breath about disobedient and spoiled children, Gwen called out, "Joan, come and get your sister and take her dolls out for her to play with."

Joan grudgingly entered. "Mom, I don't play with dolls anymore."

"You don't have to play with her. Just watch her. Please! She's been clinging on to me all morning."

Joan obediently, if reluctantly, took her sister by the hand and led her to the bedroom. She slid the box of dolls out from under the bed and told Lilly to go play on the other side of the room so she could continue listening to her albums.

Lilly played with her dolls, but the music distracted her. She turned to watch her older sister. Joan danced around, cradling an album cover in her arms. The more Lilly watched, the harder she laughed.

This was exactly why Joan didn't want to be a part of her younger sibling's life. Lilly was exasperating.

"Lilly Francis, I am going to scratch your eyeballs out!" Joan spread out her fingers, showing her long nails, and chased Lilly around and over the bed.

Lilly giggled and darted out the door, down the hallway, and back through the kitchen toward the basement playroom. Joan was close in pursuit when Gwen yelled out, "Joan!"

Joan came to a dead stop.

"What on earth are you doing? You are supposed to watch her!" scolded Gwen.

Millie mocked, "I told your mother how badly behaved Lilly is."

"She's right, Mom. Lilly is being a brat. Can't I leave her in the playroom with Anthony? She'll be happier helping him move trucks and putting smoke in the train's stack," Joan pleaded. "I would rather help you and Aunt Millie."

Maybe Anthony was the answer for the time being. Gwen had enough of the children for the morning. She handed Joan an apron, gave her directions for a recipe, and didn't give any more thought to Lilly.

❈

"Lilly, go and play with your stupid dolls," suggested Anthony.

"Can I please play with you and the train?" she begged.

"Why do you always want my toys?" he answered.

"Because they do more. They move and blow whistles. My dolls just lay there. Look!" She pointed to them in the cradle.

Anthony glanced over at them. "You're right. My toys are more fun."

They played for a good hour before Anthony grew restless. The sun was shining through the small basement window, and he felt the need to get outside with his sled.

"You're going sledding, aren't you?" asked an aware Lilly.

"It's a perfect day and I want to be by myself for a while. But I'll take you tomorrow." He waited for her objection.

Lilly thought, *I really don't want to put on my snowsuit and boots.* "That's okay. I'll play with my dolls now."

"You promise you'll stay in the playroom and not follow me?"

"I promise." She grinned. "I won't spy on you."

She understood promises. Frank made her promise many times not to tell whenever he did something he didn't want her parents to know and not once had she broken it. She was good at keeping secrets and promises.

Lilly cozied up in her child-sized rocking chair with her new doll. It had a hole between the lips where she could pretend to feed with a bottle. She was deep in the comfort of her imaginary play until a familiar sound startled her. It was a sound she recognized as danger—the jingling of the keys and coins in Frank's front pants pocket. Fright filled her tiny body.

"Did you hear that?" Lilly whispered to her doll. "Frank is down here. He's looking for us." The basement of pleasant memories of canning and freezing vegetables with her mother, watching her dad tie flies for fishing, Joan's piano music, and their toys suddenly felt dark and unfamiliar.

As quiet as a mouse, she crawled out of the chair, clutching her doll, and tiptoed to the door. She peeked out into the dust-filled haze of the dingy basement.

"I don't see him, but I know he's here. He is watching us. Don't cry because he'll hear you, and then he'll find us," she told her doll bravely.

"There's no place to hide in the playroom, but we can sneak behind the furnace. Maybe he won't look there. He does not like getting his shoes dirty and the furnace floor is dirty with coal dust. Don't be scared. I'll hold you." She pulled her doll tighter to her chest.

Hugging the wall, she slid along its wooden planks until she could dash behind the big steel fire-breathing furnace. "I know Daddy told us never ever go by the furnace, but this is the only place to hide." Her whispering stuttered with worry, and her legs felt weak.

She heard the coins again.

"He's coming; he's playing hide-and-seek, but we don't want to play with him. He hurts us and makes us feel bad. He stopped playing nice a long time ago." Her breathing grew fast and shallow.

"Now he scares me and tells me he will hurt Mommy. Then he laughs at me. He is big and strong. Hiding is our only escape. This corner is good. He can't fit between these boards like you and me." She tucked herself in, cowering to feel smaller, so he wouldn't see her. The smell of the coal was scratchy in her throat, but she dared not cough.

Smashed tightly into the corner, she remained as still as the wooden two-by-fours.

Clutching her doll to her chest she gave her final directions for safety: "Whatever you do, don't let him hear you breathing. He waits and listens for us to breathe. I think that's how he finds us."

She closed her eyes, protecting her new baby doll, and waited in the dim black corner for the coins to stop and the sound of his shoes going up the steps in retreat. That didn't happen.

"Where are you, Lilly? I know you're down here." Frank began softly singing a Christmas song.

"You know the words. What does Santa say? 'He sees you when you're sleeping. He knows when you're awake. He knows if you've been bad or good'...finish the song, Lilly. Tell me what Santa says." He walked toward her hiding place and chuckled at the mindlessness of little children and their failure to hide their feet!

He watched Lilly's black shiny shoes and lacy white anklets shift from side to side by the furnace. "Lilly, you know this game. It's my favorite." He grinned as he anxiously chewed his cigar.

"I bet you're behind the furnace where your daddy told you never to go.

I think I might tell him you were playing there. Maybe you'll get a spanking." Frank gritted his teeth and chuckled as he ambled toward her.

"Hiding makes us scared. Isn't that a fun feeling?" He breathed in the musty air, enjoying its foul smell. Lilly remained soundless except for her heartbeat and her breath.

In one sudden and swift move, he snatched her up, smothering her mouth with his handkerchief to silence her screams. He pulled her close to his chest as she kicked and wiggled.

"No one can hear you or see you. Kicking is only going to make me mad. Do you want to see me mad?" Hearing the threat, Lilly fell limp. When Frank was mad, he was meaner.

In a gruff, compassionless tone, he whispered in her ear, "Remember our secret? Just like Santa, the eyes are always watching you. If you tell anyone, I'll punish your mother. You don't want that to happen, do you?"

With a terrified look, she shook her head... no.

He forced her to stare directly at his face. In doing so, she dropped the doll from her arms, watching it fall onto the coal-dusted floor. "Now look at what you did!" Frank said. "You ruined your doll's dress. It's no good anymore."

He placed his foot on the doll and slowly squashed it into the floor, as if he were stamping out a cigarette. Then he snickered. "This is your fault!" He saw her guilty expression and toyed with her, picking up the dirtied doll and holding it close to her face.

Lilly reached for it, but he quickly moved it out of her grasp.

"I'm going to show you what happens to broken dirty dolls and little girls who don't keep secrets!" He carried them both to the door of the furnace and opened its large steel mouth, exposing the raging fire.

He tossed the doll into its center.

Lilly fought to get loose. He grabbed her by the hair, forcing her to watch the angry flames. Lilly stared in horror as her doll's face twisted and melted. With only a few breaths of the furnace, it was over. Her doll was gone.

"Look!" he commanded, moving her closer to feel the intense heat against her face. "If you tell our secrets, I'll put you in that fire myself and watch you burn, just like your doll and I'll never tell anyone. Your parents will only know that you disappeared. You will be a pile of ashes trapped inside the monster."

He laughed hauntingly and chewed his cigar with the pleasure of his cleverness. Then he sat her down and kneeled to her level, once again holding her face tightly in his hands.

"Now go, run to your mother and tell no one." He looked fiercely at her.

Terrorized, Lilly lost her voice, but her eyes said all he was looking for.

Frank released his grip and watched her little patent leather shoes tap up the steps as fast as they could, and then he slowly followed behind, jiggling the coins in his pocket.

She ran to Gwen, who was washing dishes, and hugged her tightly around the waist. Gwen stopped, bent down, and returned the hug. "There's my little Lilly. You played for a long time with your dolls. You were a good girl. Do you want some milk and a cookie?"

Frank sat down at the table. "I would like some too. I like cookies, don't I, Lilly?" he asked. Lilly feared his look. "Yes," she answered.

Gwen smiled. "I'll bring a few on a plate and two glasses of milk. It's so nice of you to help keep her busy." She directed her comment at Frank.

Frank grinned at Lilly. "Not a problem. I love our godchild. She is a good girl. Aren't you a good girl?"

"Yes, Uncle Frank."

Gwen set down the glasses and plate.

"Mommy, when I'm done can I go to my bedroom and take a nap?"

"That's a great idea. We'll be up late tonight."

Lilly left for the comfort of her bedroom, where she couldn't hear or smell him. That was when she finally felt safe.

❋

Vincent awakened her with a kiss on her cheek.

"Hi, Daddy!" She threw her arms around his neck, feeling protected in his grasp.

"That's a big hug! Did you miss me?"

"I always miss you when you go to work," she said, laying her head on his shoulder and thinking that when her Dad was home, Frank didn't play games.

"How about we go check out the Christmas tree?"

"That would be fun!" She reached for his hand. They looked at the bright-white lights shining on the strings of tinsel. "Do you like your new doll?"

Lilly tightened her lips.

"What's wrong?" inquired Vincent. "Lilly, honey, where *is* your new doll?"

Lilly stood back and, with her hands out in front, explained, "She's gone."

Her matter-of-fact face bothered Vincent. Just then Frank walked in.

"Is there a problem?" he asked Vincent.

"No, I hope not. Lilly said her new doll disappeared."

Frank glared at Lilly. "Dolls don't disappear. Why don't you go down to the playroom and look for her? She's there somewhere." Lilly did as he said.

Vincent remained puzzled. "That was odd, wasn't it?"

"Nah, she's been moody and clingy all day, probably tired from company and the Christmas excitement. Speaking of being tired, you look exhausted. How about I make you a Manhattan?"

"I would like that, thank you."

Frank returned with two drinks. "After supper I'll help you look for Lilly's doll."

"That's a good idea. I'm sure she set it down somewhere and forgot, but that's not like her. She doesn't forget anything!"

"She sure doesn't. That one there is sharp. You're going to have to keep an eye on her," chuckled Frank.

"Yeah, she's different from the others. One day she's so stubborn and independent, and the next she won't leave us alone—keeps us on our toes."

Later they searched for the doll. It was nowhere to be found.

"Lilly, are you sure you don't remember the last time you played with her?" Vincent asked. Lilly stayed with her story. "The doll is gone," she answered, shrugging her shoulders.

"Aw, I'm sure it will show up. I wouldn't worry about it," Frank assured Vincent.

"Frank's right," piped Millie. "When we leave, and the house settles back into its routine, it'll show up. Lilly has other dolls and plenty of new toys to play with."

Gwen looked at Vincent. "I think Millie's right. Let's put it aside for now." Then she turned to Lilly and added, "We aren't happy about this, and you may not get any other dolls for a while. Now go to your bedroom."

Downtrodden, Lilly walked away. Once she was alone, with her bedroom door closed, she said to herself, *"I don't like what Uncle Frank does to me. But I cannot tell. I don't want to burn up. I don't want to go into the furnace. And I don't want Mommy to get hurt."*

She sat alone, in quiet fear and worry.

1986 - SESSION TWO - OPEN EYES

Exhausted, Lilly plopped down on the overstuffed chair across from Dr. Bricks, kicked off her flip-flops, and pulled her legs up to her chest.

Her focus turned to the serenity of the waterfall outside the windows. The movement and sound immersed her in the tranquility of nature, her oldest friend. As far as she was concerned, Dr. Bricks didn't exist in this peaceful state.

He sat nearby, writing on his yellow legal pad, observing Lilly's avoidance, which he had noted in their first session. "Lilly...Tell me where you are."

His voice startled her away from the serenity. She wasn't sure of the what, when, and why of the past few moments. With a confused look she answered, "I'm right here."

"You've been staring out the window for several minutes. Tell me what you were thinking."

"Nothing, I was thinking about absolutely nothing. That's the beauty of it. It was just the rock, the water, and me. We all complemented one another, feeling safe and tranquil—I felt incredibly peaceful, existing as a beautiful feature of nature."

Placing both feet firmly against the floor, she uncurled her huddled body, took in a few deep breaths, and began scanning the room. Not much had changed from the previous week, helping her feel secure.

"How is your mood at the moment?" he inquired.

"More centered." She flushed with embarrassment, knowing she had drifted from the present, something she had done since childhood. "How often do you find yourself doing this?" he asked.

Lilly shrugged her shoulders, unconcerned. "It depends on how I feel, what I'm doing, and where I am. It settles down my overactive brain."

There was an awkward pause. "Tell me more."

She proceeded with caution. "I call it zoning out. I became aware of it as a teenager. Sometimes I don't even know I'm gone until I come back, if that makes any sense." As she spoke, she felt her anxiety taking hold and grew restless.

Noting the change, Dr. Bricks replied, "Everyone disconnects at times."

Lilly looked surprised. "They do? It's a normal thing—even you do it?"

"Yes. For example, I was driving to work and thinking about a disagreement I had with my wife. I drove clear across town to the office and didn't remember it at all, as if I had been on autopilot. I realized I had disassociated when I pulled into my parking space. It happens when I am especially tired or overly stressed."

Lilly nodded. He was normal, but more importantly, he was making her feel normal too. "So I'm not that odd or different?"

"No, you are not odd, Lilly. Have you heard of disassociating?" Dr. Brinks probed.

"Yes, in my college psych classes."

"Tell me what you remember about it."

"It's a type of avoidance or an escape from what's happening. It happens to soldiers during the traumas of wartime. Why? Do you think I'm dissociating?" To Lilly, the idea was absurd. She hadn't been in a war.

"Yes, I feel that it is an area we need to address."

"I don't understand."

"Have you ever felt trapped?"

Lilly sat back and rolled her eyes, "Many times."

"When one feels trapped in a situation that is trying emotionally and physically, the mind needs to escape. It does so by disconnecting from the body. That's dissociation."

"Did I learn to do it, or does my body do it for me?"

"The human body is amazing. Your mind recognizes when there is no way to physically escape and emotionally cope, and in order to survive, it disconnects."

"It's like I learned how to unplug myself."

"That's correct. And you learned to recognize when it was needed."

"How do I stop it from happening?"

"Learning what triggers you. When we first met, we spoke about Owen's development stirring up the feelings you had as a child. When you step away from your adult self, you are dissociating. Tell me about other triggers that usually take you away from the present."

"I'd rather not." Lilly turned her head in avoidance.

"You're safe here," he assured her.

"I would rather drift away again into nothingness than to remember. That's how afraid I am." She continued to stay clear of eye contact.

"It's scary to allow yourself to remember."

"I'm afraid that *he* will return and start all over again, or kill me, or someone I love, or take Owen away. You don't understand how dangerous he is!"

She began shaking nervously. "The idea that I'm telling secrets is freaking me out!"

"You don't feel safe, talking about the past." He engaged with caution.

Slowly, softly, and with sincere fear, Lilly leaned forward and whispered to Dr. Bricks, "He will kill. He likes to kill. He is the devil. Or worse yet, he will come after *your* girls."

Dr. Bricks remained calm. "Who is…'*he*?"

She barely said the name. "Frank." Then pulled herself into the smallest ball she could make with her body, placing her hands over her face, and waited for the end to come, for the roof to cave in and the earth to open, swallowing her whole—but it didn't. She peeked through her fingers. There sat Dr. Bricks, looking as composed as the day she first saw him.

I am still alive! She said to herself. *I said his name to a doctor, and nothing happened.* Hope replaced some of the fear of a once-promised death. She touched her stomach as she felt a wave of nausea flip and turn inside of her.

"There aren't words in the English language that describe Frank," Lilly explained. "You can try," suggested Dr. Bricks.

A lump of fear formed in her throat. Anxiously, louder than she intended, she forced out, "Frank was my baptismal godfather."

"How is it that he stirs up such anger and fear?"

"I shouldn't be here, talking to you about family secrets, but that's who I am! I'm a body of secrets and lies and make-believe worlds." She stood up and began to pace in front of the windows. "Every damn day is a chore to get myself ready in the morning, to get gas in my car, to shop for groceries, to go to a dinner party pretending that I'm like everyone else, when I'm not! Nothing in my life feels normal. I still think he is watching and he's going to get me. I'm worn out from worry." Her voice sounded heavy. "I need help."

Dr. Bricks reassured her, "I'm here to help you."

Lilly looked up at the ceiling, avoiding any eye contact. "He told me I was crazy, and if I tell you what I'm thinking, it *will* sound crazy."

"You're not crazy."

"You may change your mind about that." Lilly took a breath. "For example, I still think he is watching and knows what I do. I look out the windows every night as if he is going to be standing under the streetlight, watching and smoking his cigar! I put the knives away before I go to bed just in case he breaks in, so they won't be as easy to find, and I triple-check the locks on the doors. Sleeping with windows open isn't a possibility. The threat of him getting in the house still exists."

"How is it possible for someone to always be watching and to be everywhere at one time?"

Lilly made direct eye contact. "I haven't thought about that before. It's this stupid fear, blocking my rational thinking. Of course it's not possible. He had me believing that the trees had eyes, which I know is not feasible. However, as a child I believed they could. He also drilled it into my head that he had followers everywhere that kept watch when he wasn't around. Whenever I heard coins jingle in a man's pocket I knew that it was one of his people because it's what he did. Smelling a cigar was another. He made himself come to life wherever I was through one of my senses. That was my reality and still is."

"Does that reality need to exist today?"

Lilly sighed. "No, but sometimes I'm just not strong enough to fight off the messages he planted in my head."

"Yes, you are. Tell yourself that he is human, he has no special powers, and he has faults. Seeing him as a regular human being makes it impossible for him to carry out the task of being everywhere and seeing everything."

"I get that, but when I zone out and think like a kid he loses his human traits. He returns to a monster and a beast, nothing of this world." Lilly closed her eyes, ready to return to the waterfall.

"Lilly, I want you to keep eye contact."

She squeezed her face and forced her eyes to open. In slow motion, she looked back into her doctor's eyes. "Think with your eyes open," he gently told her.

Anger flared. "Why? Why do I have to keep my eyes open? Frank did that. He forced me to look at him. What is it with the eyes?"

"For me, keeping your eyes open helps keep you grounded in the present. You can look around the room and check out colors or movements, all of which awaken your senses to the now."

"So why did Frank make me look into *his* eyes?"

"I'm not sure, Lilly."

"Just give me some kind of explanation. I need to understand before I can let go. Why do you think he would do that?"

"Many emotions can be read from one's facial reaction."

Lilly freaked. "So he was reading me and learning what scared me, what made me cry, and what hurt. Because he kept repeating what he saw, I identified with what he was saying: scared little girl, bad little girl…It makes me sick! To this day if someone touches my face, I have to restrain myself from smacking them."

"But you are here, Lilly, not in your childhood. You must remember that," Dr. Bricks gently instructed her.

DECEPTION

"I'm ready to get back home; enough of this country life. Honestly, I'm tired of pretending I enjoy being here," Millie muttered under her breath as she folded and reorganized her suitcase. "How could anyone not like the feel of angora? Gwen doesn't know what she's missing, so far from city life! She still believes in an inexpensive collection of cotton! Imagine that!"

Her mind shifted to Lilly. *I have no doubt that Frank had something to do with that doll disappearing. He's like a jealous child when it comes to kids and their toys. He was probably teasing her and something happened to it. He couldn't let Vincent know, so he threatened Lilly to keep her mouth shut, which she did. As she should have, being our godchild.* Millie coyly tossed her long thick hair over one shoulder. *Frank's temper can get the best of him. It's wise to head home.*

Frank's weightless steps entered the room. He watched her fingers move across the material like the wings of a butterfly. He stepped up behind her, putting his arms around her waist.

"Frank! What are you doing, sneaking up on me like that?"

"I was thinking we could cuddle for a while and see where it takes us." He turned her around to face him. "I want to thank you for helping me with Lilly."

Millie stirred inside with suspicion. "Were you good to her?"

He began to explore her voluptuous body. "I play teacher, that's all. I teach her about a life that her parents don't understand."

Millie allowed his wandering hands to go where they wanted. He had a knack for pleasing a woman. "Do you know where she put her new doll?" Millie inquired, taking in a deep breath and holding back other, much-desired responses.

"I don't. Maybe I can find it somewhere under here." He lifted up her blouse.

"You're a bit sassy this evening," she chided as he laid her upon the bed. "Frank, there are children in the house."

"Do you really care about that?"

Millie surrendered. Afterward, they cuddled under the down comforter, wrapped in each other's arms. "I want to see Lilly again before we leave. You will help, won't you?" Frank's voice was calm and direct.

Millie cowered in his grip, losing the enjoyment of their lovemaking. He pulled her face up to his. "You know what you have to do. Keep Gwen busy and suggest that I take Lilly outside for a walk to see some of her and Anthony's favorite paths."

"Frank, you said it would only be once and now it's—" Before she could finish he placed a finger firmly over her lips.

"Shhh! You know how much I hate questions and whining little pleas. All you have to do is what you've been doing: manipulate your sister." His voice changed from flirty, dashing husband to dominating commander. "Can you imagine Gwen's reaction if she received a few pictures of her childless Saint Millie in the mail? Do you remember those? You know the ones where you wore—"

Clenching her teeth, she cut him off. "Yes, I remember those pictures. You promised me they were private photo shoots, for no one's eyes but yours. Now you're using them against me?"

"Against you?" He laughed. "You're very clever, Millie, but so am I. That's why those pictures remain hidden and ready to use as I see fit."

"Why do you always take the camera?"

"Does it bother you that I like to have my camera with me?"

"Why do you take it when you're with Lilly?"

"All you need to do is what I tell you and enjoy my gifts of clothing and jewelry." Tired of her questions, he stood looking down at her. "I'm going to shower. How about joining me?" He raised his eyebrows.

Millie got out of the bed, wrapped a robe around her body, and paced. "I can't. I have to plan out what diversion I can create for your walk with Lilly tomorrow." She felt bitter and hateful. *This is all Gwen's fault. She's too naive and trusting. Her godliness has left her and her family vulnerable. Perfect little Gwen wouldn't last a week in the city.* Millie slammed the suitcase shut, handing the guilt off to her sister.

Frank stayed put, amused with the tension in her face. "It could be worse."

Millie's eyes narrowed in anger. "How could my life be any worse?"

Frank picked at his nails. "You could be sitting in jail with no silk or angora sweaters, because if I am arrested, you will be too. I will sing like a bird if that happens. They'll want to know who helped me, and I'll tell them, 'my wife.' I have pictures to prove it. You pretend you're innocent when you're not. You're nothing more than a wolf in sheep's clothing."

Her eyes blankly gazed into the distance. It's true. He wove my life into his world, and I can either live with his lies or lose everything. I would be small-town gossip, which would kill me. I have no life without Frank. I have no reason to feel guilty. He loves children and doesn't have one of his own. He is a teacher, like he says.

He took her dispirited hand and led her to the shower.

�֎

The day was sunny and above freezing, not common for late December. It was a perfect morning for Lilly and Anthony to go ice-skating. Anthony took off, jumping the snowbank with his skates and entering forbidden territory.

"Anthony!" yelled Lilly. "Anthony, come back here! You're going to be in trouble if Mom sees you!"

Lilly knew how strict her parents were about skating on the river without an adult present. Vincent had checked the depth of the ice with an auger and carefully laid out the boundary beyond which, he warned, they could fall through the ice.

"You worry too much, Chicken Little Lilly! I dare you to catch me!"

Lilly never backed away from a dare made by Anthony. She once ate a worm because he dared her. She filled her pockets with baby snakes because he dared her. She carried a box of toads into the basement and put them in the sump pump because he dared her.

"Yes, I will!" Lilly narrowed her eyes in determination and took off, gaining speed to jump the three-foot snowbank. She made it, landing on her butt.

Anthony laughed as he sped along the riverbank. She brushed herself off and rebounded. It wasn't long before both of them were sitting on the ice, exhausted.

"Do you think Mom saw us jump the snowbank?" Lilly asked.

"Nah, Millie and Frank keep her too busy, Dad is at work, and Joan doesn't care." Lilly looked down into the ice. "Do you think I could see a fish?"

"No, silly, the fish hibernate deep down in the mud and cold waters."

"How do they breathe?"

"I showed you how fish breathe last summer."

"Gills, I remember now. What would happen if we fell in the river? We don't have gills."

"We'd drown unless we held on to the ice. Why so many questions?"

"Does Uncle Frank play scary games with you?" she asked, looking into the ice at the air bubbles frozen in time.

"What kind of question is that? He doesn't even like kids! You're lucky he's nice to you and brings you big-buck presents," he commented with a hint of jealousy. "Who cares about Frank anyway? Why don't we race back to the rink? I'll give you a head start."

She jumped up and, with arms swinging from side to side, speed skated back to the rink, hungry for lunch.

※

Gwen smiled at Lilly's rosy red cheeks from playing outdoors. "Maybe after lunch Uncle Frank will help you and Anthony carry wood down to the rink for a bonfire tonight. What do you think, Frank? You must be tired of watching Millie and I cook all morning."

Frank looked at Lilly. Lilly turned her head away, refusing to give him the pleasure of her attention. He bit down on his cigar. "Sure. I would love to get outdoors. I'll bring the camera and get some shots of the kids."

"Oh, Frank! That's a wonderful idea," Millie piped in. "You can take pictures of them playing in the snow, and afterward Lilly can show you a few paths that she and Anthony made in the pine forest. Would you do that for Uncle Frank, Lilly? Would you show him some of your trails?"

Lilly tensed. *Walks with him scare me. I don't want to do what he tells me.* "I'm tired from skating. Anthony can pile wood with Uncle Frank."

"Lilly Francis, don't be so rude. It will only take you an hour, and then you can come in and rest," snapped Gwen. Millie added,

"And it's such a sunny day! Are you sure you want to let Anthony have all the fun?"

Millie and Frank shared a smile. Lilly saw it. *I am not going with Frank*, she told herself.

"Can I please be excused?" Lilly asked politely.

"Yes," Gwen said. "I'll get you some dry outdoor clothes."

Lilly left the table feeling an uncomfortable sense of danger in her stomach. She had to hide and began thinking about where she hadn't tried. *Definitely not in the basement, or anywhere in the yard. He found me in the garage—where am I safe?*

Softly she tiptoed to her bedroom, crawled under her bed, and pushed her body up tightly against the wall at the base of the headboard. Breathing a shallow breath, she hid and watched for shoes—Frank's shoes.

ENTER THE DEVIL

Millie's gloating over her clever manipulation didn't last long, as she heard Gwen calling, "Lilly, come here right now! I have your snowsuit ready!" There was no response.

Gwen returned to the kitchen. "Did anyone see where Lilly went? She's not answering."

Both Joan and Anthony shook their heads no. Frank added, "I saw her walk into the living room and then down the hallway." His eye twitched as he nervously picked at his nails.

Everyone, except Frank, joined in looking throughout the house and calling out Lilly's name. They opened closets and looked under beds, but there was no Lilly. Anthony put on his jacket and checked the yard, and still no Lilly.

Gwen grew frantic. "Anthony, think hard, where could she be?"

"I don't know, Mom! Her jacket and boots are here. She has to be in the house somewhere." Anthony was worried too. This was not like Lilly. Lilly always obeyed her parents.

"Joan, what do you think? Where could Lilly be?" Gwen couldn't hold back her tears of worry and fear that Lilly may have wandered out on the ice or in the woods.

"Mom, maybe she thinks it's funny that we're all looking for her."

"It's *not* funny!" Gwen yelled. "Lilly Francis, come here right this minute!"

Millie scowled at Gwen. "If you had control over her and didn't treat her like a baby, maybe she would understand that this isn't a joke."

"Millie, not now! This is not a time to give me more grief!"

"I'm just stating a fact. Lilly has become disobedient and disrespectful toward her elders. I hope you have a proper punishment for her when… or if…you find her."

Gwen broke down in tears. The fear of losing her baby girl was too much.

Frank remained at the table, listening and growing edgy. *I know how to get her to come out of hiding,* he thought. He stood up and began to jingle his coins as he joined the search.

Millie called out with spiteful anger, "Your mother is worried silly. Come out right this moment and apologize, Lilly. This is not a game!"

Lilly remained pressed up tight against the wall. She saw Frank's shoes enter her bedroom and then leave. She heard the coins. She wasn't going to go for a walk.

Frantic, Gwen went through the house one last time, before calling Vincent, while Millie changed her song with dramatic sobbing. Not long afterwards, Gwen's loud scream of relief echoed throughout the house, "I found her! I found her!"

Everyone ran into the bedroom. "Where is she?" they asked, not seeing Lilly.

"She's under the bed, pressed flat against the wall, and won't come out!" Gwen pleaded, "Please, Lilly, this isn't funny. I am not asking. I'm telling you."

"No!" Lilly refused to listen.

Millie turned her tears off in a second. "Joan, go and get the broom in the kitchen," she ordered.

"What are you going to do with a broom?" asked Gwen.

"You, my dear sister, are going to sweep her out from under there. This has gone far enough!"

"That sounds so harsh. There has to be a reason why she's hiding and not talking."

Frank stood in the doorway, anxiously rattling his coins. "I think I know why she's behaving this way." Everyone stopped chatting, yelling, and crying. "Why?" several voices asked.

"Lilly and I play hide-and-seek. She loves the game. I think she wants to play it inside the house rather than going out in the cold." He smiled coyly.

"Frank, you should have told us this earlier." Millie smiled at Gwen. "See, dear sister, there's nothing to worry about. She's toying with you."

Joan came running into the room and handed the broom to Gwen.

Gwen reluctantly took it. "Lilly, please come out so Mommy doesn't have to use the broom." No answer. The sound of the coins filled Lilly's thoughts.

"If you can't do it, then give me the broom!" Millie snapped at Gwen.

"No, I will not let you do that to Lilly." She took the handle of the broom and slid it toward her daughter's body. Without knowing her strength, she poked it right into Lilly's stomach a little too hard.

"Ow...Mommy that hurt!" Lilly began crying and started to wiggle out from her hiding place.

Gwen grabbed her arms and slid her out the rest of the way. "You silly girl! Why were you hiding like that?" She shook Lilly, holding her firmly by the upper arms.

Holding all emotion back, Lilly answered, "I don't like Uncle Frank." Silence filled the room.

"Well, that's just crazy. Why don't you like your uncle? He's always taking you for walks and trying to help. He said you like to play hide- and-seek," Gwen said sharply.

Lilly heard the coins' jingle again. She looked away from her mother and at Frank. His head very slowly nodded 'no'. Then he addressed her. "You always want to win, and this time you did. Very clever, Lilly!"

His eyes flashed with a stern look, frightening her even more.

Lowering her head, she answered, "That's right, Mommy. I wanted to beat Uncle Frank with the best hiding place."

Millie had been waiting for the right moment to throw in one last jab. "After that little escapade, I think she should carry more than her share of wood to the ice rink. Maybe she shouldn't be part of the bonfire. Uncle Frank will stay behind and watch her."

"Millie, that's enough. Lilly is safe. That's all that matters right now. Vincent and I will take care of the consequences." Gwen found her feet again, turning all attention back to Lilly. "Lilly, Aunt Millie is right about one thing," she scolded. "You were very disobedient by not answering my calls. I am angry, and your father will be too. Go and put your snowsuit on."

"Do I have to show Uncle Frank the paths?" Lilly's mind stayed with her only thought: being safe by escaping Frank.

"Yes, you do. A nap is now out of the question."

"But I don't like him, Mommy."

"I don't want to hear you talk like that anymore. You are being silly. Uncle Frank is going to feel hurt." Gwen took her daughter's hand and got her ready for the outdoors. Then she handed her over to Frank and watched them walk to the woodpile with Anthony.

"I'm sure that's exactly what Lilly needs," Millie comforted Gwen.

With a good supply of dried logs and twigs piled up by the rink, Anthony headed back to the house while Lilly took Frank for a walk along the road. He pointed to a path and asked, "Lilly, where does that go?"

Lilly wanted to free her hand from his, but every time she pulled away he held it tighter. "It goes to the potato shed. It's an old wooden building."

"Show it to me," he ordered.

"Daddy says we can't go back there without him. It's not in our boundaries."

Frank moved his cigar to the other side of his mouth and laughed. "So your daddy has given you boundaries, but Daddy isn't here. What's one more disobedient act today from a bad little girl who doesn't listen to her parents?" He pulled her off the road and onto the lightly snow- packed path.

Lilly's heart filled with impending doom. *If I can't run away, then I'll play possum.* She let her body drop, and Frank stumbled from the dead weight.

He regained his balance and gave Lilly a strong jerk, pulling her up. "You think you're clever! I am your father, your *godfather*, so I can punish you too. Don't forget that!" He placed his hands on her face and forced her to stare into his.

Nothing she could say would make him go away. She had to keep her feelings inside, where they were safe from his scrutiny. Frank pulled a white thick cloth from his pocket and tied it over her mouth, picked her up, and threw her over his shoulder.

She closed her eyes tight, to recall happier times when she and her dad went to the shed for a new sack of potatoes. They would dance on the wooden floor, making loud thuds with their boots. They laughed as she twirled around and around until she fell from being dizzy. Now the shed was going to become another place for Frank's devil to dwell, just like the basement.

He set her on top of an old dresser that was being stored there. He took her coat and boots off, placing them neatly on the floor, next to his hat and coat. Then he set the scene for his eyes only.

When flashes stopped blinding her eyes, she knew it wasn't over. It never ended after the pictures.

"I bet you're wishing you were home with your parents, but you're not. You're here with me. No one knows you as I do." He glided the blade of a red jack knife down and around Lilly's neck and then up over her face, studying her reactions.

Lilly kept her eyes closed.

"Open your eyes!" he demanded.

Her eyes flew open, looking directly into his.

"That's better!" He returned to the play of the knife against her lily-white skin. "One day your parents will stop loving you and you'll be ours." He grabbed her hair and pulled her head back.

"Ahhhh!" Lilly cried out.

He kept a tight tug, holding her attention while he glared at her for what seemed like forever to Lilly. Then he whispered in her ear, "You're worth good money in the city."

He let go of her hair and laughed a loud sinister laugh. Then he walked over to his trench coat and pulled out a folded page of a magazine. "Before we go back, I have a story to tell you." He opened the folded paper, and held a picture in front of Lilly.

Filled with terror, she recorded the story on a movie reel—one that would play and replay throughout her life, embedded in her mind as a forever memory.

"Once upon a time, a little girl lived in the country and had a big secret. The secret was too big to keep and she wanted badly to tell someone, but who would that be? It could be a teacher, a doctor, or a priest. It could be a neighbor, or an aunt, or an uncle, but most likely she would tell her mother and father. And that is exactly what she did."

Lilly was absorbed in the picture as she listened, taking snapshot after snapshot of the picture with the camera in her head.

Frank's voice droned on, "That night she told her parents the secret she promised never to tell, but they didn't believe her. They called her a liar.

Maybe, they thought, she was crazy."

Mom uses those words when she is mad at me, recalled Lilly.

"So the family went to bed and everyone slept soundly. But there was a devil in the house, and the devil was watching the little girl."

"No!" she snapped at him. "We have angels watching over us, not devils!"

Frank laughed insultingly at her protest. "Oh, Lilly, you *are* a silly girl. The devil is much stronger than a helpless angel with wings! Birds have wings, and they fly into windows and break their necks. Angels are equally dim-witted. However, the devil? He's heavy and grounded and strong. Have you ever seen a white, fluffy, beautiful devil?"

Lilly absorbed every word, thinking, *He is right, angels are too pretty to be strong and mean.*

He smiled at the confusion he saw on her face. It was the reaction he was waiting for—doubt about her faith. "Lilly? I didn't hear an answer!" He jabbed her.

"The devil did that?" Lilly pointed to the picture.

"Yes, this is a picture of the devil's work. The little girl told her secret when she shouldn't have, so the devil punished her family. See this down here?" Frank pointed to a machine gun. "That's the gun the devil used to kill them."

Lilly's eyes focused mainly on the bloodstained wall behind each body, all dead except for one, the little girl, curled up on the floor, scared and crying. That would be her if she told and the dead people would be her family.

In the wee hours of the morning Joan yelled out from the girls' bedroom, "Mom, Lilly wet the bed again."

"No I didn't! I had a big sweat. Joan is lying," Lilly yelled back.

The two sisters stared each other down until Gwen arrived to settle the dispute.

Lilly had begun wetting the bed after Christmas, and nine months later it remained a problem, even as a kindergartener. Gwen and Vincent were at their wits' end with the early morning wake-ups.

Gwen shuffled into their bedroom. "Get out of bed, you two." She felt the mattress on Lilly's side. It was wet—wet enough to seep over to Joan's side.

"Lilly, why didn't you go to the bathroom? It's right across from your room. We keep a nightlight on for you."

"I'm scared at night." Lilly began to pick at her fingernails.

"Stop picking at your nails! You know that drives your father crazy. Nails have tons of germs and you put them in your mouth! Oh, Lilly, what *is* wrong with you?"

Lilly sat on her hands to stop the nail biting. "I didn't mean to wake everyone up and make them mad. I don't remember feeling like I had to go to the bathroom." She felt badly, not wanting to anger her parents.

Gwen and Joan stripped the sheets, blankets, and mattress pad, rolled them into a big ball, and then put on a fresh batch. "Joan, carry these down to the laundry room."

Joan gave Lilly the evil eye as she picked them up and left. "Come and sit on Mommy's lap," Gwen said to Lilly.

Lilly crawled up, hoping to find comfort. "What are you afraid of, Lilly?" Gwen asked patiently.

"There are boogeymen and monsters in my closet and under the bed."

"Daddy went through the entire room with you before you fell asleep. There were no monsters."

Lilly buried her head in her mother's shoulder. She would soon turn seven, and that was too old to have night accidents.

Joan returned. "I can't get any sleep. She wets the bed and she sleeps on all fours rocking back and forth. Just look at the rat's nest in her hair! That's from the rocking!"

Gwen tried to smooth the tangled mess, and a clump of hair fell into her hand. "Lilly, why do you sleep like that?"

She didn't know how to explain how scared she was, especially at night when it was dark. "I don't know. I just do it." The blanket of shame wore heavy on her shoulders. "Please don't tell Daddy to spank me."

"Then you must stop!" Gwen's voice grew firm, yet loving.

"Why can't I sleep in the twin bed next to Anthony?" asked Lilly. "I feel safe there. Anthony doesn't have boogeymen."

"We've talked about this before. Anthony is too old to share his room with a girl. Now go back to sleep. In a few hours it'll be time to get ready for school."

Joan let out a frustrated sigh and pulled the covers over her head. Gwen gave Lilly a kiss.

Lilly closed her eyes, pretending she was going to try to sleep again, but she knew she would lay there, awake, until the alarm clock rang.

WILD BOARS

Sunday nights were special for Lilly and her family. After supper, everyone helped clean up, and then the children got ready for bed early, anticipating the Sunday night family movie.

"What's the movie this week?" Anthony asked.

"It's about a boy and his dog named Old Yeller," Lilly answered. She snuggled up on the couch between her parents, while Anthony and Joan sat on the floor.

Lilly believed in the movies she watched. She thought often of kings and queens, princesses saved by a prince, good witches and bad ones. She watched intently, soaking up each scene as if it were happening in the moment.

She leaned over and whispered to Vincent, "Daddy, can we have a dog?" He patted her head and smiled. "Shhhh, not tonight."

In the next scene Lilly saw her first wild boar. They were mean and ugly, and they chased Old Yeller, who wasn't as strong as they were. She buried her head in her father's chest and squealed, "I don't like those pigs!"

Anthony and Joan both snapped at her to be quiet.

"Do we have those big pigs in our woods?" Lilly whispered loudly. "No, stupid, they don't live here, and they're called boars. They live in woods far away from us. It's only a movie," Anthony shot back. "Be quiet and watch!"

Lilly didn't buy it. She knew movies weren't real, but this one appeared to be because it gave life to Frank's words and pictures.

In Lilly's mind, Frank was a wild boar and anyone who helped him was part of his pack. She was the faithful and obedient Old Yeller, unable to fight them off, and in the end, Old Yeller died, just like Frank warned would happen to her if she ever told anyone.

The movie ended with everyone applauding the litter of new pups, except for Lilly. "Didn't you like it?" asked Anthony.

"No! I didn't like that Old Yeller died and I didn't like the wild boars! I didn't like anything except the friendship between the boy and his dog."

"*Old Yeller* is a movie, and the dog didn't really die. He's a movie star too, just like the people. He had to be taught to do those tricks to make it look real," Anthony explained.

Gwen moved the children along. "Pick up your popcorn bowls and put them in the sink. Then off to your bedrooms. I'll come by to tuck you in. Now shoo!"

Lilly went to her bedroom and looked out the window. In the moonlight she could easily see the old, weathered log cabin across the river, near the island's bank. The crude cabin reminded her of the house in the movie. Long ago neighbor boys had built it with logs. Now it stood abandoned. Vincent had ordered them never to go inside because of its age and danger of collapse.

"Lilly, what are you staring at?" Gwen walked up behind her to share the view.

"I was looking at the moon." Lilly hid her anxiousness.

"Hop into bed." Gwen pulled the shade down. "Did you use the bathroom?"

"Yes, and I brushed my teeth. I'm not going to rock tonight either." Lilly wanted so badly to get out of the habit and make her parents proud, but rocking relaxed her and helped her stay asleep.

"Let's say your prayers together." Gwen led Lilly in a short prayer asking the guardian angels to be at her daughter's side, to light and to guard, to rule and to guide. She kissed Lilly and pulled the blankets up to her chin.

Lilly drifted off thinking about the protection a dog would give her. Soon the dream shifted to the old cabin outside her bedroom window.

A small army of wild boars huddled around a large wooden picnic table in the center of the one-room cabin. The air inside was smoke-hazed from cigars and filled with the stench of old whiskey. The wild boars wore police uniforms and carried small guns in holsters and larger ones strapped over their shoulders. On the wooden table they studied a map, making plans to cross the river to enter the house. Their mission was to kill Lilly's family. They made a raft from old logs tied together with rope.

Quietly, in the middle of the night, they shoved off from shore and drifted across the open waters, moving closer and closer to the house. When they reached shore, they crawled on their bellies up the riverbank and slithered like snakes across the yard and into the windows.

They gathered Lilly's family from their beds, led them into the dining room, and lined them against the wall. The biggest wild boar held Lilly tightly in his arms, forcing her to watch as guns pointed at her family, tied and gagged with horror on their faces. There was a count to three, and the guns fired in unison. Lilly saw the limp bodies of her family slump down to the floor, leaving streaks of blood sliding down the wall.

The wild boars laughed and celebrated with whiskey and cigars. Lilly was now theirs and they tossed her around like a rag doll, betting on how much money she was worth. She was alone and unprotected with too many boars to outrun. The biggest wild police boar chewed on a toothpick as he approached and his yellow eyes lit up. She was now his.

※

In the soundlessness of a slumbering night, a death-defying scream came from the girls' bedroom.

Joan woke to the sight of her sleeping sister sitting straight up in the bed, screaming for her life. Joan raced to her parents' room.

She met Vincent midway. He had his .22 rifle and motioned her to get behind Gwen and Anthony as he moved toward Lilly's screams.

With gun up and ready to shoot, Vincent stepped into Lilly's room. She was rocking back and forth, holding both sides of her head. Vincent put the safety on the gun, set it on the floor, and quickly approached her.

"Lilly, this is Daddy! Wake up, honey! You're having a bad dream." At his touch, Lilly's arms and legs flailed and her screams turned into panting shrieks. Her family watched in bewilderment.

One more try, thought Vincent. "Lilly, wake up!" She remained locked in the nightmare, kicking his body and scratching at his face.

"Gwen, get a cold glass of water, quick!"

Gwen returned promptly. Vincent cupped his hand and splashed a small amount of water into Lilly's face. Startled, her eyes opened.

"There you go, Lilly. It's okay. You had a bad dream," he comforted her.

Joan brought in a washcloth, and Vincent soaked it with the remaining cold water and dabbed Lilly's forehead and face. As her temperature cooled, her screams became whimpers.

"No!" She suddenly pushed Vincent's hand away. "They're in the dining room!"

"Who's in the dining room?"

"The wild boars!" Once again, Lilly wavered toward hysteria. "Stay here, all of you. I'm going to check the house over." Gwen replaced Vincent while he retrieved his gun.

"The windows!" shouted Lilly. "Lock the windows! That's how they come in!" Vincent and Gwen exchanged worried looks. "Anthony," said Gwen, "I want you to go back to your room."

"But Mom..."

"No buts, now back to your room."

"Joan, you can help me with Lilly until your father comes back."

Vincent returned. "I checked the entire house, even the basement, and everything is locked up and safe. It's time for all of us to get back to sleep."

"Can I sleep with you and Mommy tonight?" begged Lilly.

"You can sleep at the edge of our bed, but only for tonight. Okay?"

"I promise, only tonight."

She clung to Vincent as he carried her to their bedroom.

❈

The doctor did a routine checkup with a urine test and asked Lilly to tell him about the dream. "I dreamed of wild boars coming from the island and crawling through our windows."

"What happens next?"

"I don't know." The same answer she gave her parents. However, Lilly *did* know. It was about Frank and the secrets he made her promise to keep.

"Does the dream always stop at the windows?" the doctor asked.

"Yes," Lilly fibbed.

"Tell me where you saw wild boars."

"In the movie called *Old Yeller*."

"Ahhh, you like stories?"

"I love stories."

"What's your favorite?"

"*Sleeping Beauty and Cinderella*."

"Do those stories scare you too?"

"No, they have happy endings. The princess falls in love with a prince."

"I bet you would like to be a princess."

"No, I want to be the prince who saves the princess."

The doctor smiled in surprise. "Well, I have good news for you and your mother." He turned to Gwen. "Your daughter has a healthy imagination!" Then he returned to Lilly. "Sometimes our imaginations can get away from us. That's when we need to think more clearly about what is real and not. Would you work on that for me?"

"Yes," Lilly answered seriously.

"Meanwhile keep the routine of not drinking liquids after supper and if you wake up feeling you *might* need to go to the bathroom, get up and give it a try. If you stop the bed-wetting and the nightmares, I won't need to see you again until next fall!" He shook Lilly's hand.

Lilly and her mother walked to the car. "You did very well at the doctor's office today. Did you understand what he was saying?" asked Gwen.

Lilly sighed. "I can't pretend anymore, and I have to get up at night to go to the bathroom." She lowered her head in shame. *I lied again, but I cannot tell the truth, because if I do Uncle Frank will hurt Mommy.*

"Lilly, you can still pretend, but it's important not to let it become real to you." Gwen wished she could read the mind of her distraught daughter.

"I know. My teacher said the same thing." Lilly saw the car and dashed ahead. Gwen watched, hoping this turning point would get Lilly back on her usual happy track, leaving the dream in the past. It had been going on for months, night after night.

That evening, as Gwen went about her normal routine of stories, prayers, kisses, and goodnights, Lilly asked, "Mommy, how can I not be afraid of the night?"

She answered, "When I was a little girl and had bad dreams, Grandma told me to make the sign of the cross on my pillow. That would call the guardian angels and they would take the bad dreams away."

"Did it work?" asked Lilly curiously. "I heard angels aren't very strong."

Gwen scrunched up her face. "Who told you that?"

"A boy at school."

"Well he doesn't know much about angels. They defeated the devil. They may not be muscle strong, but they are very wise, and that is strength too."

Lilly smiled. "I told him he was wrong."

"Good for you!" She patted Lilly on the back. "Would you like to try what Grandma taught me?"

"Yes, I miss her. She's in heaven, right mamma?"

"Yes, she is." Together they made the sign of the cross on Lilly's pillow.

"I like that!" Lilly snuggled under the top sheet, setting her head down right where they made the cross.

"I have another idea," said Gwen. "Wait here, I'll be right back."

Gwen returned with Vincent's black prayer book. "This is your father's prayer book, the one he reads from on Sundays. He wants you to have it."

"What do I do with it?" Lilly looked up inquisitively at her mother.

"Daddy said to place a tiny kiss on its cover and tuck it under your pillow. It's his way of saying that he is always near you."

Lilly did exactly that.

In the middle of the night, when the dream returned, she awakened and remembered the prayer book. She slid her hand under the pillow, pulled it out, kissed it again, and slid it back, leaving her hand on top of it.

Feeling her father's protection, she quickly fell back to sleep.

1986 - SESSION THREE - SCHEMES AND LIES

Lilly sat across from Dr. Bricks. "For three decades my life has consumed me in a negative way. I don't want that weight anymore. It's holding me back from being who I am."

"Who are you?" Dr. Bricks sat back in interest.

Lilly perked up. "I'm really not a nervous, anxious wreck. That's what I learned to be. The real me is laid-back and doesn't worry needlessly. I love people and enjoy being helpful in their lives. I like to be funny, making myself laugh as well as others and I completely embrace Mother Nature. The outdoors is church to me. I like the beauty of simplicity. I treasure honesty and loyalty. I am thrilled to be alive."

"I see all of that in you, and more."

"But I lost those feelings here." Lilly touched her chest, pointing to her heart.

"Remember, Lilly, you were a little girl, and you did everything you knew how to do in order to find a healthy balance in your life. As you stated earlier, you did what you had to do to see another day."

Dr. Bricks observed her slowly folding her arms and looking downward in a sad way. "Tell me what you're feeling."

"By the time Frank returned me home from his walks or rides in the car, I was reduced to the lowest level of being human a child can have. I was so ashamed and convinced that I was a bad girl and my parents would be forever disappointed in me if they ever found out."

"Do you remember what you did to cope?"

"I often went to my bedroom and took out my anger with my dolls. If I was in trouble, then so were they. I had to show them who the boss was. I would do to them what Frank did to me. That's one way I released my anger."

"That was resourceful and safe."

"Remembering makes me ache for my little girl! I tied them up with my hair bands and then tossed them all over the top of my bed. I hit them and said they were bad and ugly. I called them scared little babies. I took their clothes off and they were cold and begged me to stop, but I didn't feel bad for them. Instead I laughed. I took a sewing needle and scratched their skin. They tried to get away from me, but they couldn't. And I told them they would never be pretty, because that's what Frank told me. I actually pulled out most of their hair. That's not normal."

"You were venting your anger in role-play. That was healthy, Lilly." Anger swelled. "It's still in me...that hateful anger. He took the good in my life and turned it around to be bad. A pure innocent act of playing with dolls wasn't possible for me! Then came the nightmares of the wild boars, the same one repeatedly for years, always waking me in terror. How does that happen?"

"It's common to have nightmares at an early age. That's how a young mind processes what it doesn't understand. But trauma could have also had a hand in it; like having a flashback."

"So that's why the dream kept coming back! I was trying to put together all that was happening to me but I was too young to understand. Therefore, it went into my dream world using places and characters from a movie!"

"Very possible. Young children and toddlers are in their highly formative years and need positive modeling to express their feelings and emotions appropriately. Without that, feelings become overwhelming; and the child stops trying to communicate, or becomes disruptive for attention."

"I stopped communicating and when I did that I held more and more feelings inside. Not only that, I began to lose trust in my parents."

"It's known that love in a family can weaken and take a different course when protection and safety isn't securely set in place."

Lilly kicked off her shoes, reached behind her, and pulled out a decorative pillow, which she clutched tightly to her chest, like a shield.

"I hate Millie's schemes and lies more than I hate Frank!" Lilly punched the pillow every time she spoke the word *hate*. "I hate how she played up to me as if I were *her* daughter and I could trust *her* with anything. I hate the fact she brought Frank into our home, and I hate the way she played with my sense of guilt in obeying my parents. Never once did she take the blame upon herself. She was malicious and two-faced. I hate her!" Lilly felt breathless.

"Your Aunt Millie betrayed your trust."

"Oh, she sure did!" Lilly rolled her eyes as she gathered her long hair to the top of her head, fidgeting. "In many of my childhood years I believed Millie *was* my second mother, and a better one. Somewhere, somehow the notion that I owed her love, forgiveness, and respect is in my head. I won't cave in to it. I won't love her. I won't feel sorry for her. Does that make me a bad person? Am I not being a good Catholic? Do I need to forgive?"

"Forgiveness is a personal journey. People forgive to help themselves move forward and heal."

"All right, then, God can forgive her and Frank. God has powers way beyond mine. On Earth they knew right from wrong. It was their duty to protect me and other children. Instead, she collaborated with her sexually deviant husband and then she handed her guilt off to others. I have no remorse."

"You feel it's important to understand Millie's behavior in order to move forward."

"I do, because answers help me let go of anger. Knowing takes the blame off of Mom and me, and puts it back on Millie."

"The process of discovery demands drive, which is clearly one of your working strengths."

Lilly patted the beads of sweat from her forehead. "Millie placed me in a struggle between her and Mom. That's horrible to do to a child."

"She thought only of herself."

"I was sucked into thinking my godparents loved me." Lilly breathed in deeply, attempting to calm her nerves. "That was far from the truth. How does a family or a kid have any chance with evil people like that? Maybe it's better to avoid the truth and stop reliving the past."

"It's been hard on you, keeping these secrets…"

"Holding on to the past is destroying me physically and mentally. That's why I'm here. I need help. I have tried to heal myself, but I fail, and then I hate myself even more. That's different now. Learning and understanding is pulling me out of the quicksand and allowing me to stand up for myself. I am going to get over this. I will. I must."

Lilly squeezed her eyes shut, trying to expel all the bad she had seen and felt.

A LIE IS A SIN

"How can you love the end of summer and going back to school?" Anthony asked as he walked Lilly to her classroom.

Lilly shrugged, thinking, *the end of summer was a safe time—no Frank or Millie until Christmas. I don't have to be afraid until then. I feel safe at school and I like the rules. They are easy to follow.*

She answered her brother differently. "I like playing with all my friends, I like to learn and I love having a desk all to myself."

The desk was her little home away from home. She kept it neat and orderly, just as her teacher expected, and like her mother kept their house. Lilly took great pride in the responsibility and she was excited to see where she sat.

She walked up and down the aisles of her classroom, looking at each desk for the star with her name on it. To her surprise, she found it in the very last row, right next to the large windows. She lit up with a huge smile. It was the best row in the room.

What a fantastic year, Lilly said to herself. *Mom is going to have a baby and I'm in second grade with a seat right next to the windows. It'll be like recess all day long!*

She began unloading her bag of supplies, following the diagram on the board. Crayons, pencil box, and paper to the right; books to the left.

Her favorite new rule was talking breaks between subjects, as long as there wasn't any whispering during instruction. At that time, the classroom had to be as quiet as a mouse.

On a Friday afternoon in late fall, a solid knock on the wooden door resounded throughout the room during their reading class. The teacher stopped teaching and walked to the door, opening it only a crack, so the children couldn't see who was there. Then she called for Lilly.

Lilly flushed. *I don't remember doing anything wrong. I follow the rules and do what the teachers say. I don't like being called out in front of the other kids. It's embarrassing to be looked at. It makes me think of Frank.* Her face flushed even brighter. "Lilly, come here."

Lilly stood up, with her head lowered to avoid the watching eyes and approached the teacher.

Mrs. Wilder bent down and whispered in her ear, "You have a little sister. Her name is Eva. Your mother is doing well and your father will pick you and Anthony up after school by your bus."

A sister! I have a baby sister! Anthony can't call me the baby anymore and he lost his bet. Double win!

She walked back to her desk not caring who was watching. Life was going to change—in a good way. She was going to be a "big sister." They were going to be friends forever.

❋

Eva was baptized in a small ceremony after a Sunday mass. Afterward, Father Johan joined the family for the celebration dinner.

"I think this is a perfect time to discuss Lilly's First Communion this spring," Father Johan said, attracting everyone's full attention.

Vincent put down his fork. "Gwen and I were just talking about that. Last spring was rough on her. First she had the German measles and then scarlet fever. She missed two months of school."

"Yes, yes, of course, I remember that well and look how she has rebounded!" Father turned toward Lilly. "Are you ready to begin classes in a few weeks? You'll have more to study than your schoolwork."

"I love to study, and I'm good at it. Mom, can I make my First Communion this spring?"

"Yes, dear, you can." Gwen shared a smile with Vincent.

Every Wednesday night throughout the winter months, all three children attended religion classes, despite snowstorms and treacherous roads. Lilly's teacher was Father Johan, and their class met in the front pews of the church.

"Does anyone know what the word 'Eucharist' means?" Father Johan asked, scanning over the class for a response, receiving none. "Okay, children," he continued, "it means 'thanksgiving.' It's the most exciting part of the Mass because it's the time to be thankful."

"Thankful for what?" inquired a student.

"Thankful to Jesus because he stayed true to his promise."

"Jesus made a promise?" asked Lilly as she thought of the promise she made to Frank.

"Yes, Jesus made many promises to those who obey the commandments and those who don't. If you are obedient, you will go to heaven to live with him one day."

"What if someone doesn't obey a commandment?" asked Lilly. "Then they have sinned and need to attend confession or they may not go to heaven."

"So keeping a secret from your parents is a sin?" she asked.

"It can be."

Lilly quieted. *I'm keeping secrets. That means I've sinned and I'm bad.* If I can't go to heaven, then I'll go to hell. I don't want to go there!

Father Johan continued, "When we marry Jesus as a child, we marry into our faith and its teachings. We show him our love."

Lilly listened intently. She didn't understand what he meant by "love." *I see love between Mom and Dad, but it is about how they touch one another. Uncle Frank says the game he plays is about love.*

"Father, how can we show Jesus we love him without touching him?" she asked.

"Jesus is everywhere." Father lifted his hands high over his head. "Lilly, you love the river, right?" Lilly nodded in agreement. "Loving the water is a way of loving him. He created the earth and all that it is. The love you feel for Jesus is deep inside your heart."

The weight of sin moved into Lilly's life. *I've lied about more than the secret. I have lied about the nightmares too and the church says I am supposed to confess. If I do, Frank will hurt my family or kill me and if I don't, I'll go to hell.*

She looked around the church, focusing on each dark corner, drifting off in thoughts of Frank. *He told me that devils live in the corners of churches where it is dark, and they can hear everything. I wonder if they know my thoughts too and will tell Frank about me going to confession.*

Her nerves turned to fear. She moved her focus to the statues of the saints near the altar. They were good. They lived in heaven. "Lilly, are you paying attention?" Father Johan noticed her wandering gaze.

"Father"—Lilly pointed up to a life-sized statue of Mary on the wall—"why is she stepping on a snake with her bare feet?"

"That's an interesting question and I'm sure the class wants to hear the answer. The snake is the symbol that represents Satan. Mary is giving Satan a warning that he will be destroyed."

Lilly had an image of Frank's head under Mary's feet in place of the serpent. She recalled how he would carry a long stick, poking it into the grasses, as he walked her in the woods. He told her the only thing that scared him was snakes. She was positive that Frank's fear had something to do with the statue of Mary and the killing of the devil.

A plan came to Lilly's mind, but to make it work she needed Anthony's help.

PAYBACK TIME

"We have to invite my godparents to First Communion?" Lilly asked, disappointed and worried. "Why can't it ever be only us when it comes to *my* parties?"

Vincent gave her a warning look.

"But, Dad, you don't understand..." Lilly stopped, keeping the words she so wanted to say to herself.

"I do understand. You are being disrespectful to your mother's wishes."

Lilly looked away. "No, I'm not."

"Now you're talking back to me!" Vincent warned.

"May I be excused?" she asked kindly.

"Yes, and go find Anthony. You two have dish duty tonight."

She found Anthony in the worm garden, digging for bait.

"Anthony, I have a trick I want to play on Frank when he comes for my First Communion."

"I'm interested. What kind of trick?" he asked, continuing his digging.

"First you have to cross your heart and hope to die, promise."

"It's that serious?" He loved to tease with Lilly because she riled so quickly. "Okay, I promise. I cross my heart and hope to die."

"Pinky promise too." She put out her pinky and he wrapped his around hers.

"Now tell me what trick is?" he asked.

"Come on, let's take a walk along the river. You're going to love this!"

While they walked, Lilly told him about Frank's fear of snakes and her plan to scare him with a dead one. "When are we going to have enough time to snake hunt?" he asked.

"I was thinking of Saturday, right after our chores and promise to keep this a secret. It's important to me." Lilly frowned.

"I promise it's just between you and me. This is going to be a sight to see, Uncle Frank running for his life! A big-shot city guy afraid of a snake—you tease like Dad does!" answered Anthony.

"What does Mom say? 'Apples don't fall far from their tree'?" Lilly grinned. "Here's how it will work. We'll find a snake, let it wrap itself around a big stick, and set it free in the yard close to the chicken coop. That's when I will scream bloody murder, you'll run to get Mom, and then she'll come running to save the chickens and us. The hook is when the snake's head gets chopped off!"

"What are we going to do then?"

"One of us will throw it in the river, *but* we will only throw the head. We'll toss the body close to shore so we can pull it out as soon as Mom goes back in the house."

"Hey, sis, one problem: how are we going to keep it from rotting?"

"Oops, I didn't think that far. Got any ideas?"

"We have to keep it cold or frozen—our freezer?" Anthony grinned, raising his eyebrows.

Lilly let out a big laugh. "Anthony, that is such a funny sight to imagine: Mom goes down for fish and thaws a snake!" They laughed harder and harder until they were both rolling on their backs, bent with gut pain.

"Okay, we have to get serious. No more joking around," Lilly said, trying to get both of them back on track. "Remember when I tried to save a frog in a glass jar?"

"Yeah, and it died, smelling up the basement!" Anthony chuckled at the memory.

"I have to keep it looking fresh for a week. The basement isn't cold enough," she concluded.

"No, but the brook is." Anthony replied.

Lilly faced him. "That's it! We can seal the snake in one of Mom's Mason jars with rocks for weight, tie a rope around it, and set it in the brook." They shared a congratulatory handshake and rushed back to the house to do their chores.

The following Saturday they walked and walked in search of a pine snake, but with no luck. "What are we going to do now?" Anthony asked, exhausted.

Lilly sat down on the forest floor. "I won't give up. We'll go again after church and dinner. Are you with me?"

"Have to be now; can't walk out on a promise."

Lilly smiled. "You're the best brother!"

"Only when I'm under your command," he teased and then the race began through the woods to the ditch where their bikes lay. "Lilly, you beat me!" Anthony was huffing and surprised as he picked up his bike.

"It's all the boy-and-girl chase games I play during recess," she said between gasps of air. "I'm not racing home. You can if you want, but I'm taking my time. Maybe a snake will be sunbathing on the hot tar road."

"Right, but I bet you a nickel that you won't be able to say no to a race!"

They went about two miles before she caved. "All right, brother dear, you're on."

They were racing down their quarter-mile driveway when Anthony yelled, "Lilly, look at your back fender!"

She turned her head. In her sight was a huge, fat pine snake. Lilly didn't mind snakes, but the sight of one slithering toward her on the bike's fender scared her silly.

She screamed as she jumped off the bike and hit the dirt.

"I'll get Mom! Watch where it goes," Anthony called back as he ran toward the house.

She picked herself up, never once taking her eyes off the slithering reptile. It coiled in the dry grass next to the road.

Gwen and Anthony came running with the hoe. Gwen's face gnarled in rage, and whacked the snake's head off in one swing. It was a fairytale come true.

Then she turned to Lilly. "Look at your legs, they're all scratched up! How is that going to look for your First Communion?"

"Those little scratches will be gone by then!" Lilly replied, wiping off the gravel.

"Don't do that! You're only making it worse!" scolded Gwen and then addressed Anthony. "Go throw that snake in the river while I help Lilly."

"Mom, that snake was on my bike's fender! I should have the fun of throwing it in the river. I earned it!" Lilly insisted.

"Make it quick. You're bleeding."

Lilly could see that her mother was tired from cooking and cleaning and now this. She had to wrap it up fast. "Want to help, Anthony?" she asked.

"I wouldn't miss it!" He grinned slyly.

Lilly picked up the head, and Anthony grabbed the body. With a strong overhand throw she tossed the head out into the water, far enough so her mom could see her fulfilling the duty. Satisfied, she walked back to get her wounds cleaned and keep Gwen's attention away from Anthony.

"Anthony," Gwen yelled, "make sure you give the body a good hurl. We don't want it floating back to shore."

"Sure, Mom!"

Lilly walked with Gwen, looking back at her brother and smiling. The Mason jar was in his bag.

Every day after school Anthony and Lilly ran down to the brook to check on the snake. It was staying cold, and Anthony had put a little water in the jar to keep it moist. No animal tracks were around, and by day three they were quite confident that their plan worked. All they had to do was wait for Frank's arrival.

When the day came, they hightailed it off the bus, down the driveway, and into the kitchen, where they found Gwen and Millie. "Hi, Aunt Millie." Lilly gave her a hug. "Hi, Mom. Where's Uncle Frank?"

"He went outside to smoke his cigar," Gwen answered with a suspicious look on her face. "Did you have a good day at school?"

"All Fridays are good days!" Lilly grabbed a cookie. "I have a surprise for Uncle Frank. I'll change my clothes and go out to find him."

She ran to her bedroom, peeled off her school dress, and replaced it with a pair of jeans and a T-shirt. Then she ran through the kitchen and headed toward the brook.

Millie watched in amazement. "I see that she has come around to a more pleasant way of thinking."

"I guess so! Let's go out on the porch to see what the surprise is."

They stepped out and found Anthony already seated on a step, as if waiting for the movie to begin. "Anthony," Gwen asked, "what is Lilly up to?"

"I have no idea! You know Lilly and her imagination."

Lilly retrieved the snake and took off to spy for Frank, finding him walking up the bank and toward the house.

It was perfect timing to play the devil. Out of the surrounding woods, she ran full-speed toward Frank, holding the snake behind her back. When she was in hearing distance she called out, "Oh, Uncle Frank…Uncle Frank, I have something to show you!"

He stopped and turned with a huge gloating grin. *I knew she would come around to appreciate me,* he thought.

"Surprise!" Lilly whipped out the dead snake, swinging it in the air like a lasso and brushing Frank's belly. He faltered and stumbled toward Millie and Gwen. Lilly watched gleefully as he ran for his life, believing the snake was alive.

His cigar fell to the ground as he scrambled up the riverbank. His belly bounced. Sweat beaded on his forehead and Lilly didn't stop swinging the snake as she chased, yelling, "Here comes the devil!"

In his frantic clumsy run he suddenly tripped and fell to the ground, hitting face-first. Gwen and Millie sprinted toward him. "Lilly, throw that thing in the water right this moment!" Gwen screamed at her.

Lilly savored her triumph for a moment longer. *I wonder how he likes being afraid and trying to run away with an audience watching?* Then she felt her mother's hands snatching the snake from her grip. Gwen saw the head was missing and turned red with anger.

"You should be worried, young lady. Uncle Frank could have hurt himself. That was disrespectful and humiliating for him. Go to your bedroom, no snacks, no supper. Go!" Gwen pointed toward the house.

Lilly didn't mind a retreat to her room. She wanted time alone to replay the entire scene. She walked into the house with her head lowered, stopping only for a moment to give Anthony a grin.

Hours later, hungry and tired, Lilly heard a knock on her door. "Who is it?'

"It's Dad."

She took a deep breath as she walked to the door wondering what the punishment was going to be. Whatever it was, it was worth the revenge.

Slowly, she opened the door.

Surprisingly, Vincent stood there, quite at ease, with a peanut-butter sandwich and a glass of milk. "You must be starving, so I brought you a snack before bedtime."

"Thank you." Lilly kept her head down in hope of avoiding punishment. "I heard about the prank you pulled on Frank."

She remained quiet.

"I wish I would have been there to see it! Frank is still stewing."

Surprised, even shocked, Lilly looked at her father's smile and knew he wasn't kidding. He continued, "It was an innocent idea, not meant to harm anyone—but never again, Lilly."

"You're not mad at me?"

"Not really," he replied, "but a second trick like that will not be taken lightly. Now eat your snack and get to bed. Love you."

"I love you too, Daddy."

Lilly slept well that night knowing she could fight back.

THE PIRATE'S COVE

"Vincent, she looks so happy today, and she's so darn cute in her dress! It fits her to a tee, and the flower wreath with the veil is pure Lilly in her innocence."

"She's a beautiful girl!" Vincent looked upon his once-baby daughter with pride. "Here comes Frank." Vincent handed Eva to Gwen.

"That was a lovely ceremony," Frank said, approaching with a businesslike handshake.

Vincent continued watching Lilly and said, "Look at her with Father Johan. They have become friends, and he seems to be helping her deal with her worries. You know she frets about everything: school, friends, even church, but Father continues to meet with her, in hope of finding the underlying cause."

"You don't say! Does she see him more than on Sunday?" inquired a nervous Frank.

"Oh, yes, this winter she had religion class every Wednesday night and he was her teacher. That's when Lilly started to take her faith seriously and show more worry than the other children," Vincent replied.

Frank watched her interacting with the priest. "Has she made her confession yet?"

"Not yet," Vincent answered. "They did a mock confession as a class and in a few weeks we will go as a family. She and Anthony are already writing their list of sins together. You know, Frank, those two have a special relationship."

"You don't say! They have spent more time together since Eva came along?"

"Just about every waking moment when they're not in school."

"How's school going for them?"

"Well," said Vincent, "Anthony still struggles with getting homework done—typical boy—and Lilly, she would live at school if she could. Look, she's waving me over. She wanted a picture of her and Father in the flower garden. It won't take us long, and then we need to get back to the house for the party. See you there."

"Sure, we'll see you at the house." Frank watched the family join Lilly and Father Johan.

Millie put her arm in Frank's. "Watching the family?"

"Yup," Frank said as he studied their interactions with one another.

"Gwen has it all, doesn't she?" Millie responded as she, too, scrutinized her sister's crew.

Frank pulled her body a little closer to his. "Not everything. It's a backward family. They don't have the city with all of its magic." Frank paused. "Why didn't you tell me about Lilly's religion classes?"

"I didn't know that was important. All kids go to them for First Communion, you know that!"

"I didn't grow up a Catholic, so how would I?"

Millie heard his sharp, bitter tone. "Silly me, of course you wouldn't have."

"We should have come for Easter. That would have been the wisest thing to do. Lilly doesn't seem to care that we're here. It's been too long."

"She's not a child anymore, she's eight. She may not want to go for playful walks in the woods. You'll have to come up with something different to do with her."

Frank smiled and took one last, long glance at his cherished little bride jumping into the back seat of her family's car. "Come with me to say hi to Iris." Millie tugged at Frank's arm. "I haven't seen her in years!"

He walked with Millie into the crowd, jingling the coins in his pocket. *So many beautiful little girls*, he thought, but only one kept his interest.

※

The blinding sun rays reflected off the water, making sparkles on its surface as she and Father Johan walked along the river at their house. "Don't they look like stars?" Lilly asked.

"They are!" answered Father. "At night they shine from above, and during the day they fall to earth and onto the waters. Each one of them is watching out for you." He spoke gently.

"So the stars on the water will protect me?"

"As long as you believe in heaven and earth," he answered.

Lilly looked up at him. "I think you could walk on water, like Jesus did, if you tried."

Father laughed. "Oh, Lilly, you have such an imagination!"

They walked hand in hand back to the party. Lilly went to find her mother, and Father joined the men. Lilly skipped up to Gwen.

"There you are! Did you have a nice walk?" her mother asked.

"I did! Can I please open my presents now?"

"What excellent timing! I'll make an announcement, but first I want you to open our gift. Come along." Gwen led Lilly to the living room and pulled a large box out from under a linen tablecloth.

"This is for you, from me and Dad."

Lilly carefully untied the white silk bow, opened the edges of the silver paper, and slid the box out. She couldn't hide her surprise as she held up a smaller but identical statue of the Virgin Mary crushing the serpent.

"Mom, thank you! I love it!"

"Father told us how interested you were in the statue at church and that he often sees you staring at it. He helped us find this miniature one."

Lilly hugged her. "Can I put it in my bedroom so it doesn't get broken?"

"Sure, but come back quickly. The guests will be waiting."

She received candles, prayer books, rosaries, and cards, some with money and some without; however, her favorite was another statue.

"Mom, look!" Lilly observed its details. It was small, maybe six or seven inches tall, with a nun standing by a school chalkboard. On her shoulder sat a cute little bluebird, and other small animals surrounded her feet. On the board the Prayer of St. Francis was written neatly. "Mom, can I…?"

"Yes, go ahead and put it in your bedroom and set the cards up on the fireplace mantel."

Lilly's heart was full of joy. It was a beautiful day to remember.

※

The guests thinned out, and as the last car drove down the dusty driveway, the attention shifted to the house. It was in the typical disarray of a party. Food had to be put away, dishes washed, and tables taken down. Gwen, Joan, and Millie went to work in the kitchen and dining room while Anthony helped Vincent take down the tables and chairs, load them into the jeep, and return them to their rightful owners.

"Anthony, did you see where Frank went? We could use his help!" said Vincent.

"Nope, the last time I saw him he was down at the point, looking out at the water and smoking his cigar."

"Hmm, he seems to disappear whenever there's work and everyone is busy."

"Why doesn't Lilly have to help with cleanup? I saw her sitting on the living room floor, counting her money!" complained Anthony.

"It's her special day. That means she's excused. Besides, you don't mind taking part of her workload, do you?" Vincent flashed a grin, seeing envy in his son's eyes.

As Lilly counted her gifts of money, she thought, *I think I'll put ten dollars into my piggy bank for summer vacation and the rest into my savings account.* In the background, Millie and Gwen were jabbering in the kitchen.

"We'll be leaving in a couple of days, and Frank hasn't spent much time alone with Lilly. Would you mind if he walked the river path with her? He saw her with Father Johan earlier, and I think he feels a little jealous." Millie added a pleading tone to her voice.

"She's still in her dress. Maybe later, after everything settles down."

Millie mumbled under her breath, "Why can't Gwen just send Lilly on a walk? There's nothing else for her to do. But no, now I have to think of another angle."

The words *walk* and *Frank* frightened Lilly. A sudden wave of fear took hold, and she immediately began to think of her safety. *I'll put my money on the mantel, just like Mom said, and go to my bedroom. He never goes in there.*

She stood up and turned as Frank's hand snatched the envelopes from her and placed them on the mantel himself. Then he pulled her out of the house without waiting for Millie to get Gwen's permission.

In a stern voice he warned, "Mouth shut or that money will be gone. Imagine the trouble you'll get into!"

She slammed her shoe down on his foot and attempted to wiggle free, but her head met his fist. The look he wore told her it was better not to try that again.

Quietly he pushed her along, onto a path she and Anthony had made. It led to their secret hiding place, which they called the Pirate's Cove. Frank poked her in the back with his snake stick, making her move faster than she wanted.

Lilly's gut told her that something was dangerously wrong. He seemed aggravated, mad, and nervous. *Maybe he's still upset about the snake,* she thought.

They reached the cove where she and Anthony had cleared a large circle of dead branches and fallen tree trunks. In the center remained the stump they couldn't remove, the smooth, flat stump of a very old oak tree.

Bending down, he placed the familiar gag over her mouth and bound her wrists and ankles. Then he left her there, on the ground, amongst the dry dead leaves, to watch him set the scene.

He took out a thin white cloth, similar to the one the priest laid upon the altar at church. He opened it up and delicately positioned it over the stump. Lilly, fixated on his movements and tried to read them, but his actions weren't familiar. He was unusually meticulous. Looking back over his work with pleasure, he walked over to Lilly and seized her hair through the center opening of the veil.

"Kneel!" he commanded.

She felt a sharp pain rushing through her forehead.

"Kiss the ring." He pulled down the gag and held his hand in front of her mouth.

Lilly remembered Father Johan's words about the love between Jesus and her being private. She didn't have to *love* Frank's God anymore. She had her own who could see what was happening and would protect her. The idea that Frank's God was an all-powerful one no longer held power over her.

"*No*, I won't! You can't make me!" She drew in a deep breath and spit on the shiny gold emblem. "I hate you! You're the devil!" She glared into his eyes.

Enraged, Frank pulled Lilly up to his face. "You're a dirty little girl, full of sin." He carried her to the tree stump.

Lilly coiled into a ball of humiliation.

"Where's your Jesus now?" Frank toyed with her helplessness. "I am more alive and powerful than God, or Jesus. You think you are bound to a marriage because of a silly little ceremony in church. That's not marriage!"

Lilly's face flushed with terror, followed by tears.

"Look how pitiful you are, crying like a baby. The church has done this to you. It made you weak. The church is for feebleminded people, like you, believing in a phantom God." He paused as he removed her veil. "Jesus can't take care of you. No one can except Millie and me. Only we can right your wrongs and when I'm done with you today, you will never be like the other girls. You'll never fit in with the family you have now; not ever. You will be too sinful."

Unable to feel her body, Lilly floated in and out, coming back to reality only long enough to see his yellow, bulging eyes glaring down at her like some starving animal with a fresh kill.

Staring up into the canopy of the forest, through the baby leaves of spring against the blue sky, Lilly thought of only one thing: she was going to die in the secret cove she built with Anthony. He would think it was his fault. He would never know the truth. Frank would destroy her brother too.

She waited in paralyzed shock for him to stop; to stop touching her, to stop taking pictures.

Humiliation and shame soaked in through her skin. The only working part of her body was her brain, swarming with feelings. She was ready to die.

She had lived long enough.

The bark and growl of a dog awakened her mind to the present. It was Jess, the neighbor's old mutt. He crouched and stalked toward her, growling at Frank. *Jess will save me. He's going to scare Frank away! God is helping!*

Just then Frank picked up a large stick and threw it at Jess, hitting him in the rear hip. Jess yipped and retreated into the woods.

"Lilly, Lilly, Lilly…not even a dog can save you. No one can. You're broken and if that dog comes back, I'll kill him with my bare hands right in front of you. And then you can dig a hole to bury the old mutt."

He stroked her hair. "You remind me of your mother."

More pictures, more touches, and then he slowly and meticulously began to put Lilly back together, picking off every dry piece of leaf and bark from her clothing and hair. As he finished, he stood back and studied her.

"It's as if your mother dressed you. Even the bobby pins that held your veil on are exactly as she placed them. But we both know how different you are and the sins you made." He walked around her mannequin pose, saying nothing but touching her lightly, just enough to spark a twitch. He basked in her unprotected self.

Lilly looked down at her dress. She detested it. She would never wear it again. It was an evil dress that reminded her of unforgivable sins. He buried her that day, in a grave above the ground.

To return home and pretend that they had shared a wonderful fun-filled time on the walk was another lie, however, she had no choice. The same lie she had been telling since she was little, right down to the fake smile on her face and false carefree attitude, kept her family safe and herself from going to live with *them*.

I am what everyone around me expects me to be. I am a nothing, and I will be nothing until I can confess my sins and wipe my soul clean.

Lilly walked into the kitchen. Frank followed behind and took a seat at the table. He reached deep into his pocket, took out his pocket knife, and began cleaning his fingernails, stopping occasionally to glance up at Lilly.

"Well there you are! Millie told me that Frank took you for a walk while we were cleaning up from the party. You came back just in time for a sandwich and leftovers. But first, go and change into your play clothes." Gwen began to take the pins out of the veil. Lilly brushed her hand away.

"Are you upset about something?" Gwen stepped back. Lilly could feel Frank's piercing eyes.

"I can take the pins out myself, Mom. You've been working all day."

Gwen touched her lightly on the cheek. Lilly refrained from pushing her away again. "You are so beautiful in that dress!"

Lilly swallowed the words she wanted to say and replied respectfully, "Thank you. I better go change."

As soon as she reached her bedroom, she stripped the dress off and hung it up in the furthest, darkest corner of the closet. Her slacks and blouse felt protective and free from his stench. She walked over to her new statue on the dresser and knelt down, reading the words of the Peace Prayer.

Lord, make me an instrument of your peace. Where there is hatred, let me sow love; where there is injury, pardon; where there is doubt, faith; where there is despair, hope; where there is darkness, light...and where there is sadness, joy.

She raised herself up, repeating the words: *love, faith, hope,* and *joy.* She could try to live up to those words in hope of forgiveness. Closing the door behind her, she began to walk back to the kitchen for dinner. She came to a dead stop as she looked into the living room.

Frank sat on the carpet, dangling his keys out of Eva's reach. "She sure is a pretty little girl, a lot like you, Lilly."

A tsunami of motherly protection filled her.

Frank calmly stood up. "You better keep an eye on her," he said, as he walked away, whistling a happy tune.

Lilly ran to Eva and swept her up in her arms. "I'll do anything to protect you, Eva," she promised. "I would die for you."

Eva had to have someone to guard her from the snake that slithered amongst the family. Lilly prepared for battle. Her days of childhood were over.

Half of her wanted to die, and the other half *had* to live, for Eva.

1986 - SESSION FOUR - SNOW DRIFTS

"The ring, the one Frank wore after he became a Catholic. It still bothers me."

"Describe how it makes you feel."

"Embarrassed...I shouldn't have brought it up." Lilly cowered.

"Parts of your past are painful memories that want to keep you from moving forward."

"I know that. It's why I'm here. But some days the effects of the abuse are so overwhelming." Dr. Bricks paused. "You grew up experiencing huge snowstorms."

"Yes, I did," she said solemnly.

Dr. Bricks leaned forward. "Think of a big snowstorm and the different sizes of drifts. Some are deep and we get stuck in them: we need a plow to come and move the snow out of the way. We may remember that drift for some time, but it no longer can stop us from forward motion. Other drifts are small, and with the help of good tires we can plow through them ourselves. They slow us down, but we don't give it much thought. Imagine those drifts; is the ring a large drift or a small one?"

"The ring itself...is a small drift, but how he used it, is a maddening deep drift that hasn't been plowed yet."

"Tap into the anger you feel toward the ring and its use."

Silence filled the office. "I want to get a hold of it and throw it into the river, but then a part of me wants to walk away from it and let it go. I think of church and want to run. It's a struggle. Do I surrender or confront?"

"Talk to it as an adult."

Lilly glared at the table, bringing its image to mind. "You're a fake cheap hunk of shitty metal. You have no powers. You are insignificant, just like the person that wore you. You are trickery. You did not come from the church. Frank bought you at some cheap jewelry store. You can't fool me anymore."

"That was very good. You are coming to a realization of its origin and its purpose when you stay present. Frank used images and objects to frighten and control you, then not now."

"I understand that now, but as a child its power over me was real."

"But as an adult you know the ring had no special powers. You can let its effects go."

Lilly shook her head in disbelief. "*He* had no commitment with the church. Frank made it all up to shame me. This is so maddening!" She gritted her teeth.

"Shame hides under anger."

"The ring reminds me of what a weak and gullible little girl I was."

"You *were* an innocent child. Looking back, you expect a lot from your child self."

"My inner child was shamed to keep Frank a secret to protect herself and others. My adult shame is more about guilt."

"Think of yourself growing up when your uncle wasn't around, what were you like?"

"I was happy, giggling about anything, loving the big wide world."

"Did you feel shame in doing that?"

"No, of course not, there wasn't anything to be ashamed of. I was playing and living a child's life. If I ever did anything bad, I said I was sorry and moved on."

"Now, think of yourself growing up and spending time with your uncle. When you returned to your family, how did you feel?"

Lilly was less enthused to answer. "I felt dirty and mad. I wanted to be alone. I didn't want anyone to look at me. I didn't like anyone—especially myself. I felt guilty and embarrassed." She looked away. "Nothing was funny anymore. I wanted to be invisible because of my shame."

"The shame made you feel embarrassed, which then made you angry, and that boiled into hate."

Lilly glared at him, quietly thinking. "I didn't have the words to describe what Frank did and the truth would be his word against mine, with Millie backing him up. I believed Mom and Dad would never believe it wasn't my fault because I allowed it to happen." Lilly stewed.

"You're safe here, Lilly, and you're allowed to say what you feel."

Lilly stopped fidgeting, collecting her composure. "No one can see my anger. I have never allowed it, and I'm not going to start now." Her voice became firm and strong. "I should have been able to stop Frank. Should have, could have…"

"Is that how you felt back then, or now as an adult, retelling it to me?"

"It's me now, thinking like an adult and taking it out on my inner child."

"How do you think your inner child is feeling?" Dr. Bricks saw a hint of realization coming through for Lilly as her facial expressions relaxed.

"My poor little girl! I am emotionally beating her up! Was I this mad at myself when I was young? What could I possibly say to my inner child to help her realize I'm not angry at her?"

"Try telling her the truth."

She closed her eyes, hoping she would disconnect with the moment and travel anywhere but where she was.

"He threatened me. He disgraced me. He laughed and made me feel hideous. Even today, if someone laughs *at* me, it's hard not to regress back to being that helpless and misunderstood child."

"Explain to her how you felt."

Tears fell from her eyes. "All I ever wanted was to go home and be a normal little girl and forget that anything happened, but I couldn't get rid of the image of his frightening face and hearing his threats. And the more embarrassed I felt, the quieter I became." She tried to hide her trembling. "Frank should be the one to feel humiliated and ashamed, not any part of me. I see that, but it's hard to stay in the present. Triggers and flashbacks change everything."

"You felt powerless."

Lilly wiped her eyes dry. "I forget who I was back then. I was little, like my son."

"Yes, you were. Tell these feelings to your little girl."

Lilly wiped her tears away with the sleeve of her shirt. "I'm sorry for blaming you and letting you grow up feeling shamed, but I didn't understand back then. However, I do now, and I can protect you. Frank is responsible. Never did you do anything with him that was your fault. He spread his shame like a contagious virus, but that virus is dead forever. It is over. Right Dr. Bricks? It's over, isn't it?"

The idea that her godfather could come back into her life was more than she could handle.

THE CANONS OF CHURCH

In the quiet days that followed, Lilly began to fall out of her social life in school as well as home. She sought quieter moments by the river and under her favorite trees, examining acts of sin. The more she thought the more worried and confused she grew. *Before I started going to classes for my First Communion, sin was the last thing I thought of. Life was playing with my brother, building forts, and fishing. There was right and there was wrong and wrong had to be corrected. Church was a safe place to go with family. I didn't see or feel sin as a part of anything I did or said. Now it's everywhere I look and in all that I do.*

How can I confess to Father Johan? It will be too embarrassing! However, it's the only way to be free of sin, and at the same time I will be saving Eva from the devil that visits and sits at our kitchen table. Maybe the words will come with practice, tons of practice. It's not going to be easy, but it's what I have to do!

She studied the rules of a proper confession. The beginning and the end were easy, but she struggled to find the words she needed for the middle. Kneeling alongside her bed she rehearsed, "Bless me, Father, for I have sinned."

"Tell me your sins," she answered herself in a low, calm voice, imitating Father Johan. "I lied to my parents about where I was."

"Why did you do that?"

"I lied because I didn't want them to know about the games Uncle Frank plays."

"Tell me about your uncle's games."

Lilly stopped. *What should I tell him? How do I explain the games?*

She repeatedly started over, never getting to an end she felt comfortable with, but that didn't stop her. She knew this was the only way to break her silence and let go of all the secrets that kept her in fear of going to hell or dying.

When Sunday came, Vincent was called into work. With only one car, they would have to wait until the following week. Lilly pleaded, "Mom, we have to go to confession today. I promised Father Johan we would be there!"

"Don't worry! We will attend confession next week after early Mass. Father understands that some people work on Sunday."

Lilly walked away. Home was a veil of disappointment that she wore too often. She hated waiting. She had to wait when she hid from Frank. Waiting burdened her every breath. It played with her mind. It made her more anxious.

The following Sunday Lilly sat in the pew with her family, but her thoughts were far away from the present. Her mind kept her engaged in doubt.

Should she take the chance of confessing, or remain silent and protect her family?

The priest's voice grew louder as he began the sermon. Lilly blinked, setting her eyes upon him.

"My dear parishioners, it is with a heavy heart that I tell you what transpired this week as I met with the bishop." Father Johan paused, looking over his people of twenty years. "I am being called to further my duties in serving God and his church in another parish. I understand that this is a shock for all, as it was to me. I will be available after church for questions. Confession will be as usual, next Saturday and Sunday."

Numb, Lilly looked up and into the corners of the high ceiling. *The devils knew I was ready to confess, so they are taking Father Johan away from me.*

The car ride home was quiet except for Lilly. Rage grew inside her.

"Why would the church do this? He's family!" she shouted. "I hate church. I am not going anymore. I only like Father Johan."

"You don't know that a new priest won't be as good," piped in Anthony.

"Both of you, quiet! This is hard on all of us," Vincent scolded.

The rest of the ride home was silent, as was brunch. The usual busy table chatter was absent. The only sound was that of clanking silverware against glass plates. Its monotonous rhythm peeled Lilly's layers of patience away. Without warning, she shoved her chair back and stomped off to her bedroom. The family waited, listening for the door to slam, which it did.

"She's upset about Father leaving. I'll go and talk with her," Gwen calmly reassured the family. "Lilly was very close to him." Gwen knocked on her door. "Go away! I don't want to talk to anyone!" Lilly sobbed.

"Open the door, Lilly."

Slowly the door opened. They sat down on the edge of the bed, Lilly's face red from crying. Gwen tried to offer comfort. "I'm sorry this had to happen, and I understand how sad you must be feeling."

"No, you don't. No one can read my mind. No one knows how I feel, except me," Lilly angrily answered. "Why does he have to go? Can't he fight to stay?"

"No, Lilly, he can't. This is his calling." Lilly exploded, "What is a calling anyway?"

"A calling is something Father feels God is leading him to." Gwen patted Lilly's back. "You know, dear, things happen in our lives that we cannot change, but we learn to accept."

"I know that!" Lilly hissed. "That doesn't change the fact that I won't like any other priest and I don't need church. I'll stay home." Lilly meant what she said. She had lost more than a priest; she had lost her hope of telling the truth to the only person she trusted.

"You can make that choice when you leave home."

"You'd like to send me to Uncle Frank's and Aunt Millie's wouldn't you?" Lilly hatefully countered.

"Now that's a silly thought, of course not! What on earth makes you think I would do such a thing?"

"Millie thinks she's a better mother than you, and she's always asking for me to go to their house."

"Oh, Lilly, for a visit, not to stay!"

Lilly shouted loud enough for everyone in the house to hear, "Everything is a lie!"

She wasn't hungry. She didn't want to see her family. She didn't want to confess anymore. It was all a trick. As Frank said…church was making her weak.

"I'm going down to the river. Don't worry about me. No one does anyway."

She stormed out of the house and found refuge under the willow tree that always listened and understood. It was there she often vented her sadness.

I wonder if there really is a God. If so, how would he explain this? Who was I to think that the unknown and unseen would save me? I'm a stupid, crazy fool.

Lilly pulled further away from church and family and went deeper inside of herself.

❈

"We had another call from school today," Gwen told Vincent when the children were out.

"What now?" Vincent rubbed his hand across his forehead. His tolerance was wearing thin, and controlling his temper was a challenge with Anthony's behavior and Lilly's independence.

"Her grades and behavior in school are outstanding, that's not the problem; it's outside of the classroom."

"She's getting in trouble during recess?" Vincent raised his eyebrows.

"No, that's not it either. The teacher thinks Lilly is too concerned and worried about being wrong, making mistakes, and asking for help."

"Did she give you some examples?"

"Today Lilly was in the bathroom at lunchtime, some sixth-grade girls were pushing each other around, goofing off, and they accidentally pushed Lilly into the radiator."

"Did she get burned?" Vincent's impatience changed to concern.

"She has a second-degree burn on her elbow. They called the school nurse, who then called me. That happened at noon. At two fifteen the class had recess. Lilly didn't want to go outside. Mrs. Hanson thought Lilly was perspiring and looked pale. She barely touched Lilly's elbow to take her to the nurse and Lilly winced in pain. Mrs. Hanson then gently rolled up Lilly's sweater and found the burn. What bothers the teacher, the nurse, and me is, why didn't Lilly tell anyone what had happened? Instead, she sat for three hours in excruciating pain."

"Did anyone ask her why she didn't speak up?"

"They did; she said she didn't want anyone to get in trouble. What's going on with her, Vincent? Why would she be afraid to tell?"

Vincent's body went limp. He always had an answer for Gwen, but with Lilly, answers didn't come easy. He was out of reasons. "I don't know. She worries about everything, and she is spending more time alone. It's been like that ever since her First Communion and when Father Johan left it became worse. I don't see her playing much with Anthony, either. Do you?"

"No, they talk at night before bed, but you're right. We couldn't pry them apart six months ago."

"How about Joan? Did you ask her how Lilly is?"

"I did. Joan is indifferent. She's sixteen. They stay far away from each other."

"The older should keep watch over the younger."

"Let's not make this about Joan. It's Lilly we need to worry about."

Vincent sat back in his chair, recalling the days of his youth and what helped him get out of a bad mood. Smiling, he looked up at Gwen. "What about a puppy? When I was growing up my dog was my salvation. Maybe it's time we extend our family."

"With a dog? That's your solution?" Gwen asked in surprise.

"Can you think of a better one?"

"And where are we going to get a puppy? There is no way I am going to allow a dog in this house, and definitely not on the furniture or beds. No, Vincent, that won't happen."

Vincent laid his hand over hers. "I promise I will find a puppy that can live outside. I'll build a doghouse. We will insulate it and fill it with straw and old coats and when the weather is extreme, the dog can stay in the basement, if you allow."

Gwen looked into his green, sparkling eyes. Eyes she still could never say no to. "We can give it a try."

"It's the right thing to do, Gwen. Lilly loves animals and the outdoors. It will be good for Anthony, too. Raising a puppy will give them new responsibilities. I know a farmer with a litter of cocker spaniels. I'll talk to him tomorrow."

THE MILKMAN

"Can I, please, please?" Lilly begged.

"You'll have to hold on to the leash tighter than tight. Chipper is strong and she pulls."

"I will, I promise. I'm stronger than you think."

"Here, but stay with me. We'll walk together." He handed Lilly the red plastic leash. Chipper was now six months old and a healthy addition to the family's happiness.

Lilly held the leash proudly in her hand and kept a firm grip, waiting for the unexpected, just as Anthony had told her.

"You're doing a good job, Lilly. Chipper listens well to you. I think the two of you are close."

"We are. We talk all the time, and I brush her fur. She's the best friend I ever had."

"Do you want to play fetch with her on the side of the road?"

"Sure! Grab a stick."

"We'll leave the leash on just in case we have to grab her quickly."

They played on the damp morning grass alongside the road. Every now and then Chipper would lose her footing and slide for the stick as if she were coming into home base. Lilly and Anthony laughed at the sight.

A loud rumbling sound in the near distance stopped their play.

"Is that the school bus?" asked Lilly, confused.

"No, it's coming from the wrong direction." Anthony too was puzzled.

Seconds later, they saw a milk delivery truck speeding down the middle of the road, swerving from side to side. Anthony pulled Lilly back from the road's shoulder, and then went to grab Chipper's leash, but it was too late. Chipper had raced after the truck's tires.

Lilly saw Anthony miss the leash, so she took hold of it as it snaked across the wet leaves and hung on tight as Chipper dragged her along. Anthony screamed, "Let go, Lilly, let the leash go!"

I would rather go under the truck's tire with Chipper than let go of that leash. It's my job and responsibility to keep her safe. Lilly hung on tight.

Joan heard Anthony's yells and looked toward the commotion to see Lilly's body dragged onto the road, the leash still held tightly in her hands with no sign of letting go.

"Lilly, let go of the leash!" she yelled. The truck was not slowing down.

"No!" Lilly screamed back.

Joan sprinted forward and grabbed Lilly's legs, pulling hard and quick to drag her off the road and out of the truck's path. Lilly did not expect the jolt, and the leash slipped out of her hands. Chipper leaped forward toward the tires.

Lying on the ground, Lilly watched the front tires and then the back ones run over Chip's neck.

"Chipper! Chipper!" she screamed in horror, watching Chip's head flop. Her pet and best friend laid lifeless in the center of the road. No one had to tell her that Chipper was gone. She knew it and wished she were there, right next to her. Lilly fell into a deep state of shock, unable to look away from the sight, stuck in the dark world she associated with Frank.

Chipper was no more… One minute they were playing and the next she was dead…like her doll in the furnace, like Father Johan… They were in her life and then gone. Frank had warned her not to tell *anyone,* and Chipper knew everything. Frank was punishing her. Somehow he knew what she was thinking and doing.

"Joan, pick Lilly up and help her on the bus. Anthony, watch Eva so I can go and get Chipper," ordered a frantic Gwen. She gently lifted the warm yet lifeless body of their family pet in her arms. With haste she carried Chipper back to the house, with Eva following close behind.

Then she desperately called Vincent.

"Vincent, if Joan hadn't pulled Lilly off the road..."

"Gwen, slow down. Lilly's safe," Vincent reassured her.

"Anthony and Joan put her on the bus. She was bawling. I don't know why I didn't take her back to the house with me and Eva."

"It's probably good for her to be distracted with school. Where's Chipper?"

"I laid her in the garage. Can you come home?"

"Lay a blanket over her. I'll be home soon."

When he arrived Gwen led him to their pup. Vincent pulled back the blanket to observe the wounds. "She died quickly. Her neck is crushed. She didn't know what hit her. That damn milk truck driver." Vincent stuffed down his rage. "How long will it be before the kids come home?"

"About three hours."

"I don't want Lilly to see Chipper like this again. I'll build a little casket."

※

When Lilly stepped off the bus, she ran to her waiting father. In his arms, she felt a comfort that she greatly needed and hadn't felt all day. "Could you save Chipper?" She looked up at her father with a tear- stained face, full of hope.

"No, dear, Chipper is in heaven with Grandma. She'll watch over our pup, and it will be safe for Chipper to run like the wind, chasing everything in sight."

"There isn't a heaven for dogs," she retaliated.

"Of course there is! Why would you doubt that?"

"Because if we really had angels, God, and a heaven, bad things wouldn't happen." Lilly was serious. "I killed Chipper and I can't take it back. She was my responsibility."

It pained Vincent to hear his child take on such guilt.

"Lilly, you didn't kill her. The milk truck driver did. He was driving recklessly. He was the irresponsible one."

"You weren't there. If Anthony had the leash, Chipper would be right here with her tail wagging. I can't stand to think I will never be able to…pet her again. She was my best friend," Lilly sobbed.

"Maybe we can find a stuffed dog that looks like Chipper. You could cuddle it, and even comb its fur."

"We can't ever have another dog?" She asked with a grief-stricken face.

"Maybe someday, Lilly, but for now we need to heal."

After a few weeks of shopping in every nearby town, he and Gwen finally found the right stuffed animal, and a sparkle returned to Lilly's eyes. "Mom, Dad, thank you so much! It looks like Chipper! Where did you find her?"

"On a special shelf in a special store," Vincent grinned. "Can I put the red leash on her and take her for a walk?"

Gwen and Vincent looked at each other, not sure how Lilly was going to achieve that. "Sure," they both answered.

Lilly picked Chipper II up and carried her outside. Placing her on the ground, she began to walk, pulling the stuffed dog behind.

They settled down under the willow. *All that matters is that I have a dog again. You can't replace Chipper, but I can talk to you and Frank won't be able to hurt you, because you're not alive. We will be safe.* She pulled the stuffed dog close to her chest and buried her face in its soft, curly hair.

When she went to bed that night, she set Chipper II on the top of her headboard, looking over her bed. It helped her feel safe and protected, just like her statues and the black prayer book that remained tucked under her pillow.

※

With the arrival of spring, Lilly continued to mourn the loss of her four-legged friend.

"I don't know what I'd do without you," she told the water. "You're always here for me, cheering me up on my sad days with your lapping waves and sparkling stars."

She watched its current carry a large branch away. "That's what I wish I could do, drift away to a land of no worries, where I wouldn't feel so different from everyone else. I'm an ugly duckling. I don't fit in with my family." She began skipping stones. "I can't do anything right. There's always something wrong, no matter how hard I try. I'm angry, and sometimes mean to Mom and Dad. It's their fault. They keep letting Frank and Millie visit."

After a period of quietness, she continued releasing her thoughts to the river. "You never stop moving. Is that what you're trying to tell me to do?

"Don't give up and keep moving forward?"

She sat on the bank, pulling her legs in tight to her chest, attuned to the serenity of her surroundings, and allowing the wind to take her worries away.

Her heavy spirit lightened. "I think I'll ask Jane if she wants to take the canoe out today. That usually makes me feel better. Thank God I have her as a neighbor. She is my only friend out here in the boonies."

She stood and brushed herself off. "Thank you, river, for listening and for letting me feel how strong you are. See you later, Chipper." She looked up at the heavens.

A wave larger than the others pushed up on the shore, nearing her feet. She smiled.

1986 - SESSION FIVE - RED LIGHT, GREEN LIGHT

"Through all ages I blame myself. Even now." Lilly twisted her hair around a finger, concentrating on her thoughts.

"You believe the negative messaging that came from Frank."

"Yes. He drilled guilt and blame into my head as if they were common knowledge, like knowing your left from your right." She felt uneasy, as if a thick fog were rolling in, which wasn't unusual when anxious and stressed.

"Getting you to blame yourself gave him control."

"And it also gave *him* more power, while taking *mine* away."

Dr. Bricks paused shortly. "Let's try an activity. I want you to turn the blame around."

"How do I turn the blame around?"

"With words, try using '*accountability*' instead of '*blame*.'"

"How can a word change the way I feel?"

"A simple change in words and thinking can empower you; taking control away from Frank and back to you." Dr. Bricks continued, "For example, say, 'I blame Millie and Frank for messing up my childhood.'"

Lilly repeated his words. Hearing it come out of her mouth surprised her. "That made me mad as hell," she warned.

"Allow that feeling to stay. Now repeat, 'I hold Millie and Frank accountable for messing up my childhood.'"

She repeated the phrase, and the feeling of uncontrollable rage changed. Surprised, Lilly said, "That felt different. I sensed being older and wiser. Above Frank, and not below him...*Accountable.* It's empowering." Lilly was amused that one word had made such a huge change in her thought process.

"Now say aloud, 'I blame myself for the abuse in my life.'"

She struggled to get the words out and had to pull deep inside to release them. "I blame myself for the abuse in my life."

"Describe how that felt."

"It made me sick to my stomach and lonely. It was actually difficult to say. I had to force the words out."

"Try again, using *'accountable.'*"

"I am accountable for the abuse in my life!" Time ticked. "That is completely not true. I am *not* accountable for what happened to me."

"Explain."

"How could a child be accountable for crimes such as Frank's? He was an adult!" Lilly made another new connection.

"Yes! You were not responsible or blameworthy."

Lilly tilted her head to one side in curiosity. "When I heard myself say Frank was accountable, it sounded like he was going to jail. This works when I apply it to Millie too. But why did it have a different effect when I applied it to myself?"

"Because the real you knows the truth; you are not accountable. You are not to blame. You are releasing those feelings and getting closer to restoring who you were born to be."

"But the truth leaves behind an anger that I don't know what to do with!"

"Anger is difficult to get a handle on; still it's well worth the effort to do so. You know, many great acts of democracy started with anger, like the right for women to vote."

"Anger has always been a negative in my mind, something that leads to violence. I never thought of it as a positive."

"*You* choose how you cope with your anger. Helping others is an example of changing a negative to a positive and I believe you have been unknowingly doing so for most of your life."

"I dislike violence and avoid it at all costs. I seek out the opposite. I want to right all the wrongs. I don't want to be hateful. There is a prayer I said every night from the time I was eight until eighteen that helped me become that person."

"Do you remember it?"

"Bits and pieces. 'Where there is darkness, let me sow light. Where there is hatred, let me sow love.'" She sat in silence, remembering. "It's written on a little statue of a nun teaching. I received it as a gift on my First Communion."

"For a prayer to have influenced you with such strength and compassion is extraordinary. And as young as eight you were learning to positively empower yourself from anger."

"So is anger the same as guilt and anxiety? Are they like dominoes?"

"Interesting question. Guilt *is* an anxious feeling. It's difficult to feel guilty without feeling anxious. On the other hand, anger is tied more closely to fear or hurt."

"I think I am beginning to understand this better. Frank touching my body and using it as he did made me *angry*. He said everything he did was my fault. That made me afraid and anxious. That anxiety grew into guilt, even though I wasn't guilty."

"That's right. You were not guilty. You came to believe what Frank said about you. In psychology we call them 'introjections' or negative messages."

"How in the world did I manage? I'm not doing well as an adult, let alone a child!"

Lilly looked out the windows, over the garden. "His ugly messages never lost *their* voice; instead I lost mine!"

Dr. Bricks removed his glasses as he spoke to Lilly. "Let these words find a secure place in your mind: 'I am in the present. I am safe and protected. I am in front of my past.' See yourself standing strong and in control, while the past is behind you. Keep it there, not allowing it to creep forward."

In the silence of the room, Lilly repeated to herself, *I am safe and protected. I am in the present and the past is behind me.* She envisioned the dark world creeping up from behind, wanting to be front and center stage.

She put her arms out and shouted with authority, *"No!"*

BLACKOUT

"Lilly Francis, you are nearing eleven years old. That is certainly old enough to take the train to see your godparents. It will be fun and you'll be the only child for a week. They are going to take you shopping and to the zoo. Millie has a ton of plans to spoil you rotten."

"But Mom, I'm afraid to go on the train by myself."

"We have that worked out. Frank is going to ride the train up to our town and escort you back. A week later, we will come as a family to pick you up. You have nothing to be afraid of and it'll be fun!"

She doesn't know Frank and Millie as I do, Lilly thought. *Escort me, huh, what a lie! They always have different plans than what they tell Mom and Dad.*

"Don't I have any say in how to spend my summer vacation? Besides, we always take a trip to some other state. Aren't we doing that?"

"We can't travel this year, Lilly. Maybe next year we'll have enough money saved for a big trip. Our vacation will be going to the city to join you."

Something terrible is going to happen. I can feel it. Lilly smoothed her hand over her belly.

"Mom, why can't I wait and go with the family? I don't like the city! Two weeks will be an eternity!"

"The plans have been made. Millie has been waiting for you to be old enough to spend time alone with her and Frank. This is a privilege, Lilly. Most girls your age don't have this opportunity."

I would gladly give it up to one of them, Lilly kept her back talking in her head. *They'll never forgive themselves if I come home dead, because that's what I feel. There's no hope of being safe at their house.* She felt ill with worry and stress.

✳

"Tell us what you, Aunt Millie, and Uncle Frank did during your visit," asked Gwen on their return trip home.

"I don't remember." Lilly sat like a mannequin in the back seat and answered robotically.

"Oh, Lilly, I'm sure there's one thing you did that you will never forget."

I really don't remember. I can see myself getting on the train, but I don't remember the ride or getting off. I don't remember Millie or sleeping at their house. What I do see I cannot tell my parents about, because it's so strange. I know Frank forced a pink pill down my throat. He told me it would help my stomach ache. The next thing I remember is getting dizzy and then being in a church or a school with many people chanting and laughing. She thought hard for a *pleasant* memory.

"We went to a mall with a high escalator, and there was glass everywhere and chandeliers."

"See, I knew you would enjoy something from the trip. We don't have malls like that near us."

"We don't have a lot of things the city does," mumbled Lilly.

"I'm so happy you enjoyed yourself. Millie can't wait for you to come back next summer."

Lilly's mouth dropped open. *I will not go back. I would rather die or run away from home.* Her horns of resistance and self-protection grew stronger and sharper for her own sake.

Back in the country, her world was safe, but her constant anxiety worsened. She was obsessively on guard, in sleep and wakefulness, fearing the worst at any moment. For the rest of the summer she was lost and lifeless, trying to recall what happened that week, yet her mind remained blank. It was maddening.

One evening she sat with her back against the willow's trunk, taking in its strength and support. "My dear willow," she said, "please help me see what they did to me. Help me understand. Not knowing is like being tortured. I see faces I don't know. I see an altar. I see a stage. I see a clown and my clearest memory is two men in suits holding me under my arms and dragging me out to Frank's car. I couldn't walk. My legs were like rubber. We went through double glass doors as Frank led the way. They shoved me in the back seat. I remember feeling relief that it was over, but what was over? Where was I all that time? How can a week be gone forever?"

Lilly rammed her head against the bark, reawakened by the pain she felt.

"I have an incredible memory. I can remember Grandma's passing and I was only four. I can remember her shoes, her hair, and the dress she wore the day before she died. So why can't I remember one week with Frank and Millie?"

Uneasiness filled her head with dread, and fear walked with her every step, as if it were her shadow.

It was nearing summer's end and school was soon to begin. Gwen called out to Lilly, "You have mail! Come downstairs!"

Lilly ran down the steps with Eva close behind; even Anthony stepped away from his guitar practice to check out what the package was. Mail time in the boonies was a big event, and even bigger when there was a package.

"Is that for me?" Lilly asked with surprise, looking at a brown-wrapped box.

"Yes, it's a present from Millie and Frank!" Gwen replied.

Lilly's smile disappeared as she debated whether to open the box or not. The last gift they sent her was a stupid, ornate gold brush, comb, and mirror for her dresser. It reminded her of them and the city, nothing to do with her. She kept shoving them in her dresser drawer, and Gwen continuously returned the set to its proper place on top, in front of the mirror. Lilly knew the brush set was another way for her godparents to keep their image and memories alive. They never stopped plotting ways to get into her head.

"Can I save it for Christmas and open it then?" *It's worth a try,* thought Lilly, *even though Christmas is six months away.*

"Open the package," Vincent ordered.

Lilly refused to look at him. Vincent, the father of her dreams, was now becoming bossy and unable to manage his temper. The less she confronted him, the more secure she felt.

"Quit being so slow," complained Gwen.

Maybe I should give this gift to Mom, since she's more excited about it than me, but that would get me in trouble. Lilly opened the box. Her eyes bugged out at the neon green fabric with little blue starfish splattered all over it. It was nothing she had on her wish list.

"Take it out! Show us what Aunt Millie sent you," Gwen enthusiastically coached.

Reluctantly, Lilly pulled out a two-piece bathing suit.

"Oh, my, it's a bikini!" Gwen finally stopped raving and held her hand over her mouth.

"Mom, it's like wearing underwear in public and I'm not going to do that! Can we send it back? I will never wear it. I like my one-piece suit and feel comfortable in it."

"We don't return gifts. That would be downright rude," Vincent directly informed her.

"It's the thought that counts, Lilly. Aunt Millie and Uncle Frank are trying to please you. It's an expensive bikini. Feel the fabric! Look at where they bought it!" added Gwen.

"I don't care who else is wearing them, or what it feels like, or where it came from. You can wear it if you like it so much!" The words flew with anger from her mouth.

Vincent slammed his fist on the table, hard enough to send the box sliding to the floor. Lilly stepped back, and Eva moved closer to her mother's side.

"I don't want to hear you talk like that to your mother again! Is that understood?" Vincent walked toward Lilly.

Lilly didn't feel like a child anymore; she was raising herself and took orders from no one. "I'm not wearing it," she confirmed.

"They're coming to visit for Labor Day weekend, and we're going to the lake for a picnic. That's when you'll show your appreciation and wear it. Now apologize to your mother!" The veins in Vincent's forehead pulsated and his fists clenched tightly.

Lilly looked directly into his eyes. They were not the eyes of her father. They belonged to a beast, another monster that was trying to own and control her.

"I'm not going to apologize." She pointed to the bikini on the floor. "And I'm definitely not going to wear *that* to the beach with *them here*." She turned and ran into her bedroom, slamming the door behind her.

The bang was the last straw to set Vincent off. He ran after Lilly, punched the door open, and grabbed her by the hair.

Lilly left reality. She felt not her father's hands pulling her hair, but Frank's, as he dragged her down the hall toward her mother. Gwen sat stone cold on the kitchen chair, as if it were her throne.

"Let me go! I hate you!" Lilly fought back and screamed for him to stop, but Vincent overpowered her. She looked for Eva and saw her peeking from behind Gwen. Lilly stopped fighting. She didn't want Eva to see her that way.

"Here, now you're at your mother's feet. Kiss them and apologize!"

Lilly was back in the woods; she was by Frank's altar, spitting and shining his shoes, kissing his ring, doing everything he told her to do.

Not again, she thought. *Never will I stoop that low.* She held her stance without crying, or screaming, and spit on Gwen's foot.

She felt Vincent's open hand slap her across the face repeatedly and then move down her body. Whenever she caught a glimpse of Eva, her heart felt it was bleeding out. That pain was worse than any physical blow.

He continued waiting for her respectful apology, but she had none. *I refuse to become like him or Frank. I'll turn my other cheek; that's what Dad says we should do when we're mad at someone.* She saw the blank look in her father's face as he shoved her back down the hall and into the bedroom, shutting her in.

"Don't come out for the rest of the day!"

Lilly crawled to her walk-in closet and curled up in the dark corner. She replayed the scene, seeing her mother sitting there like a queen watching a tiger rip her child apart. *Why didn't Mom do something to stop Dad? She didn't even take Eva out of the room. I don't have a thread of love for her. I don't need a mother.*

※

Hours later there was a knock on the closet door. "Who is it?" she called out defiantly.

"Quiet, it's me, Anthony. Can I come in?"

"Yeah, the door's open." She hid her face between her knees, not wanting Anthony to see how hard she had been crying.

Anthony sat down on the floor next to Lilly and put his arms around her shoulders. "Why didn't you cry or say you were sorry so it would stop? The quieter you were, the angrier Dad got. He saw that as being disrespectful. All you needed to do was cry."

"I know that, but he went too far today. He's like Frank."

"What do you mean by that?" Anthony asked.

Lilly panicked. She had to think fast without completely lying.

"You know, all big and grown up and can do anything they want and not answer to anyone."

"No, I don't get it." Anthony wasn't buying in.

"Frank does what he pleases when he pleases. If he wants to go for a car ride, he does. If he wants to go swimming, he will; that sort of thing."

"I get it now. It sucks being a kid, but it'll get better when you start junior high and high school. Mom and Dad will give you more freedom."

"I don't see that happening. They have it out for me."

"Clean up your attitude, Lilly. You were never mean or hurtful before; why start now?"

"You would never understand, trust me."

"It's that girl thing, isn't it?"

As angry as she was, she couldn't hold back the humor she saw in Anthony's remark. "That's exactly what the problem is," she replied. It was a flawless way out.

"So are you going to wear the bikini or not?"

"I'll wear it, but just that one day, and then it goes in the river."

"You'll look great, really, sis, don't worry about that."

"That's not the point. I shouldn't have to wear something that makes me feel uncomfortable."

"I don't blame you and make sure to knot it around a big rock when you throw it in the river. Otherwise it'll float back to shore." He stood up and offered his hand to help her up from the floor.

She grabbed hold. He was the best brother a girl could ask for.

TEEN YEARS

1966-1972

TIMES OF CONFUSION

The residual anger over the bikini, and the fact that she had to wear it soon, hadn't lightened for Lilly as she prepared for junior high.

Shopping with Mom isn't fun anymore. She still wants me to wear dresses! We can't see eye to eye on fashion, colors, or styles, so we argue. Lilly fumed as she sorted through racks of choices.

"Mom," she said, "I know you want me to buy dresses, but they're not as popular as they once were. Like when Joan was thirteen. Girls rarely wear them in school now, but what about skirts?" She held an A-line skirt in front of her, smiling with hopelessness and hopefulness at the same time.

"The skirts are too short," Gwen replied.

Lilly didn't want to argue and kept the conversation light. "Yes, they are short, but we can wear them to school if we also wear tights. I like that look! We could find a few skirts, tights to match, and a couple of sweaters and blouses. That will last me all year. I'll mix and match."

Gwen watched Lilly put the skirt back on the rack and thought, *She never was a girl of lace and frills. She has always been more natural and modern. Times have changed since Joan was her age.* "Let's take a look," she said agreeably. "I've always liked the navy blue and green school plaid. Maybe there's a skirt like that!"

"There is! I saw it when we walked in. Wouldn't it be cute with a white blouse and a navy-blue V-neck sweater, and navy tights?" Lilly replied with appreciation. "Come on, I'll show you!"

A couple hours later Lilly left the department store with bags of clothes that she knew would look sharp on her for her first year of junior high. "Are you nervous about moving to a new school?" Gwen asked.

"I'm a little worried about the seniors. I heard that they shove seventh graders in lockers and take their books away; stuff like that."

"I think you'll find them much more grown up; those are just rumors. Anthony will be a junior this year. That may be helpful. How about friends? Who are you hanging around with these days?"

"I don't have any real friends since Rita moved away, except for Jane and we only get together when we're home. We go our separate ways at school." Lilly shrugged. "I don't know who I'll chum around with, but there will be loads of kids to get to know."

"That's a grown-up way of thinking."

They were encouraging words, but Lilly felt that friendships were like Chipper: here one day, gone the next, leaving her brokenhearted.

"How was your first day, Lilly?" Vincent asked, eagerly anticipating her usual creative recollections.

"It was a mess and confusing, and I got lost nearly every hour. I had to ask directions to find my locker! That was embarrassing!"

"Did you meet any new girls?" asked Gwen.

"I met a few in band class. They're nice, but they live in town, which is too far away for me to hang out with them. And then there were the boys! They don't kick me in the shins or tap me on the shoulder to get my attention. They flirt with words instead. They're looking for girlfriends, and the girls are looking for boyfriends."

"Finally, you can stop flirting with *my* friends!" teased Anthony.

"Leave the boys alone. Besides, you're too young to be flirting,"

Vincent advised. "There's plenty of time for that later. Enjoy your girlfriends for now."

She stewed over her father's comment. *Mom flirts with Dad, Joan flirts with a lot of boys and Anthony flirts with girls. He says they're beautiful. I want a boy to think I'm beautiful too*

For Lilly, going to junior high was an opportunity to pack up the old suitcase, full of childhood memories, and put it away in the attic while opening a new one and filling it with different memories; hopefully happier ones. However, she believed her parents felt differently, wanting to keep her a child.

❈

"Could I hang out with the girls from band at the malt and burger shop one day a week, after school? That's where they go to get to know one another," Lilly said, envying the kids that lived in town. "I would feel more like everyone else if I could do that."

The answer from both parents came fast and definite: "No!"

"Why not, what's the harm?" she demanded. "They're good kids from good families. Nothing bad would happen." She was beginning to boil with rage. *Mom and Dad don't trust me. They think I want to be with the wild ones. They're so wrong. They have no idea of what I've been going through and how important it is for me to be a normal teenager. They want to hold me back, just like Millie and Frank do.*

"This is a conversation we will have when you're sixteen and not a day before, end of discussion." Vincent sternly answered.

That's the stupidest rule I've ever heard of! Treating me the same as Joan and waiting until I'm sixteen to be like everyone else. Holding firm to her beliefs, she carried on. "Can you give me one chance to show you how safe and fun it would be, just one, please? Anthony, tell them about the malt shop."

"I'm not getting into this!" He placed his dishes in the sink and left. Gwen helped Eva clean up her mess while Lilly and Vincent remained seated, ready to duke it out.

"No, not until you're sixteen," Vincent repeated.

"Dad, you're not being fair. You're not even trying to negotiate."

"When you're more mature, we'll discuss this further."

Mature! Lilly's head throbbed with fury. *I've been protecting and guarding this family for as long as I can remember, and he's so blind to it!* "Isn't cooking dinner for the family mature? I clean this big house from corner to corner and do well in school. I have many grown-up responsibilities. How can you not see that? I want to be more like the other girls my age and not a role model for Mom."

"Sixteen, Lilly, no dating until sixteen and watch your tongue."

"Sixteen is an eternity away! That's a ridiculous way to think and it's not dating. I just want to hang out with other kids!" She paused to watch Vincent's reaction. There was nothing positive about it. She sat back in her chair. "So what happens at sixteen? Do I miraculously wake up on my birthday with wisdom and understanding that I don't have now?"

"It's not safe to be with a group of kids all the same age. Things can go wrong."

"So you don't trust me. That's what you're really saying, isn't it?"

"You're too young to have that kind of trust at thirteen. Trust has to be earned."

Oh, dear Lord, thought Lilly. *If they can trust any of their kids, it's me.*

"I'm going to be teen, not ten, and I know about the dangers."

"What dangers do you know about?" Vincent briefly paused over his dessert and looked up at her.

Lilly pulled her horns in. This was getting too close to her secret world. She cautiously continued, "I know about the danger of strangers, and about getting in cars, and I would never do that. I don't like older kids, except for Anthony and his friends. It's safer to be with my classmates."

Vincent pointed a commanding finger at her. "We're done discussing this."

Infuriated, Lilly replied, "Mom wants me to be with girls and act more like a girl, and I *want* to, but neither of you is willing to give me the chance. There are no girls around here except for Jane, and we are both tomboys. How can you have double standards?"

"Go to your room! You can wash and dry the dishes later." Vincent threw his napkin down on his plate.

"Lilly, do you have to always start an argument around the dinner table?" asked Gwen.

Lilly pushed her chair back and stomped off to her room. *They don't understand me! This is when I'm supposed to go to the movies with girls, while boys sit a row behind us and toss popcorn in our hair. Kids aren't going to wait for me to grow up. They'll move on, because that's how it works. You're in or out, and if I have to wait until sixteen, I'll be out. No is not an acceptable answer. I tried to reason with them, but they left me no choice. I have to take matters into my own hands.*

When I'm with other kids my age I feel a hope of normalcy, of being like them, even with my secrets. But in order for that to happen, I need freedom, which Mom and Dad don't think is important.

Her parents' twisted rope of love wrapped around her ankles.

WHAT NO ONE SEES

"Is Labor Day *this* weekend?" she asked Anthony.

"Yup, and I can hardly wait for a day at the beach. It's supposed to be warm and it's the last weekend of summer!"

"That's not true. Officially, summer doesn't end until the middle of September."

"You're just upset about the bikini."

"Darn right I am! Think of all the kids we know that will be there. It's embarrassing!"

"Chill, it's only one day."

Yeah, thought Lilly, *one day of humiliation on the beach, but what else are my evil godparents planning?*

They arrived early Saturday morning. Lilly sickened, watching their new, more expensive car pull up in the driveway. "Lilly, darling, come give your auntie a kiss."

Lilly reluctantly gave her a peck on the cheek.

"I cannot wait to see you in the bathing suit we sent. Your mother says you look like a model," Millie boasted, looking at Frank, who returned a grin and chewed his cigar with elated pleasure.

Lilly observed their glances. They were definitely up to something, and whatever it was, it wasn't good for her.

"Frank and I had such a good time when you visited. We noticed that you aren't our 'little' Lilly anymore. That's when we saw this suit in the mall and had to buy it for you!"

"You could have brought it with you; you didn't have to spend the money to ship it," Lilly suggested, catching a disapproving glare from Gwen.

"We wanted you to have it right away, so you could enjoy it before we came."

More like you wanted to torture me for a few weeks to get under my skin. Lilly stewed.

"You can come and spend time with us whenever you want—Christmas, Easter—our door is always open for you," Millie continued speaking.

Yeah, right, thought Lilly. *You'd love that. Destroy the little of me that's* left.

"The city isn't my kind of place. I like it right here," Lilly replied.

"You may change your mind as you get older." Millie snubbed Lilly and turned to address Gwen. "When will we be leaving for the park?"

"As soon as we finish packing the food," answered Gwen. "Lilly, go and get ready. Check on Eva, too."

※

Lilly felt waves of nausea. Her gut was usually right: this was not going to be a safe, fun-filled day.

The family found a table with a nearby grill that was close to the water. Vincent and Frank opened a few cold beers, while Millie and Gwen took out the snacks and started to prepare for lunch. Lilly took Eva to the sandy beach to build a castle. Her father's old white shirt helped cover up the humiliating neon bikini underneath.

The heat and warm breeze were hypnotizing. The air had a hazy fog that added to the mystical feel. It was days like this that she could write about in school—minus the bikini.

After finishing a sand castle, Lilly brought Eva back to Gwen. Then she jumped into the cool water to join Anthony in a splash fight. "Gwen, look at your teenagers. Is that acceptable behavior?" inquired Millie.

Gwen smiled, "It is, Millie. They're still kids, and they're not causing any harm. Lilly looks so darn cute in that bikini, don't you think?" Millie glanced over at her nervous husband.

"Are you listening, Millie?" asked Gwen.

"Yes, of course I am, Lilly looks cute in anything. She's going to have a lot of boyfriends!"

"Millie, she's too young to even think about boys. She still occasionally takes her Barbie dolls out."

"I wouldn't tell too many people that! She's too old." Millie gave her sister a shame-on-you look. "Why don't you let Frank take her out into the deeper water to practice her front crawl?"

"That's a good idea. She's struggling with that stroke. Maybe a lesson or two from Frank would help." Gwen waved Lilly to the picnic table. "What is it, Mom?" she asked as she grabbed a cookie.

"Frank is going to take you out into the water to practice your front crawl, just for a little while, and then we'll eat." Lilly fell speechless. *This was the reason behind the bikini.*

"Come on Lilly, I have some surprises for you." Frank took her hand and led her to the water. She looked back at her parents. They were watching, smiling and waving, clueless about Frank's true intentions.

"What do you know about drowning?" Frank whispered in her ear.

Lilly was terrified of the word. Vincent had hammered facts about drowning into her and Anthony's head, to keep a sensible fear in them, since the river was their playground.

Frank chuckled at the look on her face. "That's what I thought. Be quiet and play along with me, and there won't be an accident."

Shame was killing her as his bare hands touched her skin in the deep waters. No one could see, but she could feel. He had never taken such a risk of being caught until now. It had always been private. Lilly looked at the beach, and felt hundreds of eyes looking back. She drowned in humiliation. She believed they saw what Frank was doing to her in the deep waters. She felt disgraced and degraded. *Drowning would be a blessing*, she thought.

There was no more need to hide or try to escape. Frank and Millie were now into the thrill of going public.

Frank saw the family gathering for lunch. He had been in the water with Lilly long enough, but not too long as to arouse worry in her parents. He led her back to shore.

Lilly could think of nothing but the horror she had just gone through while her parents were right there watching but unable to see.

"There were so many bluegills in that deep water," boasted Frank, trying to impress Vincent with fishing knowledge and draw attention to himself, and away from Lilly.

"Is that so? Were there any other fish sightings?" Vincent asked Lilly.

Lilly felt eyes upon her. "Minnows, there were a lot of minnows." Another lie, the hate that filled her hissed. Frank's trying to make it sound like he did everyone a big favor in helping me with a swimming stroke. Look at them. No one sees what a fake he and Millie are. No one but me. He didn't teach me anything about swimming! I have to get away from all of them!

"Can I please be excused?" Lilly asked her parents. "I'm not that hungry."

"Drink your water and you can go." She gulped it down, gathered the big white shirt over her, and found a place on the sandy beach, far from the family, to lie down.

She gazed into the sky, watching large cumulus clouds chase one another. She sent her hate up to them and watched it drift away. Her heart began to settle and her breathing returned to a comfortable pace— until a sand ball whacked her on her stomach. It was Anthony, waiting for retaliation.

Some things had to stay constant in her life. That was vital for survival. She stood up and chased him down the wet, sandy shore, aiming an even bigger sand ball at the back of his head.

For now, she was out of harm's way.

1986 - SESSION SIX - SERIOUS CONFRONTATIONS

"My early teens were confusing because of all the changes happening. I was set on making a new life, with happy memories, so Frank wouldn't dominate my thinking. And junior high was the perfect opportunity for a fresh start."

"Tell me about the changes."

"Dad didn't trust me at all, and his temper grew short. Mom rarely listened to what I was trying to say. She wanted me to be a replica of herself, which wasn't going to happen. Then throw in Frank, who was mentally destroying me and forcing drugs into my system so I couldn't remember his attacks. It was as if the world didn't want me in it."

"You felt abandoned."

"Abandoned, misunderstood...I knew my life was not normal, but when I became a teen, I realized my home wasn't either. The only way I could see happiness was to pull away from Mom and Dad and take care of myself."

"Your new awareness brought on a need for more independence."

"You could say that. I watched and learned. I thought that if I could be more like the other kids, I would be okay. I could escape from both worlds to find my normal. No one understands how hard it was, *trying* to fit in while living with so many lies and secrets."

"It sounds overwhelming."

"My heart ached to scream the truth. It was torture to tiptoe around in secrecy. How could I feel normal after what he did to me at the beach and all the other times! I was scared out of my mind thinking of what he was going to do next—like maybe kill me! He stopped being afraid of getting caught. That changed his game and made me more terrified."

"How frightening and lonely that would be for anyone at any age."

"He said if I told the police it would be my word against his, and judges don't like kids. I would look and sound insane. They would put me in a hospital for crazy people because of my fragmented memory due to those damn drugs he forced me to take! That was his insurance plan. As soon as I became old enough to fight back, he wiped out my memory. It is frightening to lose years. Between ten and thirteen, I remember very little. It was then when I grew more insecure and untrusting with everyone, even my parents. That's when the trouble at home started."

"It was a very sensitive and emotional time of growing up."

"So I blocked it out, forever," Lilly sullenly replied.

"It helped you cope. Maybe those years are better left unknown for your own safety and health."

"Will that keep me from healing?"

"No. What you do remember is filling in for those years."

Dr. Bricks listened intently, as Lilly shifted nervously in her chair.

"I felt I could be a better parent than they were," Lilly commented as she twisted her hair around her pointing finger.

"You do realize that in your teens, your brain was not yet developed enough to reason and see consequences the same as an adult."

Lilly looked at him in disbelief. "I don't agree. I think that there were situations where I made more sense than they did, because I knew what would help. They had no clue. Their voice was the *only* voice. Mom saw me as an embarrassment and Dad saw me as defiant and disrespectful. I wasn't either. I was angry. I started to blame them for my life."

"How did you want to see your parents?"

"I wanted them to talk to me like an adult, explaining their ideas and listening to mine instead of yelling and demanding. And being physical was completely unacceptable in my eyes. They could have grounded me, or insisted that we talk until we reached an understanding and it would have made a much bigger impact. But they didn't and their actions pushed me further away."

"The majority of teens struggle with the transformation from a child to a teen *without* abuse and broken family bonds. The trauma you were dealt had to make it even more so."

"Maybe that's part of it. I gave up on hoping they would be the parents I needed."

"Tell me about your relationship with your father during that time."

"When I became a teen and grew more independent, he grew overprotective and developed a hot temper. He took everything I did personally. I was messing up his perfect world, and he had to reclaim it by showing he was in control."

"You felt he wanted you to be perfect." Dr. Bricks replied as he recalled his first meeting with Lilly.

"Dad had an obsession with cleanliness and being orderly. We had to wipe our feet off seven times on the rug in the hallway as we entered the house. Then he would watch us wash our hands before dinner, counting to numbers again. There were exact counts of numbers for using the soap and another for rinsing our hands, and another for rinsing the dishes, and so on. Sometimes he would explode just *thinking* that we weren't listening to him. It was impossible to achieve his expectations. Knowing this, I rebelled, which led to more confrontation."

"He ruled the house."

"Not really. Dad did the punishing. Mom wouldn't hit or spank any of us kids. She yelled, 'Wait until your father gets home.' Then Dad listened to her side and we got our punishment."

"You were punished, not disciplined?" he asked.

Feeling confused Lilly responded, "Is there a difference?"

"Punishment is an impulsive act out of anger. Discipline is an act out of love. Discipline builds on a child's view of what is right and wrong to help them make healthy choices, leading to being independent. On the other side is punishment, which hurts the child, taking away their control and building dependence."

Lilly replied quickly. "I received punishment. The word *discipline* belonged in school, but not at home. And when you mentioned that punishment creates dependency, I connected immediately."

"How so?"

"I think Dad felt that being a good parent meant that his children needed to depend on him. He also couldn't let go of control. Children were to be seen, not heard. I fought him on both. No one was going to control me and I could take care of myself."

Lilly stopped, looked out the windows, and calmed herself. Then she continued.

"But Mom and Dad didn't know anything about child development except for what they experienced themselves."

"Does that make it alright to be physically abusive?"

Lilly fidgeted in her chair. "No, it's not an excuse, especially now. It's all over the television, in magazines and books but I felt bad for my father. He carried some heavy weight."

"What makes you think that?"

"He would frequently come into my room, apologizing and crying with me. He told me stories about his father, who was very mean and he talked about how the war changed him. I didn't like him for hitting me, but I understood he was doing what a father did, at my mom's command. Dad hit me and had the final word. One would think I hated him more when actually that wasn't always the case. Mom watching and doing nothing was unforgivable. I felt Mom gave up on me and I blamed her for the beatings."

Dr. Bricks explained, "Physical pain heals more quickly than emotional pain. That may help explain some of your mixed feelings."

"True, the bruises healed and I carried on, but emotional messages, especially negative ones, stayed around a lot longer."

"Lilly, it's allowable to feel a full array of emotions toward *both* of your parents. They are human, and with parenting come successes and failures."

"We figure that out when we have children of our own, don't we? It sounds like our house was a nightmare all the time, but that's not true. It had balance, which kept me sane during the insane times, especially in my younger years. I saw love and felt love. That has been a key element in my survival. It kept me searching to feel it again"

"Love is an important gift to receive from both of your parents."

Lilly took a Kleenex to wipe her eyes. "This is so hard. Sometimes I want to quit, walk out, and return to a life without therapy. Crawl back into my comfortable shell and live the way I always have, that of avoiding reality."

"A healing journey isn't a timed test."

"I know that. I live taking steps forward and backward. That's not new to me; it's my norm."

"If you could go back, what would you do or say differently with your parents?"

"I would explain why I was the way I was. I would forgive them for all the things they did wrong, because like me, they were manipulated. We all suffered, but there was always love, even if it didn't appear to be so. And I would tell them how important that love is even today." Lilly held the decorative pillow tightly in her arms.

"Time continues to move forward, Lilly; it's never going to pause for a right moment. So, what's stopping you from sharing what you just said with them now?"

She was ready to reconcile, however, her stubbornness was holding her back. She stood up and walked over to a bookshelf. Eyeing a statue of a woman and a child, she picked it up and observed the beauty of its lines. "Sometimes the world is ugly, and there's not much we can do. If an opportunity comes along to make it better, we should grab it, right?" she asked Dr. Bricks.

Nodding in agreement he answered, "I think that is a healthy way to look at life."

NO FAIRY GODMOTHER

"Millie, come and look at our Lilly. I put her hair up and applied a little makeup." Gwen stood back, admiring her young daughter, as Millie rushed into the bedroom, dressed to the nines in an evening gown.

Millie paused, placing her hands over her mouth. "Oh, Lilly, you look so grown up! Frank, Frank..." she called. "Bring your camera. We have to get photos of Lilly."

"Mom," Lilly looked at Gwen with dread. "Please tell Aunt Millie no pictures. You and Dad can send the one you took."

"You have been doing nothing but complaining ever since we got here."

"I told you to leave me home with Jane's family and I warned you about making me wear this stupid dress! Weddings are for adults, not kids!"

The tightness in her chest was choking her. The nylons were suffocating, the heels made her feel unsteady, and the dress made her feel like she was eight and pretending to be a grown-up; she wanted her jeans back.

"Millie, Lilly doesn't like pictures, never has. I have no idea why she hates cameras so much. I'll send you one of ours."

"Nonsense, Frank is right here." Millie turned to him. "Take one of her by the window with the lace curtains blowing against her. It's perfect!"

Lilly didn't look at Frank or the camera. She knew that if she did he would be chewing that slimy cigar as he always did to threaten her and make her squirm. When the clicks stopped, she faced her mother.

"Is it time to go?"

Lilly's brashness upset Gwen. "Are you going to ruin everyone's day because of a stupid camera?"

"What about this stupid dress and the stupid shoes and the stupid nylons?" Lilly snapped back.

"I'm going to let this go for now, but I don't want to hear anymore back talk for the rest of the trip." Gwen glared at Lilly. "Go downstairs and make sure Eva's ready while I finish my makeup."

"What do you know about the babysitter Millie hired for later?" Lilly was wary of any plan her godparents had put in motion.

"She's nineteen and Millie wouldn't hire just anyone. I'm sure she will be fun and do a great job. Frank will pick her up when he brings all of you back here."

"Right, I'm sure he will." Lilly left in search of Eva.

What did she mean by that? Gwen thought as she watched Lilly walk away. *I have no idea anymore of what goes on in that girl's head.*

❋

After the reception dinner, Millie gathered Lilly, Anthony, and Eva as if they were her own; gloating in pride as she paraded with them through the crowd. "Here they are, Frank. Are you ready?" she asked.

"Sure am. I'll be back within the hour," Frank replied quickly. "We have to let Mom and Dad know we are leaving!" insisted Lilly.

"They're dancing to one of their favorite songs. Look at them, like two young lovers. I'll tell them as soon as the song is over," Millie replied.

"We can wait," shot back Lilly.

"Nonsense," Frank interrupted. "There's no need to worry. I know this city like the back of my hand. Millie, I'll be back before you know it!"

Lilly took hold of Eva's hand. *I don't believe for a minute that Millie and Frank aren't up to something. It is never as simple as "going home."*

It wasn't long before they were back at Frank's house. Lilly sighed with relief. Maybe this trip would turn out all right after all. Perhaps she was wrong about their plotting against her.

Frank pulled up alongside his sidewalk. "Here we are, kids! Anthony, take Eva and get her ready for bed. Lilly, you and I will pick up the babysitter. I need company to keep me awake. Anthony, here's a key to the front door and make sure you lock it as soon as you get in."

Lilly's eyes opened wide. *How could I be so stupid? How many times have I fallen for this trap? I put myself right into his neat little plan.* She continued to scold herself. *I see exactly what he's doing. He knows Anthony won't think anything of us riding alone together because he's taken me for rides before. How did I not see this coming?* Her hands began to tremble.

With Anthony and Eva safely in the house, Frank gave Lilly her orders.

"Get out!" he ordered, pulling Lilly from the back seat and shoving her into the front. He slammed the door behind him and quickly took off toward the highway.

Placing his hand tightly around her arm, he pulled her close, smiling like the Cheshire Cat. He was an ugly man. Yellow was his color. His skin and teeth were yellow. The whites of his eyes were yellow, and his nails were layers of gross yellow and as hard as stone. He looked like a week- old casserole.

The smell of booze filled the car as he sipped his whiskey and drove recklessly down the freeway. He glanced over at Lilly, looking at her more than he did the road. She tensed with fear.

"Here, have a drink," he insisted, handing her the bottle.

"No, thank you," she snapped back at him, keeping her eyes on the road.

He chuckled at her reaction. "It will help you relax and enjoy our time together."

"I never enjoy our time together."

He put the whiskey bottle on the floor.

"It's nice to see you looking more like your mother. And this dress..." He paused to put his hand on her knee. "It really shows off your figure." As his hand moved higher, Lilly slapped it.

Frank chewed his cigar nervously and gripped her leg harder. "Don't be too smart. People die on this freeway every day. You should see when a semi-truck collides with a car. That's something!" He laughed with excitement. "I saw one a few weeks ago and stopped to take a look. I couldn't make out where the people were, it was such a tangled mess. I have a picture. I'll show it to you." He made a move to take out his wallet, leaving no hands on the steering wheel.

"No!" Lilly shouted, watching the cars whiz around them as they swerved in and out of lanes. "I believe you!" *He is the last person on this earth I want to be with as I take my final breath. Oh, dear God, don't make me into pieces of flesh.* She closed her eyes and let his hand do what it wanted, as she followed his every command. When he had enough, he began to pet her like some kind of animal.

Seeing only the colors of taillights in front of her, she allowed her mind to float until Frank made a sharp exit off the highway, down a ramp, and into a residential area.

They pulled up to the sitter's house. She was waiting on the porch. Lilly watched her skip down the steps toward the car. She didn't look nineteen, wearing a low-cut sweater and taking drags off of a cigarette. Her hair was long and blonde, with dark brown, almost black roots. Her face painted heavily with makeup, especially around the eyes. Millie had duped Gwen again. There was no way her mother would allow this person to sit for Eva, let alone be in the house.

Frank leaned across Lilly and opened the door. "Get in the back," he snarled. Lilly gladly fled to the back seat, feeling the worst was over.

"Hi, Gracie, sweetie, are you ready?" His voice was all sugary and nauseating.

"Hi there, big guy." She engaged Frank in his favorite sloppy French kisses.

Frank looked back at Lilly and snickered, "Take notes, maybe you can learn something from Gracie!"

"Here." He picked up the whiskey bottle and handed it to the sitter, who took several big swallows.

It was a long ride back to the house with Frank moving at a snail's pace. She could live with the noises from the front seat and his occasional sarcastic remark about her inexperience as long as he didn't touch her again.

ONE LOOK, ONE TOUCH

The stress of feeling like a mixed-up adult-teen was sucking the life out of her, leaving too little optimism and too much sadness. She had to get out, have some freedom and be with others her age. She had to do something to help her feel normal.

"Mom, I was thinking that I would like to compete for first chair in band class and to do that I need private lessons," she explained as they made supper together.

"When do they offer them?" asked Gwen.

"That's the problem; they're always after school." Lilly crossed her fingers. "How long do they last?"

Her heart fluttered. "About an hour, maybe a little longer, it depends on the music we're working on."

"Let me talk to your father. Anthony has his license, so he could go into town to pick you up, and it would give him driving practice."

Lilly bit the bottom of her lip and grinned. This was the closest her mom ever came to hearing her needs.

At the supper table the topic returned. "Vincent. Lilly wants to take private music lessons to compete for first chair. Do you think Anthony could drive into town one night a week to pick her up?"

Vincent looked at Anthony and then at Lilly. He couldn't help but wonder what the two had up their sleeves. "I guess we can try, but only for band lessons, Lilly. Don't push it any further. And

Anthony, I'll be checking the mileage to make sure it's just town and back."

After supper, she and Anthony paired up to wash and dry the dishes. Anthony whispered, "Why didn't you give me a heads-up on this?"

"I just thought of it. Great idea, don't you think?" Lilly was all smiles.

"Yes, but I know you're going to be taking off with your friends."

"You're right, but I'm going to have a thirty-minute lesson first! It'll take you another thirty minutes or more to get to town, which gives me an hour of being me!" Lilly needed that—time to be the teenager she was, and not the child her parents saw.

"You're going to get us both in trouble."

"No, I won't. I'll always be in front of the school at the exact time you tell me, promise, cross my heart and everything else. There's no other way for me to have fun. I tried asking truthfully, that didn't work, so now I have to sneak around behind their backs. No matter how hard I try to please Mom and Dad, I can't. Lately they're not happy with anything I do. I'm not brainy Joan or loving Eva. I'm Lilly, and I'm complicated."

"Why do you have to be so complicated?"

"I just am. It's how I was born."

"That's not true."

"Well, things change and so do people. I wish they could see that."

"You're wishing for a miracle."

Lilly looked at Anthony in surprise. "You feel like me, too, don't you?"

"No, but I try to understand your feelings. I think there's something you're not being honest about, and if you were, Mom and Dad wouldn't be so hard on you."

"That's ridiculous." She refocused on the dishes, thinking about Anthony's comment.

※

"Lilly, what do you like in a boy?" asked one of her new friends as they sat in a booth at the ice cream shop.

"My dream boy has to be clean cut, smart, and polite," she answered. "He would have to pass the test of my parents, which won't be easy! I'm not interested in the wild ones."

Lilly wanted to pinch herself to make sure this was really happening.

"Are you kidding? They're so adventurous!"

"I don't see them that way. They tick me off when they disrupt class, or whistle when I walk by. It's disgusting." Frank whistled, and it always sent chills down her back.

※

With time and the help of friends—and a long break from Frank— she grew more comfortable with the boys in her class. By eighth grade, she had a new confidence and a new attraction: one boy who turned her head whenever he was near. Something about him was different, and seeing him made her stomach flip, in a good way.

He walked with confidence and had a sincere laugh, the kind that made others laugh with him. He was smart and smelled wonderful. In fact, she hadn't noticed that boys had a scent until he came along. The problem was that he didn't know she existed.

She thought about him daily in her quiet moments by the river. It was nice to have something to think about other than a troubled past and complicated home life. She went to bed early so morning would come sooner and she could get to school to see him again. There was a bounce in Lilly's step and a warm glow in her face.

One day, Julie teased, "Hey, Lilly, I've watched you checking out Blake at lunch for like the past three months. When are you going to let him know you like him? Or are you just going to gawk at him?"

"I don't gawk!" Lilly blushed. "Besides, I don't think he knows I'm alive. He's always with a group of guys, and you know how they are."

"He knows; I've seen him check you out." Julie's grin owned her face.

"No way." Lilly balled up a napkin and tossed it at her. "That's not funny."

"Look, you're totally red in the face! You really do like him, don't you?"

"I do," she admitted with an even deeper blush. "I think he's flawless and he has a laugh that makes me laugh."

"Wow, how long have you felt this way?"

"I noticed him back in seventh grade, but this year, I don't know, he looks different and more interesting."

"Oh, you have it bad!"

"What do I have 'bad'?"

"You're in l-o-v-e!" Julie said, making a kissy twist with her fingers.

"Oh, give it up. It's a one-sided crush, that's all. I'd never be pretty enough for him."

"Don't say that! You're really cute, and there are plenty of boys that would love to walk you to class or take you to a movie."

"Forget it. My parents won't allow me to have a boyfriend until I turn sixteen. That's when a magical spell will fall over me, and I'll be all grown up. Until then, forget it."

"But what about all the great times we had in town?"

"They thought I had band practice." They laughed together, recalling special memories. Then Lilly sat up straight. "How could I get him to notice me without looking or acting stupid?"

"I know he runs track, and they have a meet this Friday night. It's out of town, but you could bake him something, like cookies. You're the best cook in home economics."

"Isn't that kind of corny, handing him some cookies?"

"They say a way to a man's heart is through his stomach!"

"You're such a goofball. I'll think about it, but talking, like we are right now, makes my legs shake and my eyeballs throb."

"Like I said, you've got it bad."

Throughout the day, Lilly reviewed in her head every cookie recipe she knew, and her legs never stopped shaking. Would he think she was a nutcase and laugh at her? That would be a fate worse than Frank's laughter, and rumors would spread throughout the school. Another horror she feared.

Then Friday came, as well as home economics class, the last hour of the day. This was her chance. "Are you going to make him cookies today or not?" Julie asked.

"I am, my chocolate chips."

"Excellent; they're the best! How are you going to give them to him?"

"His locker is right outside the home ec room. I'll rush to it at the end of the day and wait. I don't want to be there when his teammates come around. That would be embarrassing for me as well as him."

"Look at you! You're a mess! You better relax a little before you bake."

"Oh, stop it, of course I'm a wreck. What if he thinks I'm crazy?"

"He's not that kind of guy. He'll say thank you, but he'll also *see* you. That's what you want, him noticing you."

"I hope this works, because I don't have enough guts to try anything else."

"You're going to do great! Wish I could be in the background to watch."

"I am so glad you can't!"

"Damn, I'll have to wait until lunch tomorrow to find out how it went! That's going to kill me!" Julie pouted. "There's the bell. We'll talk tomorrow! Good luck!"

Lilly watched Julie take off to class and then walked to her last hour of the day, hopefully, one she would never forget.

She watched the clock on the classroom wall tick from one black dot to the next as her heart raced and the flush on her cheeks moved down to her neck. She was scared, but happy at the same time—a new kind of happy, like a great ride on a roller coaster.

When the final bell rang, she bolted out of the door toward Blake's locker. He was there, putting his books away. She stopped a few feet from him. He noticed her frozen state and was kind enough to smile. The cutest smile she ever saw. Lilly walked closer and put the warm package of cookies in his hand.

"Hi, Blake, these are for you. I thought you'd enjoy them after the track meet." She tried to make her voice sound like it was no big deal and she was full of confidence, which was far from the truth. "I made them in home economics last hour."

Gently, he took them, touching her hand ever so lightly, and quietly replied, "Thank you." Then he looked directly at her. Lilly heard the track team coming out of the locker room. "Win your races," she said, and floated into the mass of students.

The smile, the touch of their hands, and the eye contact left her somewhere between heaven and heaven. The bus ride home that she usually detested didn't matter. The sun was brighter, and new blood pumped through her veins.

That night she laid in bed, daydreaming and listening to a Beatles album. This was her world of no parents, no little sister, and no older sister, nothing to disturb her dreams. She felt safe; like other girls her age. The secret world was going away, and a new world was being born. She was going to have her suitcase packed full of new happy memories and adventurous tales, without an overshadowing dark fear.

✺

"Has he said anything to you?" Julie inquired as they walked to class.

"No, but once he 'bumped' into me, if that means anything." Lilly rolled her eyes, doubting its meaning. Julie jumped in front of her.

"It does! He really bumped into you! That's a big deal in guy language."

"You're a goofball. It doesn't mean anything except that the halls are too crowded and maybe I'm not his kind of girl, but I tried," Lilly replied, feeling sad.

"Nonsense! I've been nosy, watching the two of you flirting with your glances during lunch. Don't give up quite yet. I have a feeling." Lilly sighed. "Thanks for trying to help me feel better, but let's talk about something else."

"Why would we do that?" Julie questioned. "This is much more interesting than school."

"I've got to run. I'll catch up with you later." Lilly took off to class.

Another week passed with more smiles and flirty glances at lunch. *Maybe I shouldn't give up*, she thought. *There is something pulling at us: I can feel it, and Julie can see it! Hang in there, Lilly Francis!*

Then, when she least expected an encounter, it happened. On a Monday morning, as she hurried to her locker, juggling her books in one arm and trying to open her lock with the other, she felt a soft tap on her shoulder. Startled, she turned around quickly, dropping her books and thinking of the worst—a reaction learned from all the times Frank had snuck up on her.

It was Blake.

"Hi, Lilly. You're a little jumpy this morning!" he said with a gallant look. "Let me help you pick up your books."

Lilly looked up into his hazel eyes. He was gorgeous. Feeling at a loss for words, she made do with, "Thank you." Together they collected her belongings.

"Do you have this much homework every night?" he asked, estimating their weight.

"Most of the time," she nervously replied, spinning her lock because she suddenly was unable to remember the combination. After her third attempt Blake asked, "Do you want me to try?"

Lilly blushed. "I think that would be a good idea, especially if we don't want to be late for first hour."

"What's your combo?"

My combo? I can't remember! Think, Lilly, think! She closed her eyes and concentrated. The numbers came. *Um, I'm not supposed to give them out, not even to a best friend...but this is Blake!* "It's thirty-three, seven, sixty-eight," she rattled them out quickly.

"Didn't anyone tell you not to give out your combo?" he teased.

She snickered.

He spun the numbers and opened it on his first try. "What class do you have?" he asked.

"Language arts, right up the steps and to the right—no, that would be the left." She couldn't believe how difficult it was to think. Boys usually didn't have that effect on her.

"You're having a rough morning, right-left, flipping numbers around..." He nearly knocked her out with his grin.

"Could be, I was born left-handed and made to use my right." *I can't believe I just said that!* Lilly wanted to take the words back.

"Hmm, so you're ambidextrous."

Lilly chuckled, "A man of big words!"

"No, that's just what it is."

Straightforward, I like that!

He walked her to the classroom door. "I'll see you later!" he said, and handed her books over to her.

"Yes, sure, later will be fine!" She turned and floated into class, thinking, *how long before later?*

For the rest of the morning she watched the clocks, not taking notes or paying attention to her teachers' lectures. All she could think of was his voice and that he had touched her books, and her locker; that had to be the first step of something.

Then the lunch bell rang. *The day is half over and I haven't seen him,* she thought as she stopped at her locker and headed for the gym.

"There you are!" It was Blake. "Do you want to walk to the bakery with me? They make a great burger and malt, my treat."

"Sure, let me grab my sweater."

"Not enough time, we have to move fast: thirty minutes and the bell rings." He took her hand and led her out of school.

I have never left campus during lunch before. It's fun, even a little risky! I cannot believe this is happening. Feeling the warmth of his hand, she let go of her fears and went with whatever feeling came about.

By winter, walking to classes and eating lunch with a few friends was the regular for Lilly and Blake. When spring arrived the two had formed a close friendship.

"I've never dreaded summer like I do this year. We won't be able to see each other every day," Lilly said sadly.

Blake lifted her chin. "That's true, but we'll still see one another."

"How? Neither of us is sixteen? I'll miss you. I'll miss listening to music together and holding your hand. I've never liked big changes; they make me sad."

"We'll figure something out. My job has long hours, and it's six days a week, but if we have a rainy day, I'll have time off. That's when we'll get together."

Lilly wanted to trust him, but trust was hard for her. "My parents won't allow dating until I'm sixteen." She hesitated and then lit up. "But we can meet down by the river."

"Will the bridge be a good spot?"

Lilly was once again speechless as she looked into eyes that spoke more clearly than words. "Yes, the bridge."

"I'll call you."

When she felt his hand in hers, nothing else in the world mattered. There was no Frank, no angry parents, no scary eyes watching. She found a new feeling that lifted her spirit. More than the river, more than her willow tree. She had seen the feeling before, many times, when she watched her parents dance. Now it was hers. It was possible to find love outside of the family.

IN THE MOMENT

From the first day of high school, she and Blake connected, often in the darkest, least supervised hallway in school. "How about we ditch our next class?" Blake asked, playing with the tiny braid in her hair.

Lilly hesitated. *What can be so wrong with missing study hall? All I do there is whisper and goof around. Lilly Francis, quit being afraid of life!*

She grinned, accepting the dare. "I'm game, but where will we go?"

"It's an awesome day; we'll hang out under the bleachers."

"I would love to get outside, but the doors lock and we won't be able to get back in!"

"I've got that covered."

"You're sure we won't get caught?" A flicker of worry crossed her mind, thinking about the trouble she could get into with her parents.

"We won't. It's not like we skip classes every day." His come-on look was irresistible, and her love of adventure was undeniable.

She returned a flirty glance and reached for his hand. "Then let's go!"

Laughing, they raced across the field of grass and ducked under the bleachers. She fell onto the cool ground, laughing with a sense of accomplishment in defeating authority. He lay next to her as they immersed themselves with the sunshine and sky.

"Hey, look at those clouds! What shape do you see?" She pointed out a thundercloud in the making. "I see a ship."

"Me too! I love cloud watching. Sometimes in the country, there's nothing else to do!" Lilly's expression sobered. "You know, I have never broken a serious rule in school. Well, maybe I did in fifth grade."

"What did you do?"

"I drew an ugly picture of my teacher and left it in my desk, not knowing she went through all of our stuff at night."

"Oh, wow, she did that? What happened?"

Lilly chuckled. "I had to wear a dunce hat!"

"A dunce hat?" he asked dubiously.

"To be honest, it was pretty funny. It was all I could do to keep a straight face so I wouldn't get in more trouble."

Blake grew silent.

"Why so quiet all of a sudden?" Lilly sat up, cross-legged and focused.

"I don't think there's anything else to talk about." He leaned over and kissed her.

His lips were warm and soft. The kiss was ever so gentle, as if she were breakable. No one had ever made her feel the sudden awakenings she felt inside of her. They were in a timeless moment when the warning bell rudely interrupted the magic.

"Really, we have to go back to class?" She did not know how that was going to be possible.

"We have to. I can't miss algebra, and you can't miss science." He helped her up, and they sprinted back to the door.

Once inside, he squeezed her hand tightly. "I'll see you after school at my locker." He gave her a little peck on the cheek. Lilly smiled so hard her squinty eyes nearly disappeared in her face.

"That's only two hours away," she said, wondering if she would make it that long.

They parted, and there was nothing to fill her head with but the slow rewind of her first kiss.

※

The heat between them grew stronger and harder to hold back. They each had a mysterious shyness, and down the center of that was a no-passing yellow line. It had kept them from falling too seriously into a relationship. However, the yellow line was fading as the school year neared the end. They were two shirts on one back and their spirits lively with an inexhaustible curiosity.

Lilly laid her head on his shoulder. "Time moves too fast when we're together. I wish it would slow down."

"We can't control time, but we have the moment."

She smiled. She was in love not only with Blake, but also with the life they were creating together. It was a world of safety and an energy that woke her up and put her to sleep without fear and anxiety. Finally, Lilly had found something lost in her life: happiness.

SNEAKING AROUND

Being untruthful didn't make Lilly feel good about herself, however, it was only the way to have freedom to see Blake. She had turned fifteen and the magic age was nearing. She thought she would try one more time in being honest with her parents.

With fingers crossed, she approached Gwen. "Mom, my friend Blake asked me to go to a movie with him and a group of our friends. I want to go so badly. I've been saying no to group dates and get-togethers for almost two years. Will you at least think about it before saying no again?" Lilly twisted her face in a hopeful expression.

"We've had this conversation a dozen times. You know how your father and I feel about dating." Gwen continued with her cooking.

"But it's different now. I'm close to being sixteen and I promise I'll come home as soon as it's over. You can even pick me up if you want. How's that for an idea?"

No response.

"Look, cross my heart and hope to die, I'm not lying. There will be other kids around. I'll swear on a Bible if you want me to." Lilly meant it. If she had to use the Bible, so be it.

"The answer is still no." Gwen stood firm.

"Can you at least talk it over with Dad?" she begged. The expression on Gwen's face needed no clarification.

Lilly threw her oven mitt on the table and walked away. She knew that if she didn't leave, her mouth was going to explode with angry words.

Just once, she thought, *just once could they show me the respect they demand for themselves? They don't understand growing up because they were never kids or teens. They were adults when they were born. That's how they make it sound. Home is like a prison. They are taking away precious time and memories. Healthy, happy, and innocent memories— the kind I should be having and not the ones that haunt me.*

Quietly, within her own mind, she flopped down on her bed, stared at the ceiling, and continued to release her feelings.

"So much for honesty, I guess I have to stay with lies to be happy. As much as Mom and Dad don't understand me, I don't understand them. Only Anthony understands me. He knows how lonely and boring life in the country can be, and Dad won't question him about attending a baseball game. He has Dad's respect—that's it! I'll talk to Anthony!"

※

"Anthony, please, just this one time. The game and the movie begin and end at the same time. You can have fun with your friends and I'll have fun with mine. I promise I won't involve you again."

Anthony paused, "The game would be fun. Let me ask Dad. You stay out of it and don't say a word to him or Mom. Stay in your room. Agree?"

"Mum's the word!" She jumped off her bed and gave Anthony a big hug.

On Friday night they pulled into the parking lot where Blake was waiting.

"I promise to be back as soon as the movie ends. Thank you! You're the best brother!" She gave him a big hug.

Anthony watched her practically skip toward Blake, looking happy and free. It made him smile, remembering the little Lilly he grew up with.

Blake took her hand. Lilly hesitated, remembering getting into cars with Frank. "I don't know if this is right. Maybe we should stay and watch the game instead."

"Come on, Lilly. You're worrying again." He opened the door. "I'm sitting right next to you. You'll be fine."

With his arm around her shoulders, she let go of fear and went with her heart. *If he isn't worried, then neither am I.* She slid into the back seat of the car.

Not long after they pulled into their parking space of the outdoor theatre. Blake's friends left to join others, leaving her and Blake alone.

"We're not in school or near home." Lilly's eyes filled with a daring tease as she sensed a nervous excitement.

"I know." He swept her long hair behind her ears.

Wrapped in each other's arms, the natural forces of passion overwhelmed all restraint. Their short, loving kisses grew into an eager fervor, and their hands moved wildly before slowing to an explorative crawl. Entwined, they responded to forbidden touches well past the yellow caution line.

The loud smack of a friend's fist on the metal roof brought them to a sudden stop. In a split second they went from being one to being Blake and Lilly. Disheveled, they rushed to put themselves back together.

"How could the movie be over?" Lilly asked, feeling embarrassed that they were caught making out. "Like you said, time moves faster when we're together."

"Do I look okay?" Lilly felt flushed.

Blake gazed at her. "You look dreamy, almost daring, and maybe a little flirtatious. I like it." He leaned forward for one last passionate kiss. Lilly pushed him back. "Not now…they're right out that window."

"But they can't see inside; it's all steamed up!" His second attempt was successful.

The front doors opened. "You two ready? Stop the smooching: we have to haul ass to get back before the game ends!"

She buried her head in Blake's shoulder as the car sped down the highway toward town. They were going well over the speed limit. A flash of Frank's face popped into her head. He was laughing and on a city freeway. She closed her eyes and forced the thought out, replacing it with new memories of her first time making out. She felt protected in Blake's arms. *I'm safe*, she reassured herself. *Nothing bad can happen to me when we are together.*

They pulled into the parking lot fifteen minutes late. Anthony stood waiting by his car, looking peeved. "I have to go." Lilly nervously looked at Blake.

He opened the door and helped her out. "Let me walk with you. I'll explain that the movie was longer than I thought; that's not a lie."

"No, I'm okay. I'll see you on Monday!" She sprinted toward Anthony. *I'm going to ruin his chances at going to another game, and that's not what I wanted. He doesn't deserve to lose trust with Mom and Dad over my life decisions.*

"Sorry, Anthony, I truly am. We tried to be on time!"

"Buckle up. I'm going to stop at the gas station and call Mom and Dad. I'll tell them we're on our way home," he said sternly.

"That's a great idea!" *Thank God, Anthony has more common sense than I do*, thought Lilly. *I'm too nervous to think that clearly.*

"You stay in the car. I'll be right back."

Anthony returned promptly, wearing a disappointed look.

Cautiously, Lilly asked, "How did it go?"

"Dad was glad that I called, if that's what you mean, and he reminded us to watch for deer along the road."

They turned onto the fifteen-mile country road that led them home. Lilly watched for deer, just as her father asked, while Anthony focused only on driving. The quiet tension pulled at her nerves, however, she didn't dare say anything that might upset him more.

Halfway home he broke the silence.

"Don't you think you should know about the game, so we don't get in trouble?" he asked.

"Only if you want to share, if not, I'll take my punishment. It was worth it."

"You didn't do anything stupid, did you?" He quickly glanced over at Lilly.

"No, not really, not if you call making out stupid."

He noticed her face was more pink than usual. "Be careful, Lilly; don't let yourself get away from you."

Lilly kept her eyes on the sides of the road. "Have you made out yet?"

"Nope, I haven't, and don't ruin it for me."

She laughed. "I won't, but I'll tell you this, if you're meant to be with that girl, you'll *feel* it. Your body knows and takes over. It's incredible." Lilly could smell and feel Blake as if he were right next to her.

"About the game..." Anthony told her every detail he thought Dad would ask. She listened intently, memorizing certain events. She wondered if Anthony knew how much she respected him and how much she would miss him next year, when he would be going off to college. Not having a big brother around was going to be tough.

Driving past their aunt and uncle's farm, they noticed Millie and Frank's Cadillac parked in the driveway. A cold shiver ran down her spine. "Mom didn't say anything about Frank and Millie coming for a visit!"

"I heard them talking about it last week. Mom is hurt that Millie isn't spending the weekend with us."

"Well, I'm not. They've eaten enough of our food and kicked us out of our beds."

"You really hate them, don't you?"

"I do, more than you'll ever know. They lie."

"I know that Uncle Frank does. Dad said Frank told him that he bought the ropes that he gave him to tie the boat with, but he actually stole them from his job. However, I love Aunt Millie. She's the best cook."

Lilly took a deep breath. "So she's a great cook, big deal! Why are they at Aunt Dee's?"

"Beats me, maybe it's because of Aunt Dee's baby girl. Aunt Millie loves babies, just like Mom."

"Mom's a lot of things, but she's not Millie. Don't ever say she is." They both retreated into silence.

I'm so glad they're not at our house! She acknowledged her feelings. *This night belongs to Blake and me. Not having them around will make sure it stays that way. I'm not that stupid little girl anymore. Their death threats aren't going to work. I know Frank isn't going to kill anyone. It's too dangerous, and people would start snooping around. That would expose his and Millie's world of crime and land them in prison.*

"Hey, Lilly, are you spotting for deer or daydreaming?" asked Anthony.

Lilly looked at her brother. "A little of both," and returned her focus to the road.

For Lilly, it was all about being a teenager. She was happy—deep down glowing happy—and she was in love. Her days were like the stars on the water, bright and beautiful, and she pushed away any thoughts that would make it otherwise.

CAN'T LOSE WHAT YOU DON'T HAVE

On the morning of her sixteenth birthday, Lilly awakened thinking about how long it had taken to get to this magical age. *Here I am and I don't feel an ounce smarter or different. It's been a waste of time and caused too much arguing. What a stupid rule. I guess they figured that if it worked for one of us, it would work for all. Will they ever understand that each of us is different?*

"Good morning, Lilly! Happy birthday!" Gwen greeted her at the breakfast table. "Thanks! I'm sixteen today, which means I can officially date." She reminded her mom.

"That's right. Dad and I were discussing that last night. We knew it was going to be the first thing you would ask this morning."

"So, what's the plan?" Lilly kept her eyes on Gwen, attempting to read her thoughts.

"We agreed to one night of the weekend and a curfew of eleven thirty."

Lilly didn't believe what she heard. "One night a week during the school year, fine. But all summer too and eleven thirty?" She couldn't hide her disappointment. "Blake lives in the complete opposite direction from me. Eleven thirty doesn't allow us enough time to go to a movie and grab a burger!"

"It is what it is. That was the rule for Joan, and it's the same for you."

"I'm not Joan!" Lilly gritted her teeth and then raised her voice. "This is so stupid!"

"Well, then, you don't have to date," Gwen said firmly. "That is sufficient time."

"To do what?"

"You can go into town, to the malt shop or the bakery."

"Mom, the town is a hole in the ground. There's nothing to do there or in these backwoods! I want to have real dates! I want to be able to go to Frankton where there are stores and restaurants and a real movie theater."

"Lilly, it's your birthday. Let's not start it with an argument."

Lilly poked at her breakfast. "I can't believe you and Dad don't trust me enough to give me a midnight curfew. You both know that wherever we are we will have to leave by ten thirty to get back here in an hour. It's only once a week and not on a school night. Can't you give me thirty more minutes, please?"

"Next year, but not this year and I nearly forgot! Your father wants you to start working toward your driver's license."

Lilly shuddered inside. The idea of driving had frightened her since the wedding. "I know. I already signed up for driver's ed class this summer, but I'm not too excited. I get so nervous behind the wheel that I don't think clearly."

"That will go away with practice. I was nervous too when I first learned. By the way, Dad and I do not approve of girls picking up their dates. That won't be happening."

Lilly rolled her eyes. "So it's final, eleven thirty?"

"Yes."

"Sixteen. I thought it was going to be the greatest day in my life," Lilly commented sarcastically.

"It's what you make it," Gwen flatly replied. "Lilly, I have to work late tonight. Do you want me to pick up a cake at the grocery store?"

Since she's been working, nothing is the same, huffed Lilly to herself. "Don't bother. We can have a cherry pie from the freezer instead."

"Are you sure it's what you want for your birthday?"

"I love cherry pie," Lilly muttered.

Gwen kissed her on the cheek. "Don't be so grumpy. At least you can date and not sneak around town. It's better than what you had."

"Who told you I was sneaking around?" Lilly asked in surprise.

"Millie told me that Frank's father has seen you and Blake in town together."

"Millie lies, and she has no business digging into our family's business."

"Oh, Millie is harmless."

The smiles and grins that Lilly brought to the breakfast table vanished until she walked off the bus and found Blake waiting for her.

Saturday night was their night. They parked below the river, watching the swift current of the water pass under the bridge. They talked about everything and nothing: The Beatles, cars, sunsets, and the river. They were in love, but not stupid love. They understood they had to be sexually safe, a topic that was coming up more frequently between them.

"Lilly, don't get mad at me, but do you understand your female anatomy?" Blake asked, looking out into the distance to avoid her expressive eyes.

The question took her by surprise. She turned his face to hers. "Well, don't go laughing at me, but no, I didn't pay attention to the movie in fifth grade."

"Didn't your mom talk to you when you had your first period?"

"Mom and I don't talk about much besides recipes and chores." Lilly was mortified, feeling her heartbeat in her eyeballs. She hadn't talked about sex with anyone. It was taboo in their house and oddly enough, in her mind, Frank and his behavior didn't fall into that category. What he did was sinful and violent; his actions had nothing to do with sex and love.

"Why are you bringing this up? Most guys wouldn't mention the curse of the female."

"You should know more about your body, and mine too," he answered.

Lilly felt extremely awkward.

"I didn't mean to make you blush," he added. "It's not a big deal." Blake put his arm around her shoulders. "I just read a book. It was about everything you need to know before having sex. It was funny and I thought you would like to read it too."

Lilly's eyes grew large. "If Mom or Dad saw a book like that in my bedroom, which they do inspect, I'd be grounded for life."

"Then how about we read it together?" he suggested with a coy grin.

"You're kidding, right? We're going to read a book about sex together, just what most kids do on a date!" Lilly chuckled. "I shouldn't have brought it up."

"No, I'm glad you did! But you have to admit that it is a bit odd to be learning about sex and my body from my boyfriend and a book. Not a common situation!"

"It'll be good for both of us, if we want to get more serious."

"Did you say 'more serious'? We are boyfriend and girlfriend, but we're also best friends. Would going further take that away? Because I don't want to lose what we have."

Blake thought deeply. "Someday we may want to go further, and if so, we should be prepared."

Now it was Lilly's turn to ponder the idea. "If I'm going to learn about sex from someone, I pick you. I trust you." The seriousness of his face flashed to a clever grin as he slid the book out from under the seat.

"You sneak! You've been playing with my head!" Lilly gave him a flirtatious shove.

Blake smiled at her adventurous acceptance of life. As their relationship was becoming more serious, he didn't want her to feel that he was taking advantage of her, and knowledge was the answer.

"Does it have pictures?" Lilly felt a pit in her stomach as a flash from the girl's movie crossed her mind. "Not really. A few illustrations, that's about it. I think it'll make you laugh."

His attitude convinced her to see this know-all book. Cuddled next to each other, they began.

Lilly did all she could to refrain from laughing. "I kind of like a storytelling date. No one has read me a book holding me this close since I was a toddler." She turned to look up at his face. He was so handsome—she would much rather begin making out than get involved with the book, but this was important to him, so she settled herself down.

For the next two hours they laughed. Afterwards she gave her rendition of the facts. "So I make one amazing egg a month that waits for the superior sperm to single-handedly complete entrance. If that doesn't happen then I have my period, which is the shedding of my disappointed uterus lining. No baby, return of the period. The cycle continues, month after month, waiting for that single sperm out of millions to break through the egg, which sets off the electrical spark that begins cell growth, thus creating a new life. How did I do?" she asked with pride.

"You've got it!"

"One more thing, you have it easy. Being the male, that is. All you do is make millions of sperm. No pain, no blood, no uterus, no tubes…"

"Now wait, I have tubes too."

"Oh, cry me a river! I never realized how interesting our bodies are and how they fit together, like pieces of a puzzle. I actually feel a new sense of pride in being a girl—more grown up. You were right; this was good for me. I should have learned it years ago. You won't tell a soul how naïve I was! Will you?"

"I promise my lips are sealed."

They created a finale to an incredible date night, but stopped before it became part of the book and not once did she think of Frank. The male body they read about belonged only to Blake. He filled her thoughts with his passion.

She lived for Saturday nights. Their time together was spontaneous and uninhibited. He made sure she felt safe while she made sure he felt loved.

The only time they had was the present, and that was where Lilly was living.

1986 - SESSION SEVEN - A SHOCKING AWARENESS

"When I tried to talk to Mom about becoming a woman, she told me to take an aspirin. That was my lesson on the birds and the bees. Talking about sex at home was taboo, as if it were a dirty, sinful word."

"That made it more difficult for you to try to tell them about Frank." "Not more difficult; impossible! Mom and Dad said that everything I needed to know about growing up was in a movie that I would see in fifth grade."

"Did you find the movie helpful?"

Lilly scoffed at the question. "I didn't listen to it."

"You must have had a good reason."

"I did! It was embarrassing with all of my female classmates there. I was in the first row, with the screen directly in front of me, which made me feel like the center of attention. I was choking with anxiety. The nurse directed a question at me while a picture of the male anatomy was on the screen. I was mortified, thinking she could see through me and into my secret world. Whatever I said made the girls laugh. I'm very sensitive to being laughed at, since Frank did it to me so often." Lilly placed a hand over her face to hide the shame. "I wanted to crawl under the chair or anywhere to escape."

"Do you remember the question?"

"No! The only sound I remember is the laughter."

"Tell me about the picture that was on the screen."

"I have a foggy visual of the male's private parts in a black-and-white medical-like drawing. That sketch triggered a flashback." Lilly's face reddened.

"How do you know?"

"I remember thinking it was a picture of Frank! I couldn't believe that he finally found a way to get at me in school. He always said what he did was private and secret, but there he was!" Her thoughts raced.

She took a few minutes to shake her hands out and concentrate on breathing. As she relaxed, she continued, "That film was a horror movie. I felt trapped inside a room with an audience, and nowhere to run. The only place to hide was within."

"It is very possible that you were taking in the information sexually and not anatomically."

"The movie *was* sexual. I didn't see it any other way." Lilly paused in bewilderment. "Was there another way?"

"The movie was most likely intended to be viewed anatomically, like a biology class on the human body."

Lilly flopped back into the chair. "Oh my God," she threw her head back and looked up at the ceiling. "I didn't see the physical side. I only saw it as how each body used their parts for sex. How sick is that? I was eleven!" She pulled inward.

He waited.

With her eyes still staring at the ceiling she muttered, "I feel awful and embarrassingly stupid."

"You were coming into a new awareness, most likely confused, with no one to talk about it with."

She spoke softly, as if she were in a distant world. "Physically I was underdeveloped, and sexually I was overdeveloped. The other girls weren't as naive. That was a big difference between them and me. Shouldn't I have known more?"

"Right around the age of eight, a child starts to figure out their sexual selves. However, in your case, the overexposure to sexuality may have blocked the normal physical interest. And then there is disassociation."

"I disassociated that young?"

"You may have."

"That image belonged only to Frank! I didn't see boys that way and especially not Blake. Boys were like my brother, sharing a common ground in our likes and dislikes. Blake was like me, only a boy. Does that make sense?"

"It does. You were able to separate the fact that the male who was abusing you was a forceful, unloving man; therefore, you feared men. However, you saw boys as being trusting and safe, physically different, and more like your brother, until you grew older and began to feel the natural interest and attraction to the opposite sex."

Lilly took time to sort through the thoughts in her head and then began to tell her point of view. "Frank knew that I was coming into an age of being more sexually aware, and he messed with it by comparing my body to Mom's and other women. I was a kid, told to be a woman. That hurt my self-image. Why didn't I know what he was doing? How come it has taken me decades to figure this out?"

"Let's step back for a moment. Would you as a child, react like an adult to Frank's threats and horror?"

Lilly sighed in frustration, dropping her shoulders.

"Of course not."

"Frank's introjections, coupled with your anxiety, weakened your belief system and pulled you away from trusting your parents. It's not any fault of your own."

"So much would be different if Millie wouldn't have married the devil."

"But she did, and she brought that devil into your home. That was the past. You're not there anymore."

"Where exactly am I?" she asked, looking directly at him.

"You're an adult. You have transformed into a healthier self, wife, and mother for Owen."

Hearing Owen's name changed her frame of mind to one of more hope. "Owen will never have the life I lived. I don't own him. He has room to think freely, and he can tell me anything. He knows I would die protecting him."

"Do you think Owen could defend himself from a man like Frank?"

"No, he's only a child," she responded bluntly.

"And so were you—only a child."

"I wish Frank was dead."

"What about his death would free you?"

"If he's dead, he can't hurt me or anyone else."

"That's a child's perspective."

"You can be annoying." She paused, reevaluating her comments and his. "Okay, as an adult I know that death wouldn't take away what he did to me or the damages that remain. Nothing can take them away but me wanting to make a positive change."

"That's true."

"But, I would not have to feel his touch, or look into those ugly bulging eyes, or smell and see that disgusting cigar roll around his mouth ever again."

"His physical being would be gone, but what's inside of you won't leave with his passing. Those are emotions we'll work through."

Lilly sighed. "I can get over the past, right?"

"You can. However, some emotional impacts may always be there."

She fell back onto the sofa, defeated. "So what's the sense in spending this money and dredging up the past if there are no guarantees?"

"So you can learn to accept what cannot be changed, change what you can, and move on. You have the power not to allow the past to overcome you. You are rising above survival, and finding inner peace. You're a brave, determined warrior, Lilly."

She placed a vision in her mind of the water going around, over, and under a large rock. It didn't stop. It moved forward. She could feel its determined energy. She *was* the water. There was no quitting.

UNDER THE SKIN

"Dad, it's not my fault! The stop sign was slanted, and I didn't know which road in the fork to take. I asked that unfriendly police officer, and he said, 'Do what you think is best.' There was a car behind me, and if I stopped, it would have hit the back end of our car. I made a judgment call and continued to drive forward."

"Lilly, you should have stopped. If the other car hit you, it would have been their fault for not having their car under control."

"I did everything else at one hundred percent," she huffed. "I hate driving! That's why I've been putting off this road test. It makes me nervous."

"What makes you nervous? Most kids look forward to having wheels and being independent."

"It's the city and the way Frank drives. He scares me to death, and I can't get that out of my head."

"He's just trying to be a hotshot, nothing more. Don't let his carelessness mess with your driving. A little more practice and you'll be ready for a retake."

Lilly freaked. "No way am I going back in the car with that officer! I'll flunk it again and again."

"You'll change your mind," Vincent assured her.

"No, Dad, I don't think I will. I really don't care if I ever get my driver's license. No one can force me to drive a car. I'll ride my bike. In fact, I'll do that right now." It was a wise move to get out of the house and avoid confrontation.

Coasting down the hill and feeling the wind in her hair, helped change her thoughts back to Blake. *Is it wrong to go all the way and not be married? I know the church says it is, but what do priests know about love?*

Blake says he'll respect my decision. He said that the notion of making love is about what both of us want, not just one and I should give it great thought, because it is irreversible. I think that if I lose my virginity to someone I love and he loves me back, I'll have no regrets.

She turned onto a dusty dirt trail that led to the riverbank. She stood at the water's edge, observing her reflection. *Frank is wrong. I can be pretty and others can love me. It has been so long since I felt this good about myself. I love Blake, and that's all that matters.*

She smiled at herself. The answer was as clear as the water.

❋

In the back seat of his car, eagerness and intensity consumed Lilly as she whispered into Blake's ear, "Do you have protection?"

He pushed himself up and reached into his back pocket. "Are you sure?"

She looked deeply into the eyes she had fallen for. Looking back at her was the same dreamy look she had. "Yes, I'm positive."

Their bodies enclosed like a cocoon, weaving together without space for air between them. A hypnotic silence followed.

Lilly stroked his thick hair and softly said, "I love you."

They cuddled, absorbed in the mesmerizing feelings of lovemaking, long after it was over. "A penny for your thoughts," he said.

"I have no thoughts. I don't remember ever feeling this free. It's as if all the nerves in my body flatlined. How can I be so dead and yet so alive?"

Blake placed his finger over her lips. "You think too much."

The only sound in the car was a Beatles song on the radio. Eventually, Blake grew restless.

"What is it?" Lilly asked.

He didn't want to take the moment away, but he was puzzled. Hesitantly, he asked, "Have you done this before?"

Lilly's senses went on the defensive as she pushed him away. "No, I never made love to anyone before. Why would you ask me that? I would have told you before we read the book. You know how clueless I was. I can't believe this! It was my first time, Blake. I've made love to no one but you."

Blake saw her eyes swell with tears and further explained himself. "I asked because you didn't feel any pain, and there isn't any blood."

Lilly sat up and angrily pulled her sweater over her head.

Blake gently reached out to touch her shoulders. "I'm sorry. I don't want to upset you, especially not tonight."

"Then you shouldn't have referred to me as a slut who's been sleeping around. Furthermore, I did feel pressure, it did hurt, but I wouldn't call it pain and some girls don't bleed their first time. Don't you remember *that* part of the book?" she snapped.

The magic of the night was losing its grip. Blake tried to turn her to face him, but she wrenched away, hiding her tears. "Lilly, I'm really sorry. I believe you. I know you wouldn't lie. Come here; let's get back to being us."

She could be just as brash as he was. "I have questions too!"

"Go ahead, shoot."

"How many lovers have *you* had? You seem to know a great deal about sex for your first time."

Blake's face lit up, relieved to see her feistiness returning. She had a way of changing a bad moment into a good one. "That's a fair question. There's a man I work with at Dad's factory who treats me like a son. That's where I've been getting my information." He wiped the last falling tear from her face. "You're my first too."

"What else are *you* holding back?" she continued to question him.

"Only that you're beautiful." He grinned, holding her face in his hands. A touch that would normally set her off, she now found comforting.

"Does this make us boyfriend and girlfriend?" She couldn't hold back the laugh that bubbled up with the comment.

"I think we always have been, but closer now."

They had created a peaceful loving world that existed just between them.

※

Sleep didn't come easy for Lilly as her mind filled with thoughts of their lovemaking. She felt Blake next to her, even though he was miles away. It was as if he had left his ghost behind. Eventually, she let herself drift off to sleep, until her busy mind woke her up.

"Damn it, I want to sleep. Why can't I turn my head off?" she said, tossing. "I'll open the window and listen to the hoot owl. He always makes me drowsy."

She slid out of bed and opened the window closest to her. Looking out at the night sky and listening to the sounds of nature, she wondered aloud, "What did Blake mean about the first time? He said I didn't feel pain. Is there something wrong with me? Blood, no blood, I haven't had blood since...since when?" She felt a wave of nausea and hesitated. "Why is this bothering me so much? It's the word *blood*..."

The clouds of her dark world opened and poured rain as she recalled leaning over the riverbank, trying to wash the bloodstains out of her underwear, but with no success. "I was afraid of what Mom would say, so I buried them in the woods. How old was I?"

She pulled at her hair, not knowing if she wanted to remember or not. "Was it the day of my First Communion?"

Unraveling reality gripped her mind. With her hand over her mouth, she sat on the floor in shock. "I thought the blood was from a cut, but was it? His nails were always sharp, but maybe it wasn't his nails." Her hands began to shake, and her head pulsated with a constant beat of her heart. She forced herself to stand.

"Oh my God, I was so stupid! I was so damn stupid! No wonder why he laughs at me. I didn't know what sex was. He was hurting me, embarrassing me, doing what no one should do. It was sinful. It was insulting."

She tried shoving her memories back into the darkest corners of her mind, but the black box was open and more confusion spiraled out.

She clenched her fists as she heard Frank's voice telling her: *I will always be there in the most important times of your life. No matter who you're with, a boyfriend or a husband, I will be a part of your life.* He was right! *My first time making love and now his ugly horrifying dirty face is in my head.*

"There's no God! I want to scream at the world!" Then fear raced through her bloodstream. "But no, I have to be quiet. No one can ever find out. The embarrassment of it all, Frank, an old ugly rotting man, used me for sex. I can't change that! And I can't deal with it either!"

She envisioned Frank's head on the snake that lay under Mary's feet. "Squash him, Mother Mary. Squash his neck flat, like the tires did to Chipper. Make him dead. He's not a man. He is a monster. He took everything away from me. He had no right, no permission. That was mine. It belonged to me."

She turned her conversation to Frank. "You wanted this to happen. You planned it, but just wait and see. It's not over. I'm going to get you some day. You are going to hurt, like I have. And your only resting place is going to be hell."

A deeply rooted hate resonated throughout her. She envisioned his yellow face in the center of her pillow and she hit it, again and again, until he was dead.

Still, her thoughts kept pouring out. "Maybe I'm wrong. I don't know what to think. Frank calls me crazy, because it *is* insane to think that he raped me as a child."

She felt as if a thousand red ants were crawling under her skin, and she scratched at her legs and arms. "I have to get him off of me." Then she stopped. "But Blake is on me too. How can I have both on my skin at the same time? What Blake and I did tonight had nothing to do with Frank. We made love, not sex. Blake filled me with a sense of wonderment. There was no fear or anxiety. I felt loved and special. I can still smell his scent. Maybe this *was* my first time…how can I know for sure?"

She hit her head against the wall, hoping to stop the turmoil in her head. It didn't. Through the mental battles of an inner war of three worlds—family, godparents, and Blake—she sat alone.

※

"You've been in the shower long enough. You're wasting water!" Vincent's resonant voice ripped through the bathroom door. She closed her eyes, thinking, *I cannot deal with him or Mom right now. I need space.*

"All right, I hear you! Let me rinse my hair!" she yelled back. *Why couldn't they see how upset I was at breakfast? No, probably not, thanks to Frank. He taught me to be a master of hiding my true feelings. Even if I wanted to show some emotion to them, I wouldn't know how. I lost that skill a long time ago. I can't go to church today.* She let the water beat against her face. *I'll fake being sick.*

Lilly dried off, put on her robe, and went downstairs.

"Mom, I don't feel too well. That's why I've been in the shower so long. Can I please stay home and rest so I don't miss school tomorrow?"

Gwen walked over and felt her forehead. "You don't have a fever."

"Can't people be sick without a fever?"

"You were well enough to go out on a date last night."

"I didn't feel good then either, call Blake if you want and ask him." She set her head down on the table, knowing that her mother would never make the call.

Gwen watched. That was their Lilly, up and down, but never at an even keel.

"All right, but I want to find you in bed, not out on the water. Drink plenty of fluids and stay with saltine crackers."

"Thank you, I really mean that, Mom!" Then she returned to her bed.

Wrapping herself in the blankets, she slid her prayer book out from under the pillow, and placed it on her chest.

Dear God, what have I done to deserve this? Is it true or not...Did Frank...? The pictures he took were so humiliating. That and going down to the river is all I remember. Make Frank go away. Help keep Blake in my life. I feel so ugly right now. Will he be able to love me? Will I feel the same love as I did last night?

A cold shudder ran through her. She pulled the blankets up closer around her neck and tried to reclaim the safety and warmth that she felt only with Blake. The only male in her life that she trusted and loved.

NO SAFETY LOCK

He waited for her by the school doors. She looked carefully at him from the school bus window. He stood straight, tall, and definitely self-assured. He was handsome in an earthy way with his deep tanned skin and wind-burned look from working outdoors. Lilly thought that if she could really see wind, it would look like him.

"How did your Sunday go?" he greeted her.

"It was quiet. I spent most of my time thinking about you."

"I tried working on the car, but when I heard a song from Saturday night, I couldn't stop thinking of us. I wish it was Saturday again." He moved closer to her.

"I know. I feel the same way." She filled in the empty space between them and nestled her body into his.

"Hey, get to class, you two; the weekend is over!" her English teacher directed.

Blake smirked and whispered in Lilly's ear, "See you at lunch, by the west doors. We can listen to music in my car." She blushed and gave him a nod of approval.

"Lilly, your desk waits! It's English, first hour, get a move on!" Lilly shyly brushed past her teacher.

❈

"Yes, Mom, we're going out Saturday night."

"Not unless you have your chores done."

Lilly bit her tongue to keep from talking back. *Mom was tired of being a housewife so she went to work, and now she pushes all the work off on me.* "You know what, Mom? Ever since you went back to school and found a career, I feel like I've become your slave."

"If you don't want to work for me, then work for God. He'll appreciate your labor too."

"You're unbelievable." Lilly shook her head. "But I would rather work for God! It might be more rewarding!'

"Watch your tongue, Lilly Francis and make sure the floors are clean this week. Change the water often. You know Dad will check if it was done properly."

"Anything else Mother?" Lilly inquired sarcastically.

"Last week you didn't dust under the knick knacks. Make sure you do that today. And please give the top of the door frames a quick wipe."

"Why all the fuss, is someone coming for Sunday dinner?"

"I had the strangest call from Millie this week. She and Frank are going to stay here Saturday night and leave Sunday after lunch."

Lilly put down her toast as a lump of fear stopped her from swallowing. "Why a renewed interest now? It's been Aunt Dee for over a year!"

"I have no idea, but isn't it wonderful? We have such fun when we're together."

Lilly's filter went temporarily out of order. "I don't."

Gwen gave her a better-be-careful look. "I know it creates more work for you, but they specifically mentioned that they wanted to spend time with their godchild *and* meet Blake."

Lilly turned away from Gwen, hiding the anguished expression on her face. "That's not going to happen. I don't want them to meet him," she muttered.

"Now you're being silly. They just want to see him and say hello, and then you can leave."

Under her breath she replied, "We'll see about that."

"What did you say?" asked Gwen.

"Nothing important. Can you make a list of my chores so I can get started right away?"

Gwen handed her the list.

"I think this is the most common form of our communication since you began working." Lilly sarcastically slipped in the comment.

"Is there a problem with me going to work? This is the second time you brought it up today."

"I don't like all the extra responsibilities that you have me do, and the kids at school tease me. They say that you have to go back to school to get a job because Dad doesn't make enough money."

"Well, that's ridiculous. Don't listen to them. I didn't go to work because we were poor. I went to work because I always wanted a medical career. Now, if you want to go out tonight, I suggest *you* get to work. Skedaddle!"

Lilly began in the bathroom she and Eva shared, scrubbing the shower as she considered her mother's words. "Like hell they want to see me; they're plotting something, and what is this 'meet Blake' all about? That will never happen as long as I'm alive!"

Gwen poked her head around, "Are you talking to yourself?"

"I am; is *that* a problem too?"

"Your aunt, the one out east, talks to herself. They say she's crazy. Maybe you should just think to yourself. Anyway, that is not why I'm here. Could you also change Eva's bedding and clean her room, top to bottom? That's where Frank and Millie are going to sleep."

Lilly stopped dead in her tracks, feeling tightness grip her chest, "But I sleep right next to Eva's room! Can't they use the guest room downstairs, by you and Dad?"

"The upstairs is remodeled and new, and that's where I want them to stay. Does it bother you to have them sleep upstairs?"

"Yes, it does. It feels weird. Can Eva sleep in my room?"

Gwen waved her hand in dismissal. "So touchy you are! Must be the idea that you think you're in love."

"I *am* in love and it doesn't have anything to do with that. I'm older now, and it's not right to share a bathroom with an aunt and uncle."

"That's silly! You can use our bathroom if you want for the weekend." Gwen studied the work Lilly was doing. "Can you scrub this soap scum off better?" she asked, pointing out a small section Lilly had not gotten to yet. "You're only sixteen. You have a crush on Blake and you'll have many more."

"You were sixteen when you got married," reminded Lilly.

The comment irritated Gwen. "I was two weeks from being seventeen, and it was different back then. I grew up in the Depression and then the war."

"I'll be seventeen soon." Lilly brushed past her mother, giving a little shove with her shoulder.

"Listen here: you don't have to go out tonight. That is a privilege, so change your attitude right now. And use the new white sheets in the linen closet with the light-blue blanket on Eva's bed."

"There's a lock on my door. Doesn't Dad have a key? Can I use it for the weekend?" Lilly knew she would be an easy target, all alone and so far from her parents' room.

Gwen stopped straightening and smoothing out the guest towels. "I can ask your father, but I don't see why it's necessary."

Lilly made a face at her mother's back as she turned and walked away. *I don't think I can live through another attack from Frank, not with all I've learned about myself as well as him. He has no right to touch me. My body is mine, and I share it with Blake because we love each other. Frank's world has no love: it is pure evil.*

Anxiety and fear pushed itself forward in the compartments of her mind, replacing her happy-in-love world. "Dear God, if you really exist, I need your protection this weekend."

She skipped lunch and finished her work quickly, leaving her enough time to unwind. She wrote in her journal, listened to music, and walked down to the river. *I have left the world I grew up in; now I live in my world and it's the only world that matters. Millie and*

Cynthia J. Giachino

Frank are coming to visit and want to mess my life up. I don't have a good feeling. What am I going to do?

IN DYING MISERY

Frank and Millie walked into the house, their familiar fake greeting rekindled Lilly's hatred. Frank shook Vincent's hand, gave Gwen a kiss and then Eva, and when he came to Lilly, he slipped his tongue into her mouth and pinched her waist. He was quick and sly, creating no suspicion. Lilly's gut churned as she stepped away.

"Lilly, take the suitcases upstairs to their room," instructed Gwen.

"Gladly," she said, wanting to get as far away from Frank as possible.

Picking up the small makeup case and a larger one for clothing, she turned to Millie. "I'll show you your room."

Millie hobbled up the steps as if she were a hundred years old and complained nonstop. "I'm not young anymore, and these steps are steep." She huffed out her words. "It's been too long since we've seen you. You're too busy with that boyfriend to think about your aging godparents."

Years ago I would have felt badly for her, thought Lilly, *but not anymore. She is a sick old witch who deserves to live in her own misery.*

"The bathroom has fresh towels, and you can open the windows if you want." Lilly kept the conversation short and didn't respond to Millie's whining.

"You know you're the only one who understands how hard my life is." Millie's remark grabbed Lilly's attention. She stopped and turned to face her aunt.

"I just heard you telling Mom how wonderful your life was." As soon as she opened her mouth, she realized she had stepped into Millie's manipulative conversation.

"Oh, I don't want to worry your mother; besides, you and I have more in common."

She's trying to get under my skin. "I don't think that's true."

Lilly was ready to make a fast exit when, out of the corner of her eye, she saw at least a dozen bottles of pills in the top organizer of Millie's makeup case.

Millie had hoped her godchild would be curious and quickly explained, "Oh, my dear Lilly, my heart is failing. The doctors don't know what is wrong with me. I have had so many tests, and still no answer as to why. Now I have to take these medicines to ease the symptoms. Let me show you."

As Millie explained each bottle and its purpose, Lilly counted twelve pills a day. *She should be dead—or maybe that's what she's trying to do: kill herself. I would too if I had to live with that sick freak.* Lilly paused. *No, this whole scene is too obvious and rehearsed. Millie is up to something in order to help Frank.*

"I'm too young to die," she said and began to cry. "Come here and comfort me." She patted the bed beside her. Lilly backed closer toward the door.

"You are sick, that's for sure, but I don't think it's your heart."

The tears stopped instantly and Millie's face turned to scorn.

"You are an unappreciative godchild! After everything I've done for you, you can't offer me an ounce of sympathy. You are too bold, and I told Frank it was that boyfriend of yours. You think you don't need us anymore, but you do. We're going to meet him tonight."

"Like hell you are. You'll never set eyes upon him."

Millie walked over to the large suitcase and opened it, her voice trembling like a witch as she said, "And look how ungrateful you are! We shopped for this and it was expensive, but we wanted you to feel special." She held up a black bra with a matching bikini bottom.

"This is the type of under garments your uncle likes to see on women, and you are old enough to wear more fashionable lingerie, like all the other girls your age. Maybe you could wear them tonight for your uncle. When he's happy, my life is better."

Millie ignored Lilly as she jabbered about Frank and his needs and wants and how unhappy he had been because they hadn't been able to visit, laying the blame on Blake.

Lilly stood frozen in disbelief. Nothing could have prepared her for this brazen act and the jolt of it all was that Millie didn't appear to be uncomfortable talking about sex, Frank, and their sixteen-year-old goddaughter! The pressure in Lilly's head felt like an imminent implosion.

This is insane, she thought. She pressed her hands firmly over her ears and shouted, "Stop!"

She balled up the undergarments and threw them back at Millie, watching them float down into the suitcase where they belonged.

"How dare you talk to me like that!" called Millie as Lilly stormed out and ran down the steps, thinking of her own safety as well as Eva's. Frantically she scanned the house and caught a glimpse of her sister through a window. She was on the swing in their front yard.

She ran to Eva. "Come on, we're going to dig some worms and go fishing," she said as she pulled her sister into her grip.

"I don't like to fish, you know that!" Eva tried to yank free, but Lilly tugged her along in a fit of rage, stopping only to grab the pitchfork to dig with and the worm bucket. She was livid.

How dare Millie put me in the position of a prostitute giving pleasure to her husband? She is a psycho, like him. They are the same evil. They have become too unashamed; nothing seems to bother them. They are not afraid of anyone or anything and her talk about Blake ruining me is nothing but lies to put pressure on Mom and Dad. She's behind the fights and yelling at home. My godparents don't want me to be happy because they're not. I... hate...them.

Using every muscle in her skinny little body, she drove her foot down on the pitchfork and into the moist ground. *It would be so easy to put this fork into Frank's fat gut, or better yet, through his eyeballs.*

"You're scaring me, Lilly." Eva was standing a good six feet from Lilly, watching with caution.

Lilly realized she had gone off into another world, the dark, hurtful world that *they* brought with them. She had to fight to keep her mind out of it, or she would fall limp into their grasp.

She turned the rich black soil, exposing the worms, and calmed her voice. "Here, Eva, there's enough in this one dig for us. Help me pull them out."

"I don't pull worms out of the ground. I don't like the way they feel. Can we go back to the swing?"

"Eva, we're going fishing, didn't you hear me?" Lilly scolded, though she felt guilty doing so. She never yelled at Eva. In fact, she tried to be the opposite, to teach Eva that people need not hurt one another. Lilly put the fork down. "I'm sorry. I'm not myself. I don't like my godparents being here."

"I don't like them either," Eva replied quickly.

Lilly stopped her tantrum and sat down on the pile of dirt. *I know what that means. There is no need to ask. I thought I protected her, but I was wrong.*

She has felt Frank's touch. Shock waves ran through her body.

How can this be happening? I woke up excited for tonight, and in nine hours my world has come undone. Eva, precious little Eva.

Just then she heard Gwen's high-pitched call.

"There you two are! Lilly, what in God's name did you say to Aunt Millie that upset her? She's in the kitchen, crying and complaining that her heart is skipping beats, maybe a heart attack, because of what you called her!"

Lilly clenched her teeth and answered, "Why don't you ask her yourself?"

"I did, and she cried harder. What did you say?" demanded Gwen.

"I told her she was sick. Go upstairs, look in your sister's makeup case, and ask her to explain *her pills*. Ask her whose fault it is, and if she says mine, she is lying to you as she always has. I'm taking Eva fishing." Lilly pulled Eva's arm again, and this time Eva didn't resist.

Lilly batted around her head as if she were shooing away flies, pushing away the image of Millie throwing the lingerie at her and saying she should please Frank by wearing it. Then Eva telling her she didn't like Frank either and Mom's screeching voice yelling, "Wait until your father comes home!" She shoved the rowboat off the bank and beat the oars against the water until home was out of sight.

Dropping anchor, she turned her focus to her sister. "Eva, do you want to hold the pole? It doesn't matter if we catch anything. Peace and quiet is what we both need." Lilly baited the hook and held the pole with Eva. "Do you want to tell me about Frank?"

Eva shook her head no. Lilly sickened.

"Eva, you can tell me. I know about Uncle Frank and his games." Her sister turned her head away, avoiding Lilly's eyes.

If I can't get her to talk, I can at least give her some ideas on how to protect herself. Lilly reached out. "Make sure you stay by Mom's side. Do not go for walks or let Millie convince Mom you need one. Speak up for yourself. Say no! They are not going to hurt me or anyone else in the family. When he says that he will, it's a trick. You understand?"

Eva nodded yes.

"Good, and tell me if he ever lays a hand on you. I am not afraid of him, and I believe you. You don't have to be scared all the time. I know how that feels."

"But you're going out tonight." Eva looked up at Lilly.

Lilly's heart was wrenched. "Yes, I'm going out and you'll be safe sleeping next to Mom and Dad. And I'll check in on you when I get home." Eva sat like a statue, promising nothing. Lilly knew he had already put the fear of death into her sister's head.

Softly, Eva asked, "Aren't you scared to sleep all alone upstairs?"

Lilly took a deep breath. "I'll be careful and keep myself safe."

She could not help but judge herself. *I failed to keep Eva safe, and the only end to Frank and Millie is to tell, but who will listen? Mom will never believe me. She would defend Millie and Dad's fuse has been so short. He would probably whack me for some dumb reason.* She leaned over the boat and vomited.

Black undergarments: there they were, a flash in her head. *If Millie would stand up to him, she wouldn't need the pills, but she expects me to do that job for her. How can I? I am sixteen. Millie is fifty and the fact that she speaks Blake's name infuriates me. Blake is never going to be a part of this twisted life. I will protect him at all costs. Frank's vile evil fills our house, but it will not spread any further. I promise.*

"Are you sick?" Eva asked.

Lilly sat back. "No, it must be the rocking of the boat. We'll pull up anchor and head back home. I need to shower and clean up."

"Will you be home late?"

The worry in her sister's voice was stabbing. "Not any later than usual."

"I'll lay awake until you come home."

Lilly closed her eyes, feeling the pit in her stomach growing larger. "Aw, Eva, that's so sweet, but don't worry about me. Blake is a responsible driver, and he protects me. I'm safe and happy when we're together."

"I like him." Eva smiled.

"He likes you, too."

By the time they docked and tied the boat, Lilly had little time to think about their date. That night her mind filled only with ideas on how to break her promise of silence.

I could ask Blake to take me to his house for the night. I would tell him and his parents about Frank. They would help, however, I would be putting them right in the middle of my mess, and how do I know what the outcome would be? The unknown scares me and keeps me quiet. Maybe this is really my fault and I'm the guilty one. I don't know anymore.

"No way are they setting eyes on him," she muttered to herself as she finished dressing. "I'll duck out of the house and wait for him on the road. Millie and Frank are having drinks with Mom and Dad. They won't notice until it's too late."

She tiptoed down the steps and slipped out the back door.

AMBUSHED

Blake slowed down at the sight of Lilly plucking petals off a wild daisy on the side of the road. "Love me, love me not?" He cruised up alongside her.

"Are you trying to pick me up?"

Blake laughed. "What are you doing out here?"

"I just wanted to get out of the house a little earlier." Lilly opened the door and slid in.

She envied him. He had a comfortable, normal life, one she wished belonged to her, but it didn't and maybe it never would. She felt doubt in herself and a sense of unworthiness.

"You're unusually quiet tonight."

"I had a rough day with Mom."

"Do you want to talk about it?"

"No, not really. How about we drive to the city?"

"We may not get back in time for curfew." He glanced over at her and noticed her distant look. "But we can try, if that's what you want to do."

"I want to be with you, and that's about it."

"I know a lake close to town. It has great sunsets. How about hanging out there?"

"Sounds good." She put her head on his shoulder and allowed herself to get lost in their world.

The lake was picturesque, with waters so calm it looked like ice. They carried a park bench out to the sandbar, where they sat and watched the horizon's blues and pinks come together.

"This is the coolest thing ever! Look how far we are from shore, and we're sitting on a bench, in the water. What a great idea!"

"Thought you would like it, but it's kind of cold."

"Not as long as you're next to me." She slyly smiled.

Her mind returned to the present, leaving the afternoon where it was. Blake did that to her. He filled her mind with thoughts of the good in the world and how beautiful it was.

"I wish I could go home with you tonight," Lilly thought aloud. "That wouldn't work with either of our parents."

"I know. It's just that..." She grew quiet.

"Go on, it's just that... what?"

I can't do it! What will he think of me? How could he ever love me the same way again? "Just that...I love you so much that it hurts to be apart. I feel like you would protect me from anything, or anyone."

"I would!"

"Can we make love?" She looked up at him.

They returned to the car and the chill of the water was replaced with the heat of passion.

�֎

Blake pulled into her driveway. Immediately she looked up at the second-floor windows. The house was dark except for the kitchen light. Worry and nerves renewed themselves. It made her quiver.

"Are you sure you're okay? Something is bothering you. I can tell."

"Everything is good." She kissed him gently. "I worry about you driving so far late at night."

Blake squeezed her hand. "I'll call you tomorrow when I'm done with work, probably late afternoon."

"Thank you for the beautiful night. I'll sleep with the feel of the waves lapping against my ankles." She held onto him, not wanting to ever let go.

"I better hit the road."

"No, wait." She pulled his hand toward her. *Why can't I just come out and say what I want to?* The words sat on the tip of her tongue.

He saw her concerned look. "Hey, don't worry. I'll keep the radio on and make sure the windows are open." He clicked his tongue, winked, and pointed at her. He did that often, and it always made her grin.

She watched him pull away and then quietly walked into the kitchen, relocking the door behind her and proceeding with caution.

Her first thought was Eva. She carefully tiptoed into the guest room to peek in on her. She was asleep, nestled tightly in her comforter with her striped tiger cradled in her arms. She loved Eva, maybe too much, like a mother, but she couldn't help it. She loved deeply and too easily except when it came to herself.

She stared at the steps that led up to her bedroom.

"I should crash on the couch, but then Mom and Dad will think I was drinking or doing drugs." Again, she looked at the stairway.

Light on her feet and carefully listening to each of her steps, she walked to her room. Once inside she leaned against the door, feeling the pounding of her heart and a choking sensation in her throat. *I can't breathe! I need air. I can feel his hands on my neck.*

Shaking her head, she scolded herself. "It's a memory, stupid, that's all. I'm safe in my room." She moved to the window and opened it for fresh air.

Looking out into the night, she tried to think her words to Blake. *Please come back, I have to tell you the truth about why I was so moody tonight. It's important enough that our parents would understand why curfew was broken.* A regretful sadness fell over her.

I can do it. I really can. I am brave with you by my side. Please hear me and turn around. By tomorrow at this time Frank and Millie will be in jail, and I will accept whatever fate comes my way, even if it means that you will no longer be a part of my life.

She stared at the phone on her desk. It was useless. He wouldn't be home this soon, and she wasn't going to awaken his parents. *Letting him leave was a huge mistake. I wasn't able to make a decision, and here I am, looking out the window and feeling the tentacles of death wrapping around my throat.*

"Snap out of it!" she said aloud. "I've been in this room for fifteen minutes, and I'm perfectly safe. Frank and Millie are sleeping and I will wake up tomorrow morning with the memory of our date and no nightmares. I'm overreacting because *he's* so close. It gives me the creeps!" She changed into her pajamas and slid into bed.

As soon as they leave I will wash down the walls for Eva, clean the sheets and mattress pad, and wash everything else in her room. She reached under her pillow and slid out the black prayer book. She placed it on her chest, feeling its comfort.

I'm safer if I stay alert and awake until morning. She stared at the ceiling and walls. *I can tough it out and there's no school tomorrow, so what does it matter if I am exhausted?* However, the exertions of the day took over, and she caught herself drifting deeper into sleep and fighting harder to reopen her eyes.

"Come on, Lilly, stay awake. Morning is only a few hours away." The night breeze blew softly across her face and again she nodded off. The next time she opened her eyes she was no longer staring at the ceiling. She was looking into the bulging eyes she knew too well.

He straddled her, smothering her with a plastic bag while whispering, "You're not good enough for that boy you're sleeping with." Whatever else he said or did was lost as her eyes rolled back and his hands wrapped tightly around her throat.

※

She awakened to her mother's knock on her bedroom door. "Get up, sleepyhead, breakfast is being put away."

"What time is it?" a groggy Lilly asked.

"It's after nine!"

"After nine?" she asked, alarmed. "All I want is a glass of juice. I'll come down after my shower." Lilly looked at her clock. *This is strange. I never sleep late. I wake up at six or seven like an alarm clock.* A flash of Frank on top of her sparked panic. She jumped out of bed and looked at the sheets, her pajamas, and around the room.

"Don't use all the water. We have company and everyone is showering. Are you listening to me?" shouted Gwen at the door.

"Yes, Mom, don't use all the water. I got it!"

Frank was here. I remember him smothering me. I couldn't breathe. Oh my God, what did he do? She picked up the golden brush Millie and Frank had given her, the one her parents wouldn't let her get rid of, and threw it at the bed. Then she picked up the mirror. She saw two red marks on her neck.

Dizziness overcame her and she reached out for the dresser to regain her balance. *My head feels wobbly, like it is going to fall off.* She slumped down, cowering to the floor.

I don't feel anything. I can't think, I can't remember. Blake, where are you? I need you; I need to know I will be alright. Her fear and anxiety turned to tears of helplessness. *This has to stop before it kills me.*

She threw on her jeans and a shirt, slipped out of the house, and headed to Jane's. As she rode her bike, she couldn't help but think about Eva.

I left her unprotected, but how could I stay in that house another minute, or see him *grinning at me. He knows what he did and that I can't remember. If I show Mom and Dad my neck, he will deny he had anything to do with it. He'll say it came from making out with Blake. My parents would believe him over me. They trust him more. I love you, Eva, but today I can't be there.*

As soon as she turned onto Jane's driveway, Lilly shut down her feelings, which was easy to do when they overwhelmed her. She had at least a decade of practice.

She knocked on Jane's front door.

"Hi, Mary, is Jane home?"

"I'll get her for you."

In minutes Jane was outside with Lilly.

"You look like you saw a ghost! What's up?" she asked.

Lilly took a deep breath and answered, "Not a good morning. Will you go out on the river with me?"

"Sure, let me tell my parents."

"Can you ask them to call my mother and tell her I'm here?"

"Are you sure you're okay? Your eyes are weird."

"Yeah," Lilly forced a smile. "I need some time to cool off."

They canoed to the inlet and explored the woodsy area until they heard the cowbell ring. It was Jane's mother telling them lunch was ready. By midafternoon, Gwen called for her to come home.

"Do you have to leave?" asked Jane. "I'm not sure you've calmed down."

Lilly shrugged her shoulders. "We had a disagreement over my godparents again."

"You told me they were visiting."

"They are, or were. They left after lunch. That was their plan. Once they leave, our house returns to normal."

"I've never told you before, but we think your uncle is creepy. My mom doesn't want any of us kids near him. He prowls along the roads with his overcoat and city hat, smoking that cigar. Dad said he's not right in the head."

Lilly looked down at the gravel, rearranging the little stones with her shoes. "Your dad's right." She looked up at Jane. "You helped me a lot today. Thanks for letting me hang out, and thank your mom for lunch."

"Do you want to call me when you get home and let me know you're safe?" Jane asked.

"Not necessary, I'll be fine. See you Monday morning on the bus."

Lilly hopped on her bike, feeling in a much better place. All she needed now was to see Eva.

The wind against her face felt freeing, but as she neared home the turbines of her mind went from a comfortable purr to an increasingly loud hum, bringing to the forefront more unanswered questions.

This is my body and he walks into my room, drugs me, and does what he pleases. Was he after pictures or was it rape? Did he use those black undergarments? I can't remember,...no matter how hard I try, there's nothing there. I feel so dirty and...used.

In deep thought, she paid little attention to the road and automatically turned into her driveway, coasting down the hill toward the house. That's when she saw Frank standing in the middle of the road.

Panicking, she slammed on her brakes and skidded to a stop, only a foot away from him. "Stay away," she warned, shaking in terror.

He sneered, "You're not going home."

"Stay away or I'll scream bloody murder! I will!"

He yanked the bike out from under her. Lilly hit the gravel and immediately pushed her body up, prepared to run, keeping her eyes on the front porch of her house. *It's less than a quarter mile. I can make it, and if I scream loud enough, someone will hear me.*

Their eyes locked. He reached into his front shirt pocket and pulled out a small brown bottle and his familiar white handkerchief. He poured a liquid onto it.

Lilly made her move, taking off with one big leap, but his strong arm grabbed her around the waist, pinning her arms. She kept her eyes on the porch. It was still reachable as she kicked and twisted in hope of an escape. She could smell her mother's cooking. She had to get home.

She bit his arm, angering him more as he firmly pressed the handkerchief over her mouth and nose. The sight of the porch grew hazy. There was no smell and she couldn't hear anything. Then her life disappeared.

In the darkness of her mind she was dead, except for the sensation of the tall, prickly grasses brushing against her legs. Lilly fought within her thoughts as her body submitted to unconsciousness.

※

She awakened to sunrays filtering through a small opening in the canopy of a tree. Bewildered, she watched the light dance from branch to branch. "I know this tree." She stared into the blue sky. "It's the old maple at the bottom of our hill. I'm close to home," she whispered, trying to pull herself up, but her arms and legs wouldn't respond.

In a weak but determined voice she snarled, "Get up, damn you, Lilly. Get the fuck up!"

She tried; it was impossible. Her body and brain were working in unconnected planes. She could think, but she could not act. She lay trapped within herself.

"Help." She strained her voice to shout, but barely a murmur escaped.

Weak and afraid, she allowed her head to fall back onto the ground, sensing a return to the dark. "No, I won't pass out. I have to get up. I have to get home."

Breathing heavily, she forced her memory to the forefront. "I remember seeing the front porch and smelling Mom's cooking. I was riding my bike and thinking about last night and then…"

A tear trickled from her left eye. "It was Frank. I remember a brown bottle and his handkerchief. Then the long weeks scratching against my legs. He must have brought me here."

Her breathing grew rapid and erratic. "Breathe, Lilly," she told herself. "Just breathe. All you have to do now is breathe. Don't think!" The filtering sun rays that danced between the leaves captured her attention.

"*Get up, Lilly!*" Her head whirled as she saw flashes of Frank's ugly face. *You can't let him make you weak. That's what he wants. Show him how strong you are—stand up!*

Leaning forward, she held onto the pain at her core. It felt as if she had fallen and smashed against a rocky ledge. She looked down at her body. It was as she had suspected. The buttons on her shirt were out of line. He had primitively redressed her.

Overwhelming guilt shamed her, releasing a swell of retching tears. She imagined her naked, defenseless body exposed to his lust and camera lens.

She lay on the cool earth among the damp dead leaves, reflecting. *There isn't a complete story to tell. Whatever I say, Frank and Millie will make fun of it, and they will create some ridiculous story to defend themselves. Then all the blame will fall on me. I will be the one who looks guilty. Mom and Dad will send me back with them to save face.* Lilly felt trapped. *I couldn't fight him off; he ambushed me and used me like some kind of…toy doll. I swear to God I will get back at him.*

The hate in her hissed, realizing they had returned to knock her down from happiness and love. They had reintroduced her feelings of being scared, insecure, weak, and shameful. They were trying to stop her from getting any closer to Blake in fear that she would break her silence.

"I fucking hate them." She pounded the ground with her fists. "Stand up, you bitch. Stand the fuck up!"

She warily stood up, rearranged her clothing, and fixed the buttons on her shirt. Her unsteady legs wobbled as she staggered from tree to tree, holding on to the strength of their trunks as she moved toward the river. The woods she could count on to find respite were now leading her to the healing waters.

Reaching the bank, she splashed its cold water on her face. Thoughts took her from place to place; the past, the present, school, family, church, and Blake. She looked for her reflection and saw none.

The sun was setting itself up to retreat. It was getting late. She never got home as her mother requested. That would land her in trouble and again it would be her fault because she couldn't tell the truth. She never would. Her shame was too deep. He had finally broken her. She was tarnished and ruined. Not the girl Blake loved; not anymore. That girl just died.

Lilly retraced the trail he had dragged her down and ended up on their gravel driveway. Her bike was alongside the road, buried under a heap of dried brush. She pulled it out and began a slow pedal to the garage. Their big black car was still there.

She knew exactly how to walk and talk as she entered the house. She could perform this lie flawlessly. There was never a time where he abused her and didn't stay around to enjoy watching her afterward.

Sluggishly, she walked up the steps, opened the kitchen door, and laid eyes directly on him. He sat at the kitchen table, sipping on a drink, watching Gwen and Eva cook. His glare could start the fires from hell to swell out from under the floorboards.

He looked at Lilly and scoffed. "What's wrong with you? Cat got your tongue, or did you see a ghost?"

Gwen turned around and in her friendliest voice said, "Well, there you are. We were beginning to worry, but Uncle Frank said he saw you riding with Jane onto a logging road. You know you shouldn't go that deep into the woods so close to sundown. Go clean up and ready for supper. Frank and Millie want to leave right after we eat."

Lilly's thinking was still foggy as she fought her way through the façade. "Are you okay? You look scared," her mother asked.

Frank jingled the coins in his pocket.

"Lilly, I'm talking to you! Go clean up and then help Eva set the table. She's been by my side all afternoon, being such a big helper. You can thank her for that!"

Frank worked to unnerve Lilly with a sinful glare and Lilly returned it with a crafty look. He took out his pocket knife, the one he often used against her neck, and began to pick at his fingernails, removing dirt from the forest floor. He was pushing every button he had built into her since childhood.

Lilly looked over at the butcher knife on the counter: it shined among the yellow fat and red blood from the butchered chicken they had prepared for supper. His eyes followed hers.

She fed her feelings. *I want to grab that knife and gouge out his eyes, ending this nightmare. Dad will run to protect Mom and Mom will grab Eva.*

Millie will scream in terror and cry, but me, I'll fend for myself. I won't stop stabbing him. Not until I know he is deader than dead. Frank won't be alive to question and without him, Millie's stories won't hold up. The only way I can tell the truth is to kill Frank.

She heard her mother's muffled voice ordering her around again, but it didn't matter as Lilly stared at the knife. Frank sat as cool as a cucumber, looking at the knife, then at Lilly.

I can imagine what he is thinking. He wants me to do it. He wants me to snap and go crazy. I can hear him saying, "Come on, and give it a try. Oh look, you are afraid! You're scared! You don't have the guts. You're a weakling."

His threats and taunts echoed throughout her mind. *He's in my head without talking. It's what he does: the glare, the grin, the pocketknife, and the coins. He wants me to lose control. That would make me a lesser person.*

The commotion of the kitchen came at Lilly from all sides until Vincent's voice overrode everyone else's, directed at her. "Act your age! What's wrong with you?"

Her head filled with overwhelming chatter. Lilly bolted. She ran out of the house hearing the faint outcry of her father's voice from the front porch, "Wait until you get home!"

She was going home, to the woods, to the dancing leaves, and the waters of the river, to her refuge.

Sitting by the riverbank, she kicked her heels into the wet moss and fell backward to the ground, smelling its sweet evening scent. Looking up, she focused on the stars, which hung on the backdrop of a pitch-black sky. She had no fear of Frank finding her there. He feared the woods at night because of the snakes. "I curse his eternity to be one filled with serpents slithering up his legs, entering every orifice, and weaving in and out of his eyes. He would feel their scaly moist skin and muscles contract as they slither over his body. He would be helpless. The same helplessness he left me to feel." She took comfort in the image. "That would be an agreeable hell for Frank."

Under the dark sky she confronted herself.

"I can't cave in to his demands of becoming him. I have to stay a better person. My revenge cannot be one of violence or anything that resembles him. My revenge will be the opposite. He says I won't succeed, but I will. He says no one will love me, but I already found love. Revenge cannot be falling into his deceit and sins. It will be the opposite of evil. For as long as I remember, I have struggled in this world; so little has come easy. There has to be a reason and purpose for my existence. I have no idea what it is, but I have to be patient. Time will show me."

1986 - SESSION EIGHT - STORAGE COMPARTMENTS

Lilly shifted nervously in her chair. "Face it. Seventeen was the last year of any possible normal existence for me."

"You feel this way because…?"

"Chloroform, dragged like a dead deer over a grassy path, and then God only knows what. Pornography? Sex? He had no boundaries. That changed me forever. I never felt my 'female self' again with anyone other than Blake."

"The impact it left was life-changing."

"Because of my age and awareness, what he did demoralized me and the unanswered questions that it left behind were frustrating and troublesome. Throw in the chloroform that made me dead and alive at the same time, with my brain working, but my body unable to respond to my commands—what was there to live for after that?" Lilly shivered with the memories. "There aren't any words to explain that Saturday and Sunday. It was so horrifying."

"Words don't often have the power to express our feelings."

Lilly pressed on, furrowing her forehead in concentration. "That entire weekend was my life mistake, and there's no one to blame but me. I should have never walked through the kitchen door. I should have gone home with Blake. Time provided me with opportunities, but I was too afraid and ashamed. I hated myself before he pulled me off the bike, and afterwards, it was deeper than hate."

"Should-haves are of the past. Step back and revisit the memory, thinking as the adult you are today."

"All I see is that if I had loved myself when I was young, there would have been no reason for me not to tell my parents about Frank, long before I was a teenager."

"You're taking the blame again."

"No! Yes! I don't know!" She threw her hands up in the air. "But before that weekend, the love I felt with Blake was greater than any of my fears and I felt more confident having someone to talk with. I hadn't experienced that since Father Johan. However, by the time my godparents left, it was gone. I was shattered, and simply could not get a grip on my thinking."

"Your godparents felt insecure because of *your* security. Keeping you from getting to that point was part of their ritual."

"That's exactly why they visited. Frank and Millie were hell-bent on destroying any good that came my way. Millie spied on me through letters with Mom and relatives in town. How was I doing in school, who were my friends, was I dating, did I get into any trouble? If they sensed a change in my self-assurance, they returned."

"It was a pattern," responded Dr. Bricks.

"I call it a ritual," Lilly shot back.

"Using patterns is a form of ritualistic abuse."

Lilly contemplated. "They liked to tie their visits with religious events such as baptisms, weddings, and Christian holidays." She flushed and reached out for a drink of water to ease her anxiety. "Frank and Millie were horrible people who knew many others like them in the city."

"How are you able to recall so many of the attacks?"

"I'm not sure. I know I grew up being very hyper vigilant and aware of my environment and I think I remember the ones that embarrassed me the most. I created a filing system in my head and put them in there."

"Tell me about that." Dr. Bricks leaned in with interest.

"It's a stack of labeled boxes that I move through, looking at each one's story, trying to make sense of the memories and finding connections. My toddler belongs in this box, my early childhood in that one, and so on—all of my developmental stages and traumatic attacks are neatly separated, so I can refer to them quickly."

"You placed each age memory into a filing system to help you function. Now you are connecting them, finding that each box is an important lead to the next."

"That's it: you understand."

"It's referred to as *compartmentalizing*. It's a lesser form of disassociation."

"I disassociate and compartmentalize?" Lilly inquired, not liking another label attached to her mental health.

"That isn't unusual, Lilly, especially during trauma. Both are instinctive skills for survival. Compartmentalizing is a coping strategy."

"How is that different from dissociating?"

"Disassociation allows the *mind* to *escape* while disconnecting from the body. An example would be how you felt during the movie in fifth grade. You referred to feeling trapped with no escape."

"So I left my body, and mind, to cope."

"Exactly, remembering nothing but the last image you saw."

"And when I compartmentalized, I stayed with my body, but my mind avoided the traumatic feelings." Lilly squinted with uncertainty.

"By placing what bothered you in a box, you were able to separate the different values of your parents and godparents. That made it easier to move on. You were quite clever."

Lilly took time to process. "I created boxes to hide away what scared me or made me feel guilty. Once I tucked them away, I could carry out my life as normally as possible."

"Exactly, compartmentalizing kept your physical and emotional being intact and allowed you to pack away what was not good for you."

"That worked as a kid, but not as an adult." She felt downhearted.

"Correct. When you were a child it was natural to push memories out of your mental sight. That type of coping gave you the present. The problem with compartmentalizing is that it only works for short periods. Eventually all that was pushed away will return to the forefront, needing to be readdressed."

"And that's why I felt I was a bad mother when I first came here. Memories that I shoved away started sliding forward as I interacted with Owen." Lilly hesitated. "Do they stop? Or when he turns sixteen, will that compartment of my life come forward too?"

"It may, but it will be different, because you're working at opening them now. You have begun processing. You're not waiting for a specific age and you're staying in the present."

"But as I open these boxes, it's easy for me to slip back and lose my protective adult. Then I go back to feeling all the negativity in my life. Will I ever be able to see the whole picture *and* stay in the present?"

"As you accept the past into your present and manage what can and cannot change, you'll reach a point where you have only one box. And in that box is where you will live as a whole."

"That would be a new normal."

"Coming to healthier terms with a hidden past takes patience and hard work. Think of it as a self-rescue plan."

Lilly gazed out the window and into the waterfall. "No more secrets to hide away in those boxes and I know for a fact that I won't die if I open them.

That's Frank's way of thinking. I can rationalize them and rescue myself." Lilly's mood picked up with the positive thinking. "Correct, and your determination will help you with the challenges."

"I have to be strong to get through this, and patient, not only for myself, but also for Mick and Owen. I've wasted too much life by living in fear."

"To recognize that is powerful."

Lilly remained quiet and then responded. "People say, 'Forget the past,' but how can the past, present, and future exist without one another? I feel that's impossible to do or ask."

"Interesting, explain that thought further."

"I feel that we can have a present without a past. However, we cannot have a past without the present. And the future seems to propel both."

"That's an interesting point of view. You are quite insightful, which is another resource of your survival."

THE RAGING MONSTER

Lilly looked at herself in the mirror. "A few months ago I loved my shoulders. I thought they were sexy. Now they look bony and deformed. I hate myself. My country-girl cuteness is too vulnerable. I have to toughen up. Dad said my eyes barely sparkle anymore. He's right. I have become a complicated person in a complex life with no one to understand me. I'm really alone in this world."

She changed out of her school clothes and joined the family for supper. Vincent began badgering her about taking the ACT.

"Dad, why do I have to go to college? There are many jobs that don't need four more years of schooling."

"If you don't go after high school, you'll never go. I see that time and time again," he answered.

"Just because you and Mom did that, doesn't mean I will too," she snapped back.

"That is disrespectful, young lady. When I was your age, times were different. There was a war to fight," Vincent snarled.

"Well, there's a war now too. We see it every night on the news… It's called Vietnam. Maybe I should join the air force, like you did. Is that what you would like me to do? Would that be a respectful career choice?"

"Now you're talking silly! You would make a fine teacher like your brother. It's a good career with health benefits and a pension."

"I hate little kids. They annoy me, and they cannot speak for themselves. See, this is what I mean. I need time. I don't know what I want. Maybe I would like to be a psychologist or maybe a stewardess— then I could travel the world."

"Girls don't become psychologists, and a stewardess is nothing more than a waitress. Nursing and teaching are worth the money you spend for a college degree."

"My gut tells me to stay around here for a year, get a job, and then go if nothing works out."

"So you have more time to date Blake? Then you'll be pregnant, and all hopes of a career will be gone."

"What on earth are you talking about? Blake and I haven't even mentioned marriage. I don't want to get married until I'm at least twenty- one. I don't want to be a child bride like Mom and look at Joan! She went to college too young, dropped out, and got married. Now she has kids! Blake and I aren't like that."

"Go to your room—that's enough back talk and make that appointment for the ACT Monday morning! I'll be calling school to make sure you did!"

"Right," Lilly mumbled as she walked upstairs. "I'm tired of his bossing me around and controlling my life. College is the law of the household, but not one of my choosing. I'm sick of grown men trying to own me and stop me from being who I want to be."

Looking out her window and into the forest she continued, "I would be happy to be a wife and mother and maybe have a part-time job as a secretary. I love to type, file, and keep things orderly. That's my comfort and safety zone. It's a simple happiness and what's wrong with that?"

"But no, I have to go to college. So much could change! What if Blake and I come to be engaged, or what if we break up? Oh, God, I don't think I would live through that. I have given him my heart and my soul. He wouldn't break it…would he?" Behind each question was a mountain of anxiety and unanswered questions.

"I can't keep worrying like this. It's rotting my gut and making my head swarm with confusion, one thought building onto another until I'm dizzy. But I have no idea how to help myself."

❇

The answer came one Saturday morning, as she wiped out the medicine cabinet in her parents' bathroom. "What's this prescription bottle doing in here? There's never anything but aspirins."

She read the bottle's label. "Hmm, Mom is having migraines. I know she comes home with maddening headaches from work, but I didn't think they were serious."

Curiosity overcame her as she held the bottle. "If these pills help Mom, then maybe they'll help my headaches too. I have one nearly every day. Mom says it's because I don't eat lunch, but I think it's my nerves."

She opened the cap and saw many broken pieces of white pills, far too many for anyone to notice if a few went missing. Lilly grabbed five of her mother's little helpers and shoved four deep down into her pocket. "Tonight I'm going to go out with Blake feeling like I'm sixteen again, making love with nothing else on my mind. No more out-of-control thinking and being scared." She put the chip of the pill on her tongue, threw her head back, and swallowed.

Within an hour the pounding shores of her brain silenced to a quiet ripple. She could see the big picture and not only fragments of an idea. Her chronic worry and deep sadness lessened, and she could feel the old happy excitement of Saturday night.

As usual they ended up on another road to nowhere, making love. Afterward they talked more about the future than the present.

"Dad is pressuring me about college so much it's become a daily lecture!" Lilly avoided eye contact, knowing college was a touchy subject.

Blake immediately responded, "I don't want you to go to college, period."

"You could go with me and get a business degree."

"I'm not going to college. I'm staying here and working with Dad."

"Then am I supposed to wait for you to marry me? Do you think about that?" This was the closest conversation they had about the future since he gave her a diamond in a white gold friendship ring. She recalled the pride she felt when he slipped it on her finger. Maybe that was a feeling she would feel again. Only this time it would be a forever commitment. That was her dream, her Cinderella ending.

"Maybe. I don't know, we're not even out of high school. But college…" Blake left the sentence open.

"It makes me mad too. Teachers and parents want me to make adult decisions. I'm only seventeen. I have no idea what I want to do for a living."

"Then why is this weighing on you?" Blake asked with little sensitivity.

"Because I already missed the first round of ACT tests and I have to take that test to get into a college." Lilly felt uneasy. Blake had never been so irate and uncaring about an idea.

"I don't want you to go to college!" His eyes narrowed over a serious frown. "I don't want you to have more education than me. My wife won't need to work."

Lilly slid away from him. She was afraid of the anger she heard and saw in him "I may want to go to college someday. Cleaning the house and taking care of kids can get darn boring. What else would you want me to do if I *was* your wife?" she asked with a sneer.

"Be by my side and look good."

"Are you for real? You want me to be your Barbie doll! That won't sit right for very long. I like to be doing, seeing, learning…"

He leaned over and opened the passenger door. "Guess I'm not good enough for you if I don't go to college!"

Lilly returned the fire. "Maybe I'm not pretty enough for you to flaunt!" She stepped out of the car and slammed the door shut. "Go, get out of here!" She began walking down the dirt road toward home.

Blake took off, spinning his wheels and spewing gravel with the anger of a two-year-old.

Stammering to herself, she steamed down the road. "Does he see me in his future as his wife and that's why he doesn't want me to go to college or have I become an object of his control? Am I nothing more than a replaceable toy? If he only understood the pain I am going through. I'm fucking everything up with my fake life."

In her self-blame she fell susceptible to dark memories of Frank. The usually soothing sounds of the night owls seemed to be stalking her. Heart pounding against her chest, she began to see eyes watching from the dark rings in the white bark of the poplar trees. She could feel the stalking of Frank.

Lilly's pace rose to a jog and then to a sprint, until she fell to her knees alongside the road. Fear stifled her tears as she frantically looked around, preparing herself for his attack.

She heard the distinctive sound of Blake's car and saw the glare of its headlights. She wiped her face and watched him turn around, pulling alongside her.

"Get in." He leaned over and pushed the door open. "I'm sorry I got so pissed off."

Lilly was angry that he put her in the situation she was in. "Go home. I don't know what you want from me! I don't know if you even love me."

"I'm sorry, I am really sorry. Please get in the car! I won't leave until you do. Come on, Lilly, we had our first fight and you're shaking. I'll come and get you." He opened his door.

"No, I can get up myself and save you the trouble." Lilly brushed off the dead grass and sat down on her side of the car, slamming the door shut. Blake tried to touch her shoulder. She moved it out of his reach.

"Lilly, please don't be mad. Come on, slide over, and let me warm you up."

"Just take me home."

"Okay, home it is, but we have to fix our problem."

He slowed the car to a snail's pace, which made Lilly angrier.

"I'm not going to sit next to you. You'll get me out of this mood, and I want to stay in it."

"That's not allowed."

Lilly wanted to slide over—it was hard to resist him—but she chose to stay with her anger, instead of her heart, and diverted all emotions by focusing for the reflection of deer's eyes alongside the road.

"Quit looking at me, and watch for deer," she scolded him.

"So you still care about me." He looked at her with a devilish grin.

Lilly caved. "Yes, I'm mad at you, but I still love you."

"Come here."

Lilly slid across the seat.

"It felt terrible to fight. I hated it. Never again?" she asked. "Never again." He put his arm around her shoulder.

In a flash of a second she saw the reflection of eyes in the ditch. "Watch out! Deer!" she screamed.

He hit the brakes while Lilly braced herself for impact. They swerved sharp left, hearing the brakes squeal and smelling the hot rubber of tires grabbing the pavement.

Lilly screamed and threw her hands over her face as the large buck slammed into the windshield. Blake swerved the opposite direction, sending it sliding off the hood and back onto the pavement. The sounds of screeching tires, bending metal, and shattering glass were surreal. What seemed like minutes was only seconds before the car came to a dead stop.

Blake immediately looked for Lilly. She sat in shock, staring at the broken windshield. Another few seconds and the deer would have been on her lap.

"Are you okay?" He turned toward her, looking for injuries. "Lilly, you're not hurt. Neither am I." They looked at each other.

"Come on, we need to get out of the car. Careful, there's glass everywhere." Blake helped her out, and together they picked the glass off their clothing and the car seats.

Lilly saw the huge buck lying in the center of the road. "Is it dead?"

Blake, in his own numbness, bent over the deer and checked. "He's dead. I'll drag him into the ditch."

"I'll help," Lilly automatically responded.

"No, stay on the side of the road and watch for any cars coming. If one comes along, wave it down to warn them that our car is in the middle of the road."

Blake dragged the bloodied deer to the ditch and began to assess the damage to his car. The entire front end was a mangled mess. Eventually he was able to pry open the hood.

"Well the engine appears to be okay, but we have only one headlight, no windshield, and one tire is barely drivable."

"We can walk to the nearest farm and call for help," suggested Lilly.

"Actually, I think your house is just as close. I'm going to knock out the rest of the glass, pull the metal away from the tire and try to make it."

"If we had landed in the ditch, there's no telling how long before someone would have come by. We were lucky, Blake, but I feel awful about your car."

They both glared at the damage. "Me too. My parents aren't going to be happy either. Insurance will go up and Mom's been pissed off about me driving so much."

Lilly's heart sank. "You never told me that."

"Not now. We're damn lucky to be alive, like you said."

They inched their way to her house in silence, giving Lilly's mind time to wander.

He's right, I should drive to his place every other weekend, but I never retook my road test. I have to stop being so dependent. I never was. I'm tough on my own. Tomorrow I will talk to Dad about getting my license.

They quietly pulled into the driveway.

"I can't turn the car off. It may not start again and I have to get home. We're late."

"You can come in and call your mom and dad, and get some water. Look! Your hands are still trembling," she said, holding them in hers.

"Can you call Mom for me? Maybe Dad can meet me halfway and follow me home."

"I'll do that," Lilly said. "This is my fault. If I hadn't brought up college, none of this would have happened."

"That's not true. I shouldn't have left you in the first place." He held her. "You're all right and so am I. The car can be fixed."

"Should I ask Dad to follow you home?"

"I can make it, but I've got to go."

They shared a brief farewell kiss, he drove away, and she walked down the sidewalk, opened the front door, and walked into the kitchen, where she immediately saw her parents at the table.

Lilly looked at the clock on the wall above her mom's head. *Oh no, curfew, I forgot all about curfew!* She looked at her parents. Dad appeared to be steaming mad, and Gwen's face was stained red from crying. "Dad, I can explain, but first I have to call Blake's mom."

"You're more worried about his mother than your own?" he belted out.

"That's not what I said! You're twisting my words. We had an accident. There was—" Lilly stopped short as Vincent grabbed her hair and forced her toward Gwen. "Look at how you make your mother suffer."

"I'm sorry, Dad, but the accident was out of our control—"

"You don't think of anyone but yourself and Blake! You should have called. You have to learn the hard way, always the hard way!" She couldn't get another word in through his shouting barrage.

Tempers flared. "It's not my fault! I couldn't call, there's no phone in the middle of nowhere…let go of my hair!" Lost in his daughter's irresponsibility and defiance, Vincent maneuvered her up against the wall.

"Every damn weekend you do this to us," he spat. "Your mother can't take it anymore."

"That's a lie! I am home for curfew all the time. We can't go out for dinner because it could make us late. I'm going to be eighteen, and I still have the curfew of a sixteen-year-old!"

"You're screwing him, aren't you? That's what the gossip is in town!" Vincent put his hand around her neck and pushed her head into the wall.

"Let go, you son of a bitch!" The words came out before Lilly could stop them.

In the second of silence she prepared for her father's retaliation, slapping her hands over her temples before he struck her with his fist.

When her eyes opened, the room was spinning. "Stop, Dad, we hit a deer!" More blows. "WE HIT A DEER!" she screamed louder, with no one listening. "Mom, stop him!"

Lilly took hit after hit as Gwen watched.

Hate swelled in Lilly's heart. "I'm sick of being your slave to *earn* a date."

Another blow connected with her head, snapping her neck backward. Her father was gone. He was out of his mind, lost in his own violent days of youth.

Screaming, Lilly slipped away and ran upstairs, seeking shelter in her room. Vincent followed, blocking the door as Lilly tried to slam it shut. "Stop!" Lilly cried, trying to push him away.

Vincent pinned her again, this time against her bedroom wall, and punched her repeatedly as Lilly coiled downward like a snake. Again she yelled, "We hit a deer!" Still, no one listened.

"Mom, stop him!" Lilly pleaded, looking at the doorway.

Gwen stood like a mannequin and watched, until with one last punch Vincent leveled Lilly flat to the floor, a speck of disgrace on the bedroom carpet.

The next sound was of his feet moving quickly down the steps.

Lilly lifted her head and saw Eva standing in the doorway, cowered behind Gwen, with a gut-wrenching look of horror on her face. *Why did they allow Eva to see this?* Lilly's heart moaned.

Gwen turned in disgust, taking Eva's hand, and shut the door. Lilly lay on the floor and wept.

I have wanted to die so many times before, but not as bad as I wish I could tonight. If not for Eva, I would walk on the water and never feel again. I am tired of this life. I can't handle it anymore.

She cried. She cried for herself and the one feeling that was an unbearable weight in the center of her chest: her parents hated her.

Angrily she wiped her tears and toughened up her heart. "I don't have any parents," she told herself. "I'm an orphan, and in some ways I always have been. I'm done trying to earn their love. They say I'm a failure, so that's what I will be. After all, Frank created me to be unlovable."

"All I care about is Eva. I have to show her what strength is. It's the only way she'll be able to forget what she saw. I'm the big sister; I will pick myself up as I always do and life will go on as it always does. A life of lies and secrets, fear and pain, and being scared every day."

Putting on her pajamas, she saw the red welts over her back and legs and a huge one on her shoulder. Running her hand through her hair she felt several golf-ball-sized lumps. She went to the bathroom and placed a cold washcloth on her face and head.

It took the heat out, but not the sting. She went to her drawer and took out two of her mother's magical pills.

She caught a glimpse of the phone. *I never called Blake's parents! I let him down. I let Eva down. I let everyone down tonight.*

She threw her head back and swallowed.

DISCARDED

The next morning, Gwen entered Lilly's bedroom.

"I told you we hit a deer. Why didn't you listen?" Lilly asked for the last time, hoping her mother would have an answer.

"There's always an excuse with you, Lilly," Gwen replied. "It's hard to know when you're telling the truth or when you're lying. The names you called your father, well, you had to have been drinking. And the fact that you didn't deny you were having sex..."

"That's how an adult is supposed to act? By hearing what they don't want to? It's better to beat the crap out of someone than listen?"

"See, that right there is an example of how *not* to talk to your parents."

"I don't get it. This is who I am."

Gwen cleared her throat. "This might help. You and your father cannot live in the same house anymore, and I will never send him away. He came before you, and he will stay. But you, Lilly, must go."

The words hit her worse than her father's fists. "Mom, I've been home on time. We had an accident. Call his parents!"

"It's not only about last night. You have been disrespectful for years, and we cannot tolerate it anymore, not under this roof. Your father doesn't sleep, he's terribly depressed, and I can't take it anymore."

Lilly's head filled with her worst fear; complete abandonment. She fought to stay out of the dark world of runaways that only people like Frank enjoyed. "Are you telling me I have to leave? Where will I go?"

"I spoke with Millie. They are more than happy to come and get you. You can live with them until you finish high school. That's only one year, and the schools there are far better than the ones we have here."

Swallowing her vomit, Lilly looked intently at her mother. "You called Millie last night?"

"No, I called her this morning. I needed someone to talk to, and she is your godmother. Lilly, she and Frank want you to be happy. They can give that to you. It'll help everyone."

Lilly fell into silent thought. *My godparents' final plan is coming to a reality. This is exactly what they have always wanted: me as their daughter. And the last time they were here, they did their best to ruin me, so they could come sweeping me up in some kind of saving grace act. No way in hell is this going to happen!* Lilly's thinking went into overdrive.

"There has to be another option! I will be a senior in high school! I won't leave!" Lilly stated directly at Gwen.

"Millie's offer is wise and kind. I agree with her. You should go live with them and enjoy all the benefits of city life. Dad and I can drive you to their house next week and help you pick out a school."

"This is Millie's plan, not yours. I'm staying right here! I love the country." Lilly grasped for different options. "What if I promise to leave after graduation instead of now? That's a year away and I'll apply to a college, take the test, and do whatever I have to. Dad stays away from me and I stay away from him. I graduate from high school and leave the next day."

"Millie and Frank want to be your legal guardians. Think of Eva! You're not being a positive influence."

Is she out of her freaking mind? Going to the city is a death sentence for me and it frees up Eva for more attacks and control by Frank. He hates that I am around here. I don't stop all of his plans, but more than he likes. I have to be taken out of the picture.

She could hear Frank's voice sneering at her: *You know why your parents cannot help you. They don't listen and what would you tell them when you can't remember yourself?* She heard his insulting laughter.

I have done nothing to make your parents believe I'm anything other than a good uncle. It's your word against mine, and you're the one with a history of lying.

Lilly gasped for air, as if she had been drowning, and looked into the angry face of her mother.

Gwen stood up, prepared to walk out of the room. "You'll go to Frank and Millie's as soon as school is out."

Lilly pulled herself together. "Fine, if that's what you want then I'll leave now. I'll run away and find a friend to live with, but no way in hell am I going to the city."

"Listen to your swearing."

"Mom, I learned every swear word in my vocabulary from being sworn at."

Gwen sternly replied. "You can't run away in the community. What would people say? What would you tell them? That is not an option! What happens in this house stays in this house!"

"You're making it my only option, and I can lie. It can be my fault. Let people say what they want. I don't care. I'll defend you and Dad. Keep your image clean. That's what's important here, right?"

Gwen quieted. "I'll give your idea some thought, but this is for sure: it's you who needs to straighten up, not your father." She shook her pointer finger at Lilly until it nearly fell off.

"What about school tomorrow?" Lilly asked, under her breath.

"You go as always."

"But I have gym, and I have to take a shower."

Gwen looked at the fresh bruises. "I'll come up with a written excuse. You fell horseback riding and hit your head. Remember, what happens at home, stays at home. That includes not saying anything to Blake."

"You would like to see him out of my life, wouldn't you?" Lilly shot back with hateful eyes.

"I think you should date other boys, not just one."

"You don't realize what a good guy he is. We don't drink, smoke pot, none of that. Other boys do."

"You asked, I answered. You're on your own, and if you mess up, it's the city."

When Gwen was out of hearing range, Lilly threw her shoe at the door. The movement made her dizzy. Falling backward onto her bed, she looked up at the ceiling and shouted, "God, are you listening, or have you left me too? Maybe Frank was right when he said God isn't real, he exists only in our imagination, because no God would abandon a kid."

Once again she turned to nature, climbing up into the big old pine tree that looked over the split in the river. Far from the ground and close to the sky she freed her feelings.

"Mom has no idea of what I face every day and how hard it is to stay positive while faking happiness in this house." She ripped a twig off a large branch and watched it fall to the ground.

"I lie and pretend that everything is fine, and people think that's who I am, but it's not. I hate myself because of it. It makes me a fake like Frank. If only I could put tomorrow on hold and have the power to stop time, then maybe I could figure something out, but time is moving too fast."

The wind picked up, howling through the pine needles. Lilly allowed the branches to hold her, like the strong arms of a mother holding a child and she heard its whisper, "Never lose hope, always look forward, and keep moving."

It was a long, grueling week. Every time Blake put his arm around her shoulder, she had to swallow the pain of the bruising. Making up a story about the horse brushing her off was unbearable. Lies, all lies. Lies about her parents, lies about Frank, lies about herself, but lying to Blake struck deeper and hurt the most.

How was she going to hide the bruises from him, especially the handprint on her thigh! She remembered that blow. It had knocked her legs right out from under her.

Saturday night she picked out a pair of knee-length shorts and a T-shirt with three-quarter-length sleeves to hide the bruises. Looking in the mirror she saw her fake reflection with Frank standing behind her. Laughing and chewing on his putrid cigar. She was scared, worried, and anxious. How could she explain herself to Blake without mentioning the truth or upsetting their relationship? He and the world they built together were her only joys.

As she slid into his car, her shorts rose up revealing the imprint of her father's hand in purple, green, and yellow. Panic hit. "That's not a bruise from falling off a horse. What happened?" Blake demanded.

Lilly remained silent. He put the car in park and began to step out. Lilly pulled him back, fearful of what would come if he faced Vincent. "Blake, let it go. It's over. Please?" Her eyes floated in tears.

"This isn't right, Lilly. When did it happen?"

"When I broke curfew last weekend," Lilly exhaled, feeling a sense of pride. She had spoken truthfully for once.

The anger was all over his face. "You didn't break curfew. We hit a deer in the middle of nowhere. Where else are you hurt?"

"It doesn't matter," she weakly replied, thinking, *yes, it does! It does matter. He should know how I really feel. How much I need him right now.*

Blake took his place behind the wheel and hit the road with controlled anger, driving to one of their special places in the pine forest. "Let me see," he asked, staring her down.

She pulled up her shirt.

He softly held his hand over each bruise. "Why didn't you tell me? All week I have been holding onto your shoulders. That had to hurt."

"No, your touch was comforting." Lilly looked down and away. "I'm not good at telling people my problems. Since I was a kid, I have been told to work them out on my own, or don't get into any." Then she returned her focus on Blake. "I am tougher than you think. Bruises heal."

"I should have gone inside with you and explained what happened," he said. "Then I could have called my parents."

"And I should have made you come in or rode back with you and spent the night at your house but we were shaken up and not thinking straight. It's wrong to look back and rethink. That only makes both of us feel guilty, and we shouldn't."

Blake sat quietly in thought, far removed from their date.

Lilly dreaded seeing such pain on his face. "Blake, there's a chance that if you did come in with me, the situation may have been worse. Dad and I have been walking on a fine line. He is obsessed with his thoughts about me having sex and drinking booze. The two of you crossing tempers could be a matchstick waiting for a strike, and that's a fire I never want to see lit."

"Lilly, it hurts to know you took a beating like this over one of our dates."

"The date was an excuse for him to let go of everything. I don't think either of us will be going near the other for quite some time. And Mom, she did nothing. I'm angrier with her."

"Lilly, if he ever touches you again, I'll call the police. That's a promise."

"Don't say anything to him, please?"

Blake didn't respond.

Lilly felt a stabbing pain. Their relationship was becoming complicated, like her hidden self. Something she once could keep separate was no more.

The parallel lines had intersected.

Time healed the bruises, but not Lilly's frame of mind. Life sucked, and her replenished stash of Gwen's freedom chips was withering away as stress mounted.

"Lilly, come to the kitchen table. We have to talk," called Gwen.

Stopping her chores and wiping the sweat off her forehead, she went into the kitchen. She and Gwen hadn't been speaking and the same held true with Vincent. Throughout the house there was a restless silence.

"Where's Dad?" Lilly asked. Gwen never had a conversation without Vincent when Lilly was involved. "He's outside. This is between you and me." Gwen's body language was nervous.

Finally, she thought, *Dad has enough guts to tell his queen to deal with some of the female problems by herself!* "What is it?"

"I noticed that there are pills missing from my prescription bottle. Do you know anything about this?"

Lilly had rehearsed an answer, just in case this day came. Getting caught would be an immediate excuse for Gwen to send her off to Frank's.

Bowing her head in wrongdoing, Lilly spoke calmly. "Last Saturday I was cleaning the bathroom medicine cabinet, wiping out the shelves, and I picked up the bottle by its cap. The cover wasn't on tight, and it fell out of my hands and into the sink. I stopped as many as I could from sliding down the drain."

"Why didn't you tell me?" asked Gwen.

"I freaked out about getting punished or sent away, so I said nothing and hoped it wouldn't be noticed. Mom, it happened so fast! I couldn't see how many were lost. They're really tiny."

Gwen bought it hook, line, and sinker. Lilly sat back, letting out a sigh of relief.

"I can see how that could happen when I take one at night. It would be easy not to put the cap back on tightly."

When Lilly looked in the medicine cabinet that Saturday night, the pills were gone. All that remained was a bottle of aspirins, not exactly a replacement for the freedom chips but they would have to do. Lilly threw a few into her mouth.

INTO NOTHINGNESS

As much as she wanted to stop the negative chatter in her head, she couldn't. *You're unlovable, you're not good enough*, the words screamed constantly inside her, even at school and on dates.

Blake was clueless as he boasted about his weekend fun without her. "On Sunday, my brother and I went into the city. I bought a few mini-cassettes. Wait until you hear them! They have an amazing sound!"

"Sounds fun," Lilly answered, feeling jealous. *He's been spending more time with his troublemaker brother, who I don't trust an ounce, but there's no way I can hang out with Blake all weekend. Maybe I should* run away.

"What is this fabric?" he asked, rubbing the collar of her dress between his fingers.

"It's called 'embossed.' Why don't you like it?" she asked, flustered that now she couldn't dress right either.

"Not really," Blake replied.

"What else don't you like me wearing?"

"I don't like that long-sleeved black sweater. It's too tight and it makes your arms look too skinny."

"Fine, I won't wear it again," Lilly said bluntly, her already low self-image absorbing the blow.

"Do you mind going out Friday night instead of Saturday this week?"

She felt her stomach flip, in a bad sort of way. "I don't mind, but I need to ask my parents if I have to babysit."

"I could come over and hang out with you."

Lilly's mood lightened at the idea. "That would be fun! Eva goes to bed by ten. But what's wrong with Saturday?"

"I have plans to go to a race with a few guys."

Why doesn't he want to bring me with? He always has. Maybe he's seeing another girl from the city. The idea nauseated her, *But then why lead me on with coming over Friday night?*

"Sure, I'll check with Mom and Dad," Lilly said, thinking she was reading into it more than she should. Besides, it would be a good opportunity for them to talk.

Friday night came and there was no talk.

❋

"Lilly, you have to take your road test again," insisted Vincent. "When you go to college, you'll need a license for identification. I'll call Officer Jones and set up another road test."

Two weeks later Vincent drove her back to the police station. He must have arranged something with Officer Jones, because after a single ride around the block he passed her.

Embracing her new feeling of independence, she drove out to see Blake. His parents were out for dinner and she had big plans to walk the beach and have a romantic night.

Much to her surprise, that's not what greeted her. Instead, she ended up on the couch, with Blake's brother in the room, receiving another unexpected blow.

"It's not that I don't like you. I do. But I think it's time both of us move on," Blake stammered uncomfortably.

"If you *like* me, then why do we have to break up?" Lilly tried to hold herself together as her mind wanted to leave. "I asked you six months ago if you wanted to date other girls and you freaked out. You were totally upset. You even cried. Now, out of the clear blue sky, you decide it's a good idea. After you made me feel *I* was the only one?"

She had endured many horrific feelings in her life, but none this deeply painful. She drifted in and out, not wanting to hear any more.

The wrenching rejection was too much. He was the sun in her life and everything she did revolved around him.

She looked down at the promise ring, remembering the ring Frank wore. Hatred swelled in her. All rings were fakes except this one. This one came from true love—or so she thought. However, as Blake said such painful words, she realized it too was another lie.

"Here, take it." She handed it back.

"No, I had that ring made for you. I could never give it to another girl!"

Does that mean he still cares for me and wants me to know that? Or is he messing with my head? Does he love me or not?

"What am I supposed to do with it? Wear it every day to remember you?" *How dare he think like Frank!* She fumed inside, struggling to stay in the moment, but she was still trying to deal with her mother's decision to send her away and now this. Her head couldn't take it anymore.

"I don't know Lilly, but it's yours. It doesn't belong to anyone else."

"Fine, I'll give it to my mother. She always admired it." Lilly put the ring in her pocket. She was mad and hurt. She was empty. She felt a sinking feeling in her core.

Lilly left the soul of her hopeful joyful world sitting on the couch without her. Her whole heart pained with a crushing heaviness. Life was over.

There were no more reasons to wake up, and she did not give a damn about tomorrows. Her walls of safety and comfort had fallen.

My body is for everyone to use; to beat, and punch and enjoy. I am nobody. I'm a ghost, haunted with a dying loneliness. Why do I live? Damned if I know. A deep, dangerous sadness tore through her.

※

Her continuous weeping, day after day, wore on Gwen's nerves.

"For heaven's sake, Lilly, he's only a boy. There are going to be many more in your life. You need to grow up and act your age. You were both too young to know what true love is. Get over him, and stop carrying on like a fool."

"Don't tell me that I don't know what love is!" she gritted her teeth.

"When you go off to college you'll be happy that you don't have a boyfriend back home."

"Mom, I love him. How can you not see that?"

"It was puppy love; you'll be over him by the time school starts."

"Oh my God, school!" Lilly buried her face in her hands., "It's going to be horrible! All the other kids will be watching and gossiping. I won't make it. We were like posters in the hallway."

Lilly thought about the shameful day at the beach and how humiliated it had left her. It wouldn't be much different walking the halls alone, no longer Blake's girl and the eyes following her every move.

"Well, there's time to enroll you in the city. Millie still asks me when you're coming. She even bought a new bedspread and curtains for the guest room, just in case."

Lilly felt dead. Nowhere was she safe and protected.

"Talk it over with Anthony; he's coming home this weekend," Gwen informed her. Lilly awakened, taking in a deep breath. "Is he coming home Friday night?"

"Yes, and leaving Sunday morning. I knew that would cheer you up." Gwen watched Lilly's face light up for the first time in weeks.

He'll tell me that it's going to be okay and that I'm not going to feel this horrible forever. I don't want to be spoiled, but some special hugs would be nice, especially now. Without Blake, I have no love!

After their Friday night dinner, Lilly and Anthony sat on the front porch, in the dark of the night, while she told him all that had happened. "We hit a deer. We had no way to tell them and I took the beating for breaking curfew."

Anthony shook his head, enraged with Vincent. "He had no right to hit you."

"And Mom just watched. She even let Eva watch! I can't get that out of my head."

"If he ever hits you again, you have to call me."

"That's not all. Mom told me that one of us had to leave, Dad or me, and it wasn't going to be Dad."

"She kicked you out?"

"She wanted to send me to Frank and Millie's to finish my schooling."

"No way! You've never liked being around them!"

"Exactly. Then I asked if I could stay and just behave, leaving the day after graduation. She agreed after I threatened to run away, but where am I going to go? I don't know what to do!"

"Have you told Blake?"

Swallowing hard, she began phase two, the breakup.

"I'm so sorry, Lilly. I know how much you love him. How are you doing?"

"I'm a wreck. I feel awful, and I'm so sad I can't stop crying." Her tear faucet opened. "It's like there's no more me! My heart will never heal."

"Love happens, sis, and it hurts."

"I know, but I didn't think this would happen. We rarely fought. We were friends and lovers."

"Lilly, we can't control love." "I wish we could."

"You and millions of others! You know I'll help you any way I can. We had a lot of closet time after our spankings, remember?" He tried to pull a smile from her and bring back her once bubbly outlook on life, but it didn't appear to be working. He tried another avenue. "After graduation, why don't you come up to college and live with me and my roommates for the summer? You'll have to find work—apartment living isn't cheap—but it's a plan."

"How do I get into the same college?"

"Make sure you fill out two of the top three choices of schools, naming mine as first choice. Then wait and see what they offer. You should get a break in tuition, being that Mom and Dad already have a child enrolled. Besides, academically speaking, what college isn't going to take you?"

"Thank God for my grades." She paused. "Can I stay with you when school starts?"

"No, campus policy, all freshmen must live in a dorm. You'll have to move on campus in late August."

"Who will I live with then?"

"The school chooses a roommate for you."

"Oh, that sounds lovely." Lilly didn't like changes, and that was what her entire new life was going to be, one change after another. "I'm scared, Anthony."

"Don't be. Just mind your behavior, graduate, and get out of here."

"Don't you worry about Eva?" she inquired.

"Dad and I are going to have a talk. He won't be using her for a punching bag, or I'll turn him in."

"Don't mention me; please don't tell him I told you."

"I won't. I have my own plan. Do you have any girlfriends to hang out with?"

"What girlfriends? It's been only Blake for two years!"

"Julie still talks to you, doesn't she?"

"Yeah, but…she's a cheerleader now. I don't know if that group will take me in. I haven't been in the clique for a long time."

"You can't stay home and cry your heart out night after night. Focus on college, thinking of being free of this small town, with no parents and ten thousand kids."

"But it's so far from Blake. I won't be able to try to win him back."

"Let him go, Lilly. If he really loves you, he'll come back to you; no matter where you are, he'll find you."

Lilly didn't answer. Instead, they sat listening to the sounds of their youth and Mother Nature.

"I can't," Lilly confessed.

"What can't you do?"

"I can't let him go."

"Lilly, you'll get over him, trust me."

"I don't think so. He was my morning and night. Now I don't care about either. Days are for calendars, not for me. I walk around watching the pavement. There's no more reason to look up and feel grateful. Heaven is part of my childhood imagination. There was a time I thought there was someone or something looking down and getting me through life, but I don't feel that way anymore. When I look up, it's black, nothing else. No one is watching over me; they never have."

"Lilly, you don't believe that. I know you. You have faith."

She shook her head no. "Not anymore."

1986 - SESSION NINE - NEVER TOO LATE

"Most of my life I felt some sort of abandonment or rejection from my family, but when Blake walked away, his rejection was the worst. I could live without parents and siblings, even friends, but I didn't see life beyond Blake."

"Your world didn't include a network of friends."

"No. I found friendship *and* love with Blake. Girlfriends would have added more complexity; I wanted simple. With Blake as the center of my life, that was possible. Our world came with no baggage attached. It was built from day to day. I was the most grounded I had ever been and then, bam! Like an idiot, I thought we would be forever." Lilly looked away. "Guess I had our love wrong too."

"You feel that he wasn't who you thought he was."

"Maybe he never loved me. He saw me as his property."

"You believe that."

Lilly tilted her head downward. "Not really, but then I don't know, because we never spoke again."

"Not ever?"

"I tried, but in all the wrong ways, each one making me look more desperate and out of control than the last. All I wanted was one more talk to tell him how I felt and what I was hiding. But it never happened."

"Bringing closure to *both* parties is important. However, the reality of breakups is that one person stands in left field with a ton of unanswered questions, while the other is at home plate with a clear view of their future. And with Blake being your first love, it had to be even harder to accept and move on without finalizing your feelings."

"It was like torture to wake up and have to go to school. I disassociated and buried myself in living out the negative messages of my lifetime."

"Even those of Frank?"

"They were the strongest. His way of thinking fed off of my depression."

"Once again making you feel at fault."

"I wasn't pretty enough; I wasn't tall enough…I wasn't honest. The list is endless."

"And Blake was without faults."

"No, but I accepted them and some I found entertaining, even cute. Loving someone deeply means accepting the whole person as they are."

"And because you felt unloved at home, you loved Blake entirely."

"That I did. But now I wish I hadn't."

"You're willing to give up all those wonderful feelings you had?" He asked in the silence of the room.

"No, and because I haven't let go, it still feels open-ended, creating a forever raw ache in the pit of my gut."

"Let's attempt some closure. Ask me anything about how you felt or what you did when the relationship was over," Dr. Bricks offered as he sat back, putting his pen down.

"No one has asked me to do that." Lilly sat back too. "First, what good comes from losing one's first love?"

"Actually, there is good."

"I can't wait to hear this!" Lilly rolled her eyes.

"The fact is that the majority of people do not marry their first love."

"Is that for real?"

"Yes, for most, finding love and a life partner means risking the loss of the first. It's a positive stage in our lives."

"Oh, please, positive? I can't think of one positive factor, and it nearly killed me."

"Did you never find love again?"

"I did fall in love, several times, and yet no one could replace the feelings I felt with Blake. That is, until I met Mick."

"That there is the positive about first love."

"I don't get what you're saying."

"How did you know that Mick was able to heal the hole in your heart?"

"I knew by how I felt when he touched me."

"The electricity you felt with Blake."

"Very similar."

"That's why first love is a positive stage. You rose above rejection and learned what made you feel love. Then you searched for it again, finding it in Mick."

Lilly remained quiet.

"Do you still love Blake?" Dr. Bricks bluntly asked. Lilly looked up in surprise.

"I can't get him out of my heart. Is it love or the fact that I had no closure? Our relationship ended at one of the most emotionally delicate times in my life, and I never had the chance to explain."

"If you could, what would you tell him? Let your eighteen-year-old hear you stand up for who you are now and then. Use your voice."

"It makes no sense to do an imaginary breakup with a boyfriend from years ago." Lilly rolled her eyes.

"I'm offering it to you as another tool to move forward."

"I think this is silly, but I'll try." Lilly cleared her throat, sat up tall and confident, as she glared into the imaginary set of eyes she once could read like a book.

"You know what, Mr. Blake? You are making the biggest mistake in your life. You will never find another girl who loves you for who you are, from the inside out, as I do. We balance each other and you need me to keep you moving forward. To help you build your life. Nothing will be the same without me. You will always try to fill the void that *was you*. However, that will be impossible because there's only one me and you're letting her go. If you choose to be that idiot, fine. I'll walk. And just so you know, it won't be easy to get me back."

"How did that make you feel?"

"A little better, but I left out Frank and how he had changed me. I still can't go there when it comes to Blake."

"Life is all about learning how to make yourself a better person, and then moving on to accomplish that goal. Think back from the time with Blake to now. What did you learn to take forward with you?"

"Nothing but heartbreak."

"I don't believe that. You came out of each attack stronger. You came out of this relationship stronger and wiser too. You loved him completely, but maybe he didn't know how to return that love to you."

Lilly centered her attention out of the window and over the waterfall. "I *did* learn a few things from his rejection, such as resiliency, keeping an eye on the future, and that drowning in sorrow is destructive, almost deadly. It also became important not to keep my emotions hidden for very long anymore, and never with Owen or Mick. I often wonder what it would be like if I was a normal person. Would I have still blanked out when Blake was talking to me, or would I have said what I wanted? Would we have been able to work something out, or stay friends? We had a great friendship. Another 'I'll never know' moment."

"It's important for you to feel acknowledged."

Lilly reflected on the statement. "I never thought of it that way, but you're right. I do seek out acknowledgment of who I am, and what I have to say. My parents saw me as an extension of them and never allowed me to be me. Their one-size-fits-all routine was maddening. Maybe my sisters and brother felt differently. But I felt I needed to be seen and heard as an individual."

"The abuse can play in that feeling. Victims can also experience stronger emotions than normal in life's upsets. Trauma victims need *more* protection, *more* love, and *more* guidance to help them find themselves again."

"Which didn't happen; instead, I *lost* most of that." Lilly sat back, letting her shoulders relax and moving her neck lightly to release the tension. "The fact that I was born with an incredible drive to exist, no matter what I had to confront, has been a saving grace."

"Lilly, you are not that defeated teenager."

"No, I am not," she said, looking out the windows. "And thank you for saying that out loud. I need to hear it more often and get it here." She pointed to her head. "And in here!" She pointed to her heart.

"You will. You are determined."

"That I am. Trying to swim out to my ocean where all the tributaries and rivers become one. That's a strong mental image for me."

THE GOLDEN ALE

Lilly sat by the river, throwing pebbles into the water, watching the ripples disperse. *This is how pathetic my life has become. Senior year is supposed to be the best. What a joke that is!* She turned up the volume on her portable radio and sang along to a song about mending a broken heart. She no longer wiped away her tears. Her life had given them reason to stain her face.

I may as well start the party life. Without the headache pills, I need something to curb my mood. Maybe beer is the answer. I can drink Blake away, drown him out of my system, and maybe forget about him. I turned down a date to a party, but I think I'll call him back and tell him I've changed my mind.

He's not one of Blake's friends. They *still see me as his property; hoping they can pick up where he left off. That's small-town life.*

She walked back to the house and called LeRoy. "Hi, this is Lilly. I was wondering if you still wanted to take me to the party next weekend."

"I'd love to."

"What time?" She broke out a slight grin. "How about seven?"

"I'll see you then."

Lilly hung up the phone.

Gwen watched in disbelief. "Lilly, you were so frank with that young man. No one is going to want to take you out with that attitude."

"Not true, we're going out next weekend."

"Be home by one."

Lilly blew out her frustration and replied, "Yes, Mother. Like Cinderella, I'll turn into a pumpkin!"

When I was with Blake I had to be home at eleven and then midnight. Lilly mumbled to herself. *Now that I'm a senior I can stay out until one. Maybe if she hadn't put so much pressure on being home and let Blake and me have real dates things may have turned out differently.*

※

LeRoy pulled into her driveway at seven sharp.

"Mom, I'm leaving!" Lilly shouted as she walked out the front door to the car and slid in. He began talking about their date. "The party is at the Willbergs' cottage."

"Wow, that's a nice place. How many kids will be there?"

"I'm not sure, maybe thirty or forty."

"Those many kids drink around here?"

"You have been sheltered."

Lilly agreed. "Guess so. This is my first beer party."

"You've never drank before?"

"Nope, not ever. Any tips?"

"Take it slow, don't slug it down, and stop at three or four tonight. You have to build up your tolerance or you're going to get pretty sick."

"What do you mean by sick?" Lilly asked innocently.

"Vomiting, not being able to walk, everything spins like you just got off the merry-go-round."

"I wouldn't like that. I need to feel in control and that sounds just the opposite."

"Stay close to me. I'll watch out for you."

"You are really sweet!" She flashed him a smile.

LeRoy pulled onto a dirt road. "Here we are. Ready?" They locked eyes.

Lilly's heart rate accelerated. *Am I ready? No, I am scared silly, but here I am. Move forward, Lilly.* "Let's go." She took his hand. "But stay close."

"I won't let you out of my sight."

She was surprised to see so many of her classmates. Quickly, she began conversing about their earlier school days, paying no attention to the constant refilling of her beer mug.

"This is good stuff." She tried to talk smoothly, but the words came out slurred and choppy. "It goes down easier than I thought."

LeRoy reminded her to slow down.

"Why? I'm not drunk," she insisted, enjoying the new sensation of no inhibitions and spontaneous laughter. "I don't even know what drunk is because I have never been drunk!" She giggled, standing on her tiptoes for a kiss. "You're really cute!"

LeRoy picked her up in his arms. "It's time to go home."

"Put me down!" Lilly grew angry at the idea of being controlled. "I'm having fun! Look at all my friends. Hey, friends, tell him to put me down and let me party!" Lilly cheered the crowd on, feeling no fear, not even an ounce, as they hailed her to chug. LeRoy put her down.

"Thank you, Sir Lean-a-Roy!" She bowed to the applause of her classmates.

LeRoy saw that there was no stopping her as she continued to down one beer after another. The once shy Lilly, who avoided crowds of kids and appeared interested only in intelligent conversation, was now the main attraction in a wild, drunken party.

He stayed sober for her sake. "Hey, buddy," a friend said, throwing his arm over LeRoy's shoulder, "I never thought she had this wild side in her. She's hilarious! Thinks she's walking on fire and it's only a wooden floor."

"She's drunk. I have to sober her up before she gets sick."

His friend patted him on the back. "Good luck with that!"

LeRoy approached Lilly again, and this time she didn't resist.

"Hey, Lean-a-Roy, where have you been? I missed you." Then, in an almost inaudible voice she whispered in his ear, "I don't feel so good." LeRoy took the mug out of her hand and set it down. "We should go for a walk."

He threw her coat over her and carried her outside.

"You're so charming! I bet all the girls are in love with you." She twisted his long hair around her finger. "Uh-oh, I think I'm going to puke." LeRoy set her down and held her hair back as she vomited.

"That's not fun," she garbled.

"Come on, up you go." He offered her a supportive arm.

"Wait! Look!" she pointed to her vomit. "There are minnows everywhere! How can they swim without water? Can you see them?" Lilly picked at the leaves on the ground that held the contents of her stomach.

"Lilly, those aren't minnows; it's what you've been eating."

Lilly stopped poking. "These aren't little fishes?" she asked in surprise.

"Not even close! Come on, up you go."

"That's funny, isn't it, Lean-a-Roy?" She laughed and laughed until she puked again and passed out.

A half hour later she woke up in LeRoy's car. "Do you have to drive so fast? My head is spinning and the world is passing by too quickly. It makes my stomach turn."

"Welcome back, Lilly! Glad to see you're coming out of it. Try not to look out of the front windshield."

"Where am I supposed to look?" she whined. "How fast are you going anyway?" She placed her hands over her eyes.

"I'm doing thirty-five."

Lilly chuckled, "Oh, it's my head…so woozy!"

"That's normal for the amount of beer you drank. I'm taking you to my house. My mom will make us coffee and some snacks. That will help you sober up."

Lilly looked at her clothing: everything was exactly as she had put it on. "You didn't try anything with me, did you?"

"You passed out. I'm not one of those guys."

"I had no idea what too much alcohol could do, but it was fun. I felt free, as if I was a kid again with no worries."

"You had a great time, no doubt about that!"

"Thank you for staying sober and watching out for me. I would like to go on another date, but not to a party. However, I get it if you don't want to."

"No, I would like that. You're special, Lilly, you really are."

"You can say that after watching me puke?" She caught a whiff of her vomit. "Did you say you were taking me to your mom's?" Her voice increased a few notches.

"Don't worry; she's cool."

"I will be so embarrassed. Can't we get coffee somewhere else?"

"We could, but trust me, this is the right thing to do."

She was too sick to argue.

After they drank a pot of coffee, snacked on homemade goods, and talked about everything from the moon to high school, Lilly cleaned up and LeRoy took her home, like the polite young man he was. After a friendly kiss goodnight, they made plans for the following Friday.

Vincent heard the car pull out of the driveway as he rocked in his chair, waiting for his daughter's safe return. He had vowed not to touch her again in any hurtful or harmful way. He had done her wrong and his guilt sat heavy in his heart. He hoped that someday she would forgive him and until then, he had to prove his love with patience and guidance.

The kitchen door opened, and it didn't take long for the stench of alcohol to fill the room. *I am not surprised,* he sadly told himself. *She's hurt and angry. I should have never accused her of doing wrong. She was always a good kid. I created this. I pushed her away when she needed me.*

He watched Lilly journey up the stairs, stumbling and falling, but always getting back up and making it a little further with each attempt. Finally, she reached the top and wobbled down the hallway to the bathroom.

She brushed her teeth and absentmindedly popped out her contacts, rinsing them with saline and dropping them into their containers. Vincent saw it differently.

She turned off the light and shuffled her tired body to bed. Vincent closed her door, lowered his head with the weight of a wronged father, and walked downstairs to his and Gwen's bedroom. He was relieved that his Lilly was home and safe.

Lilly opened her eyes to the sunrays pouring through the open shades.

"Damn, I didn't shut them last night." She rolled over on her stomach and put the pillow over her pounding head. Just as she was falling back to sleep she heard Eva's voice at her door.

"Mom says you have to get up and get ready for church. Breakfast is almost over."

"Thanks, Eva, I'm getting up," she said into the pillow.

Lilly could feel Eva's eyes glaring at her. "What is it?" Lilly rolled over to look at her sister.

"You came home late last night."

"Are you waiting up for me?" Lilly had forgotten about that little secret they shared.

"Blake doesn't come around anymore, and he kept you safe. Who's watching you now?"

Lilly mused; *she's a smarty, that little Eva.* "I'm old enough to watch myself now. You don't need to worry about me. Besides, it won't be long and I'll be going off to college."

"Do you have to go?" Eva pleaded.

"I do, Eva. I have to learn a career, like Mom, but I'm not *leaving* you. I would never do that. We can talk on the phone, and you can write me letters." Her head throbbed with every word she said.

"I will." Eva skipped off, satisfied with life.

Lilly put both feet on the floor to stabilize her spinning, "To be young again, and I hope she never drinks as much as I did last night! This feels worse than any flu I ever had!"

She walked to the bathroom to put her contacts in. Running her fingers around the container, she realized that the slippery discs weren't there.

"I'm positive I took them out last night," she reassured herself. "Maybe I put them in the case I keep in my purse. I dropped it by the dining room door, I think."

She brushed her teeth, put her hair in a ponytail, and took a deep breath to relax. *I cannot let on that I was drunk last night. Get it together, Lilly,* she demanded of the image in the mirror, holding her shoulders back and practicing a pleasant morning smile.

Once down the steps, she saw her purse exactly where she remembered leaving it, not far from where Vincent sat reading the Sunday news. Quietly she began feeling for her contact case.

"Good morning, Lilly. Feeling a little tired?" he asked, peering over the paper.

"I swear I took my contacts out last night, but they're not in their cases." She shuffled through her purse and then began to empty it.

"Maybe you should try looking down the drain," he suggested, eyes moving over the headlines.

"Why the drain? What drain?" She was confused. "Do you know something I don't?"

He put down the paper. "I saw you wash them down the drain last night. You thought you were putting them in their vials, but you didn't."

Dread fell over her. They were her eyes. She hated glasses. They made her feel uglier than she already thought she was. Suddenly her heart sunk. "Why didn't you stop me?"

Vincent shrugged. "You wouldn't have believed me. Not in the condition you were in."

He was right; she wouldn't have. The sick feeling continued to grow.

"What am I supposed to do now? They cost a hundred dollars! I can't use money from my savings account because I need it for the summer."

"I would suggest you start wearing your glasses again."

"Dad! You know how much I hate being called four eyes!"

"We could try taking the pipes apart."

"Will you do that for me?"

"No. I'll do it with you, not for you."

Successfully they recovered one lens. The other was history. "Now what? I'll only be able to see out of one eye."

"Talk to your mother. I think Aunt Dee is looking for a babysitter on the weekends."

Lilly sighed, again disappointed with herself. "Thank you for helping me, Dad. I'll talk to Mom about Aunt Dee."

She wanted so badly to put her arms around him and feel the love of a parent's hug, but she refrained. It would be too hard to leave home if she didn't keep her hate inside.

THIS IS HAPPY

Graduation. For twelve years I couldn't wait for this day and now I dread it! All that I had hoped for is gone. Even the person I thought I would be is gone.

Lilly's depression crept to the forefront of her mind as she tried on her cap and gown at Julie's house.

"I think the robe looks cheap and feels like plastic and these hats are ridiculous. What idiot insisted that this event requires a square hat?" Lilly kept tilting and turning it to see if she could possibly compliment her face with its shape.

Julie watched in amusement. "It's weird not to see you and Blake together. I'm sorry. It just is. I thought for sure you two would be the first couple to get married from our class."

"Tell me about it. Whenever I see him he looks edgy, like he's upset about something."

"Maybe he's mad about your partying. Or maybe he's jealous of you dating other guys."

"If he was jealous, wouldn't he say or do something about it? What kind of man would let someone he loves walk away without even trying to win her back? All he has to say is 'Boo!' to me and I will be back in his arms."

"Guys are funny that way. They act all big and tough, but when something like this happens, they don't know what to do."

"And neither do I! Do I talk to him in school, corner him somewhere so he can't escape, or wait for him to make a move?"

"That's a tough call. All I see is that he's not happy, you're not happy, and I don't know why the two of you can't work something out."

"When I try I screw everything up. I called when I was drunk and his mother answered."

"That's stupid," Jane affirmed.

"I know, but at least I tried. He doesn't do anything. He has moved on, and that's that. Wish I could feel the same."

"The two of you are so stubborn!"

Lilly didn't respond. The topic made her feel sicker than being too drunk. "Are you going to the graduation party tonight?" asked Julie.

"It would be nice to say good-byes, but I don't want to drink."

"What do you mean 'good-byes'? We have summer for that. And of all the parties to drink at, this is the one!"

Lilly could feel the tears trying to break through. *I can't tell Julie about leaving home. She doesn't know that we have today together and that's it. There will be no summer for me.*

She stuffed down the truth. "I'm silly! Of course we have the summer. It should be fun!" Lilly took off the hat and tossed it next to the gown. She felt no pride as she looked at it. Her achievements, awards, scholarships and acceptance to Anthony's college meant little to her. Her broken heart stole the stage.

"Hey, Julie, do you want to go and get a Coke or something? I have the car!"

"How about we take a walk around town?"

"Perfect, let's enjoy being irresponsible youths while we can!"

※

After the graduation ceremony, she changed clothes and headed out to the field where the party was. She found a boulder away from the crowd and rested her back against it. She had a full view of everyone. They were the people she grew up with. And now it felt like they were strangers.

Julie saw her sitting alone and joined her. "Who are you watching?" she asked curiously.

"Blake. Look at him. He is beyond intoxicated. That's not who he is. He's always in control. He's strong and not weak. It hurts to see him in that condition."

"Maybe that's how he felt when he saw you drunk."

"I have a reason to drink. What reason does he have? I should talk to him, get him sober and make sure he doesn't get into his car."

"Do you want me to walk over with you?"

"Would you?"

"Sure."

When they were about six feet away, one of his friends approached. "Stay away from him. This is your fault. Can't you see how miserable he is without you?" He acted as if Blake was a rare white tiger and she was the poacher.

"Me? This is my fault? He is the one who broke it off. He's the one running around with some fancy city girl. He knows where I live."

"Stay away." His friend turned and continued to help Blake.

"Wow, I'm sorry that had to happen," Julie said under her breath.

"Does it make sense to you?" asked Lilly.

Julie watched Blake, who was barely able to stand on his own two feet. "I don't know, Lilly. Does Blake ever know what he really wants?"

"He's changed. That's not my Blake." Lilly's heart was too full of grief. "No offense, but this party isn't for me. I'm going home. You want a ride back into town?"

"Thanks, but no thanks. I'm going to stay a while longer."

Without good-byes or explanations, Lilly walked back to her car. She turned around for one last look at her classmates of twelve years. "Time to put everything behind: home, school, friends, the river and woods, Frank and Millie, Blake, even my willow tree. This world and this life are over. I have to build another with whatever is left of me. Funny how no one truly knows who I am after eighteen years. Hell, I'm not sure if I do! I never had a chance."

She drove away, down the dark country roads, to spend her last night at home.

"Can I come in?" Vincent asked outside Lilly's bedroom door. It was early in the morning and he knew she would be packing.

This isn't the time to apologize. That should have happened months ago. Maybe then I wouldn't be packing now, Lilly thought with mixed emotions. "Come in," she answered.

"Mom and I bought you these. You'll need them for college." Vincent held two new suitcases in his hands. *They bought me luggage after kicking me out of the house! How ironic is that?* Lilly shook her head in disbelief. "I guess I should say thanks." She placed them on the bed. "But plastic bags and boxes would have been fine."

"Do you need help?" He wrestled with the correct words to say, not wanting to upset her more.

"No, Dad, I can do this on my own."

He chose to stay, hoping to mend some of their differences. "Lilly, I'm sorry it has to be this way."

Expressionless, she answered, "It didn't have to, Dad. Not if you and Mom listened instead of attacking me."

"What I did was wrong," he grappled, trying to face up to his failure. "I want to explain myself."

"There's nothing to explain. You did what you did, and Mom said what she said. I got both of your messages loud and clear."

"Please, hear me out, Lilly. I'm not making excuses. But I do want you to understand."

"Understand?" Lilly looked up at him. "You won't listen to me, but you want me to listen to you?"

"My father was an angry, bitter man who would beat me for no reason. I hated him for that, but after the war I realized how short life is and I found it in me to forgive him. I know you're not feeling that way now, but I hope that someday you can forgive me too."

Mercilessly, she answered, "I'm happy you forgave your father, but I'm not you. I'm not ready to forgive, and maybe I never will."

Lilly recalled the sting of his hand. *I don't need to forgive. I need to get out of here and start over.* Her body language made it clear she didn't want to see or hear about *his* misfortune.

Vincent left, quietly closing the door behind him.

Lilly filled her suitcases, carefully wrapping her statues in her sweaters, and then sat on the edge of her bed, taking one last look at her room.

"If these walls could talk, they would have quite a story to tell. They know the secrets I hold and the truth of who I really am. They know what I've gone through. Over there is the corner where Dad pinned me down."

She looked at the closet and smiled. "And that's where Blake and I once made love."

The smile faded quickly as she glanced at the corner behind the door. "And that's where Frank stood watching me."

She glanced at her windows, where she would listen to the whippoorwills, the night owls, and the loud exhaust of Blake's car.

She closed the shades and curtains. She put the gold brush and mirror in the drawer, for the last time. She would never have to look at it and deal with its memories again. She picked up the suitcases and walked downstairs.

Gwen sat in the kitchen.

Lilly detested looking at her. *Dad does the hard work so she doesn't have to feel the pain or explain a difficult farewell to Eva. She may think it wasn't her fault, but she's wrong. She is like her sister, pushing blame onto anyone but herself.* Lilly felt a chill run through her as Gwen hugged her good-bye. It was cold, just as she expected.

Vincent put the luggage below the bus and in an unprepared moment gave her a hug. Lilly pulled away. She didn't want him to see the ocean of tears she was fighting off or the desire to hug him back.

She looked out the window of the bus and saw the silhouette of a defeated man. She couldn't stop loving him, and she couldn't stop hating him.

Lilly sat. This was her punishment; she had to learn to live with it. No one was going to rescue her. Blake didn't even know, let alone care. This was not a happily-ever-after fairy tale. It was sorrowfully real.

She reached into her backpack and pulled out Vincent's black prayer book. She held it over her heart and pulled the hoodie on her sweatshirt over her head. Home for eighteen years was over. Now it was just a place to visit.

She thought of leaving for good, but death was not an option. That would bring pleasure to Frank. He would gloat in her weakness, her inability to stay strong. She had to accomplish more than surviving. She had to fight. She had to succeed. She had to be strong. That was the only way to defeat Frank. But she was tired, so very tired.

She wiped her eyes. *From here on, life is mine. It's what I make of it.*

1986 - SESSION TEN - CRUTCHES

"You *reflect* your own insecurities in your own psyche from how you felt when you were with Frank, your parents, and Blake."

Lilly grasped the idea. "That explains a great deal. When I allow myself to live in the past, I remove myself from the present, and that changes reality. In a way, disassociating became a crutch of avoidance. Just like drinking and drugs."

"You drank to avoid the anxiety of being social?"

"Sort of," she confessed, not feeling proud of her once drunken life. "All I wanted was to be like the kids who *loved* the attention of a crowd. You know, the kids who were confident and comfortable with who they were, what they wore, and how they acted. Other people's judgments or comments did not bother them. I saw them as normal and I badly wanted normal."

"You were self-treating your anxiety and depression, as you did with your mother's medication."

"Come on. I always knew what I was doing."

"You did?" He took on a look of a sly weasel, and Lilly slid back in her chair, putting distance between them. "Yes," she confirmed. "You think I drank to escape from my pain and depression!"

"Did you?" he questioned.

"No. My first drink was with a date my senior year of high school— the first date I was excited about since Blake."

"And you chose to drink because…"

"We were both of legal age. He was drinking, I was drinking, and so was everyone else."

"What if your date hadn't rescued you?"

Lilly grew increasingly aggravated. "I get it. You want me to see how vulnerable I was before I went to that party. Mom's pills weren't accessible. I was in emotional pain, so I planned the whole thing. I wanted to hurt myself and took the risk that my date would save me."

"That's an interesting perspective."

"That night I was with a group of kids, at a social event I had never experienced. To blend in I took a bottle of beer. I thought that would make me *less* vulnerable. I was tired of the constant grind to stay alert and safe. I didn't want to feel different anymore. Is that escaping from reality?" She paced in front of the windows.

"You're feeling angry."

"Don't tell me what I'm feeling!" she snapped back. "I'm not angry. I feel dejected. I wanted someone other than myself to see *me* hurt, but everyone thought it was all about Blake, which was not true. It was about me! Even my own parents couldn't see that!"

"You wanted to be known as someone other than 'Blake's girl.'"

"People can change; why can't I? I wanted to get far away from the Lilly they grew up knowing. And on that particular night, beer was the answer."

"You wanted 'a change'."

"Yes! I wanted to change immediately. Like a magic wand waved over my head," she snarled. "Poof! All of a sudden I become someone else."

"Most eighteen-year-olds still need adult guidance and supervision. The parts of the brain that deal with impulsivity and risk don't develop until the early to mid-twenties."

Lilly stopped pacing and faced Dr. Bricks. "What are you saying? That my brain wasn't as developed as my parents' were. Right! They threw me out of the house. They pushed me into a scary dark corner."

"Your parents did not make a good decision."

"No, they didn't, and at eighteen I knew what they were doing was wrong, but they didn't see it. So, don't tell me that my brain power was lacking!"

"I'm not. What I want you to think about is the fact that teens are more tempted to indulge in risky behavior when there's peer pressure or strong emotional stress."

"If I'd had a happy, comforting home I might have not accepted the date in the first place. My heart was broken by Blake and Dad, while Mom abandoned me."

"You felt you were left to fend for yourself and didn't need parental supervision."

"You could say that. Call it payback, or call it a cry for help; at the time it felt necessary."

"Exactly: your brain wasn't developed to the point of making a more rational choice. I've heard the teenage years referred to as a repeat of the terrible twos."

Lilly's anger changed with a visualization of a bratty eighteen-year-old, acting like a two-year-old, wanting life to go her way as soon as possible. Then she placed that teen in a room filled with others just like her. It was a no-brainer for disaster.

"If that's true, why does society have us graduating to fill adult shoes when we aren't ready until we are twenty-one? Aren't we set up for failure before we begin?"

"It is hoped that a parent's teachings will carry you through until you can figure it out for yourself."

"Funny you say that. As much and as little as my parents guided me, there were times I saw my father's face, or heard his words, and I did make a wiser decision. However, when I cut Dad out of my life, I left those teachings behind too. I was only eighteen. I didn't know about the dangers of drinking. I was alone and scared. I wish I could relive that year."

"Being twenty-one?"

Lilly plopped down in the big overstuffed chair. "Yup…a very wise one. At eighteen, I was out of control, freaking out everywhere and anywhere there were people. Total aloneness was my only comfort and sense of safety."

"Being alone helps you control and avoid triggers that set off your anxiety."

"Those damn triggers were firing nonstop."

"Tell me about them."

"There were many…cigar smoke, especially if it was sweet; people staring at me for any reason; the sound of coins jingling; the sense of being followed; people laughing while looking at me—to name a few. The triggers stopped me from seeing the whole picture. My mind scattered, and all I saw were bits and pieces. Then I went into a panic and wanted to run. It was nearly impossible to let my guard down."

"What did you think would happen if you did?"

Lilly glowered. "Someone would attack me. People would see my past with Frank. I would look stupid, or worse yet, crazy. Maybe I would die."

"It would be difficult for anyone to stay grounded with such catastrophic thinking," Dr. Bricks expressed with deep concern.

"That's just it! When triggered, there is no present, only the past. There is no rational, only the fear of irrational," Lilly shot back.

"Are you rational now?"

"I am *trying* not to fall back into the thoughts of my inner child. I *try* not to let the past get to me! But I fail, over and over."

"You are defending yourself now, not failing, but growing into a new reality," reassured Dr. Bricks.

If only I could sincerely believe that, Lilly quietly thought.

YOUNG ADULT

1972-1976

AFTER HOURS

The bus slowed as it cruised through Main Street toward the station. Redbrick stores, stone banks, and rugged wooden restaurants caught Lilly's interest with their resemblance to a city in the early 1900s. However, the true beauty was how the street sloped downward, looking upon the vast, aqua-blue waters of a massive lake that lifted Lilly's spirit.

Stepping off the bus, she spotted Anthony standing at his car. She quickly walked toward him, her backpack strung over her shoulder and the weight of the suitcase pulling her sideways.

"Hey, sis, welcome to Black Rock!" Anthony gave her a gentle hug. "What do you think so far?" He pointed toward the lake.

"She's a beauty: white-tipped waves and all. Like an ocean! It feels like she is calling me to play in her waves. She's alive and feisty. I think we're going to be friends!"

Anthony took her suitcase. "Lesson number one, be careful. She has her own personality, which can be dangerous at times with waves eight feet tall, even bigger. They'll snap your neck *and* she has a tide. Don't be fooled."

Lilly looked at Anthony with disapproval. "You're so much like Dad, always assessing the dangers. Look!" Lilly twirled around. "It's gorgeous! Smell the water! Embrace the view!"

That's Lilly, he reminded himself, putting her luggage in the trunk.

"How did it go with Dad and Mom this morning?" he asked.

"Don't want to talk about it. That part of my life is over," Lilly bluntly cut him off.

"Sorry." Anthony opened the passenger door for her. "I thought I would show you where a few popular restaurants are. They're always looking for waitresses and we can stop to pick up some applications."

The idea of getting a job made her nervous. "What if no one likes me, or thinks I can do the job, then what?"

"Lilly, you know how to work. Mom and Dad taught us well. Be confident and believe there's nothing you can't do!" Anthony pulled up to the entrance of a resort on the lake.

Lilly's eyes lit up. "This is where I want to work!"

"I thought you would love it! So do all the other college kids. It's hard to get in, but give it a shot!"

"I will, most definitely!" Lilly had her mind set. She had found her place of employment.

After a few more stops she was bored with running in and out to collect application forms. "I think this is a good start. Where next?"

"The campus," he replied.

A lump of fear formed in her throat.

"Do you think I'll be able to pass the classes? I didn't take college prep in high school."

"Why in the world didn't you?"

"It was my choosing and college wasn't my first choice. I thought Blake and I would be together, working at his family's business. Then my life collapsed. It was hard enough getting through senior year without the extra stress of college courses."

"I didn't mean to bring up memories. Don't worry; I'm not sure if our school back home prepared anyone for college. It's completely different than high school," Anthony remarked. "You have good study habits and you should use the free tutors. But be careful with the parties."

"Yes Daddy," Lilly grinned. "You're always pointing me in the right direction."

"I try, but sometimes you're not easy to guide."

Lilly rolled her eyes. "If you knew me, you would know that's not true. Hey, I'm starving. Can we grab something to eat?"

"First, let's drop off your luggage at the apartment. Then we'll pick up my roomies, and get a bite to eat."

"You're lucky to have kept your high school friends. I won't ever have a high school friend that I was that close to except for you-know-who."

"You'll make plenty of girlfriends here. There are thousands of college kids. Hey, what do you think of going out for a hamburger and a beer?"

"Are you for real, a burger and beer? You don't have to ask me twice!"

"Do you have your license?"

Lilly beamed. "Dad insisted that I get my license. Reluctantly, I agreed and I'm so happy that I did."

"Wise move. You can't do much in college without a driver's license!"

❈

Lilly ordered another pitcher. It was their fourth.

Anthony took hold of her elbow. "Come on, sister, it's time to get back to the apartment. You've had enough to drink."

Lilly pulled her arm away. "Don't touch me!" she commanded.

Anthony let go. "You're getting drunk, Lilly," he reprimanded.

"Nobody cares but you!" She drawled the sentence out and gave him a little shove in the chest.

"We're going back to the apartment— now!" Anthony was not amused.

However, Lilly was. Once she was wound up, there was no unwinding until she blacked out. "Bill, Tom...Do you boys want to go home with Anthony or stay and drink another pitcher?" she asked flirtatiously.

Tom replied, "Why don't Bill and I walk you to the car? We'll pick up some beer and finish it off at the apartment."

"That's an idea. Captain Anthony, will you drive the ship back home?" Lilly joked while looking at her brother.

Both roommates gently guided her out of the bar. "You guys are cute. I never said anything in high school because you were my brother's best friends. But now we're old." She stopped at that thought and laughed. Her laughter was contagious and soon everyone was laughing except Anthony.

Back at their apartment, an upper flat of an old, white, two-story home, they guided Lilly as she trekked up the steep and narrow stairwell. Once inside, she stumbled toward the makeshift bedroom the boys had made for her in the corner of the living room, using sheets for walls. She flopped down on the bed, feeling the spinning of her head from too much alcohol. When she opened her eyes, she saw Anthony staring down at her and yelling.

"Anthony, I don't know what you're saying!" She giggled.

He wasn't her brother or her fishing partner—not anymore—he was a young man. The thought continued to tickle her imagination, and she could not hold back the laughter.

She looked and focused on his mouth, which moved faster and faster without any sound, as if she were watching a silent movie. Her laughter filled the room. Anthony stopped, and that's when she saw the anger on his face turn to hurt.

It was too late to take anything back.

He walked away, slamming his bedroom door behind him, as his friends followed suit.

"Fine, be that way," she muttered to herself. "You're all grown up, but I'm not. I don't know if I'll ever grow up. I'm too much of a Lilly-tangled mess!" She laughed at her metaphor. "I need to go and play with the lake." She rolled to the edge of the bed, steadied her legs, and slowly staggered across the living room to the steps—the zillion steps that led to the outdoors.

"Holy shit!" She looked downward at them and then over at her bed, which now seemed to be a mile away but a much easier path to travel. On all fours, she crawled her way back to safety.

She threw one leg off the bed and onto the floor to help stop the room from spinning, and then she passed out, falling into the sleep that a good drunk brought on. It had no nightmares of Frank or the constant doubts of what she could have or should have done differently with Blake. She only slept.

Bliss ended the next morning as the pounding headache of no sympathy arrived.

"Where is everyone?" She threw on her robe and shuffled to the fridge, where she found a note from Anthony: *We are in class all day or at work. See you tonight.*

"This is convenient, the entire apartment to myself," she said, feeling smug.

With one hand holding onto her head, she made her way to the shower. After breakfast, she felt more like herself and noticed that the apartment needed a female touch. She washed the dishes, polished up the kitchen, cleaned the bathroom, and then headed out for a long walk along the lake.

Once she hit the sandy shores and breathed in the moist, cool air, her head began to clear.

"Oh, man, I laughed at Anthony when he was trying to help me," she recalled, feeling guilty for being disrespectful and hurting his pride.

Lying on one of the black rocks near the shoreline, she closed her eyes and listened to the waves. She was right where she needed to be and she didn't have to leave. She was on her own, no curfew, no list of house chores. She simply soaked up the sun's rays and contemplated how to make the mess she created last night go away.

"Why can't I get it into my hard head that the past isn't going to change? It's an impossible feat and yet, day after day, I think Blake is coming back and we'll be in love again. I think my parents are going to apologize and ask me to come back home. I'm a fucking fool!" she cussed at herself. "And I have to stop looking over my shoulder for some mental case sent by Frank to watch me. Frank isn't coming here. Grow up, Lilly. Get a hold of yourself."

"What's gone is gone!" she continued. "So pick up your lazy ass and start looking for a job. Maybe Anthony will be more forgiving if he sees that I didn't waste the day." She brushed off the sand, walked back to the apartment, and prepared herself for an interview.

As she walked the five-mile trek to the resort, she recalled the advice Vincent had given her about getting a job. He said to speak to the manager and not to accept anyone else. She did exactly that, and soon she was talking to the man in charge.

She hadn't realized how helpful the strict work ethic her parents had given her would be in the job market. As the interview wound down, the manager threw in one last question: "Would you consider working after hours?"

"Would I be paid my hourly wage?" she asked and then worried she was too blunt.

"No, it would be more than that because you wouldn't be receiving tips."

How could I go wrong? They'll probably have me clean the kitchen and set up for the morning. Hard work doesn't bother me, and it's easy money. "Sure, I'll work after hours."

"Great! Then I will see you tomorrow night. Check with the hostess for your uniform and she'll answer any other questions you have. Take a menu home to memorize. You'll follow a waitress for three days and then you'll begin taking orders by yourself." He held out his hand. "It was a pleasure to meet you."

Lilly firmly gripped it and returned a sincere thank-you shake.

Once she was out of hearing range, she jumped into the air with a celebrating shout. "I did it! I have a job!" The walk back went faster as she gloated in her accomplishment—a feeling she had not had for quite some time.

CALIFORNIA DREAMING

Lilly was a quick study of the ins and outs of the restaurant and resort business. By night four she was working six tables with confidence and smiles. She loved conversing and meeting new people. As a result, her tips were generous, pushing her hourly rate of one dollar and twenty-five cents up to a minimum of seven dollars an hour. She opened a savings account for the school year, paid rent, and still had pocket change. She was learning how to survive on her own, based on hours of hard work.

After her shift, she did the usual routine: check out with the hostess, report how much money she made in tips, and declare what was suggested. The rest was her extra spending money.

The hostess was a matronly woman with a British accent. The girls called her "Mum."

"Mum, what's this?" Lilly asked, holding up a napkin and key in her hands.

"Where did you get that?" Mum questioned her. "Some guy slipped it in my apron pocket."

"Lilly, did you agree to work after hours?" Mum's face went from surprise to regret.

"I did—after hours, you know, overtime, to make more money, right?" Lilly scrunched up her face. "Not right?"

"No, dearie, you are the cutest, sweetest waitress, but after hours is exactly that. The key is to a room where you are to 'service a guest's needs.'"

Lilly stood back, horrified, and immediately heard Frank's voice telling her what a cute little country hussy she was, worth some good money. "Oh my God, Mum, that is never going to happen! What should I do?" Lilly frantically asked.

"First, I'll return the key and tell him there was a misunderstanding."

"What's second?" The size of Lilly's eyes swallowed up her face.

Mum put her arm around Lilly. "Don't worry, honey. I'll handle it."

"But I need this job! I've worked so hard and I'm finally making enough money to live on *and* save for school."

"I know you are. You are one of our best, but the night shift won't be possible. I'll get you switched to morning."

Lilly's shoulders fell in disappointment. "The morning shifts don't make the tip money like the evening dinner."

"That's true, but you'll still do well. I'll see if you can work into the lunch hours. That'll make up the difference. Morning is better than no job at all," Mum answered.

"I know. Thank you."

"Don't look so defeated! You'll love the morning once you get into the groove," Mum said, trying to cheer her up. "People are generally in a good mood and you'll meet many more guests, but Lilly, you must promise not to tell anyone about the key. Can you do that?"

What's one more secret in my life? She thought. "Trust me," Lilly answered, "I am an expert at keeping secrets."

"We should be good then. Take tomorrow off and I'll see you Sunday morning. The one big difference about breakfast is that it moves very fast. Study the new menu. I'll put you on training for only a day."

"That will help, thank you."

"Remember, just between us."

"I understand."

Lilly hopped the bus and headed for home. She held her hands together to stop their shaking. *That was too close*, she thought. *I could have ended up just as Frank said I would. The city has its dangers. I need to remember that.*

She said good-bye to wine and steaks and good morning to bacon and eggs. She filled the syrup cups with prune juice and the prune juice cups with syrup. That was her first day. Shortly after she dropped a Reuben on a man's lap and tried to assist him in cleaning it off. With another customer she delivered the bill before the food, but slowly, Lilly fell into the morning mania and lunch madness. Her drive and ambition earned her a head waitress position and new friendships, including a young girl her age who sat alone, near a window, morning after morning.

"Hi, what would you like today, coffee or juice?"

"Neither, I'll have water and an order of toast."

"Sure." Lilly looked up from her ordering pad. "Is everything okay?"

"No, living in this resort is getting boring. My father's job transferred him here from California. I had to drop out of college and move with." Her eyes slanted downward like a disappointed puppy dog.

"I'm sorry. It must be lonely."

"You could say that. We have to stay here until my parents find a house."

"Oh wow! I get it!" Lilly felt a bond growing. She, too, didn't have a real home. "Do you have wheels?" she asked, with a twinkle in her eye.

"I do. Why?" The young girl returned the same look.

"My name is Lilly. I'd love to show you around the town after my shift."

"That would be fun! My name is Ann." She offered her hand.

Lilly gently shook it, "Hi, Ann."

She had finally met a girl her age who felt as lonely in life as she did.

This had to be a good sign.

❋

Following an afternoon of rock climbing, drinking a few beers, and talking, a friendship ignited between the cute country girl and the tall lanky California blonde.

Ann's exceptionally laid-back demeanor was an ingredient missing from Lilly's life. Their friendship blossomed, and it was a rare afternoon or evening when they weren't together. They often hung out at the lakeshore with a bottle of liquor and snacks as they talked for hours.

When Ann's parents moved into their new home, Lilly sat at their dinner table almost as often as their own children did. She soon found herself spending more nights with Ann and her family than with Anthony at his apartment. She cautiously allowed herself to feel happy and to start believing in tomorrow again, with the love of a true friendship in Ann.

Thoughts of Blake lessened and she stopped looking for a replacement. Ann filled that role. During one of their quiet times, Lilly felt an emotion she had put away a long time ago, trust. She wanted to take a chance at accepting it again.

"Ann, I want to tell you something that explains me."

"Is that possible?" Ann laughed.

Lilly smiled. "It is. Can you keep it a secret?"

"Sure. You're really serious; that's not like you."

"What I have to say *is* serious and not easy." Lilly let out a sigh and continued, "I think I'm unlovable; first by my parents and then by Blake. Mom and Dad saw my behavior as intolerable and kicked me out. Blake saw me as being an old toy and wanted something newer and shinier. I had nowhere to go except the streets. That's when Anthony suggested coming here and going to college."

"I'm sorry, Lilly, but you shouldn't ever call yourself unlovable. You're the easiest person to love that I've ever met!"

"Thanks." Lilly paused. "But there's something else."

"You don't have to tell me if you don't want to. You look worried."

"I want to and I need to." Lilly hesitated, recalling the dangers of going any further with the losses she had experienced throughout her life.

"Ann." Lilly leaned forward. "I have a sick uncle who is evil and dangerous. He…he has touched me in ways I haven't talked about… ever. He threatened to hurt me and anyone I told. I would die if anything happened to you or your family. That's why I want you to hear me and then forget."

Ann saw and heard Lilly's fear. "Are you saying he abused you?"

"Yes," Lilly responded, waiting for the earth to open up and swallow her down to the hell beneath—but it didn't.

Ann's soft, comforting voice kept her in the present. "I won't say anything, Lilly, but are *you* safe? Can this uncle find you here?"

"No, his name is Frank and his wife's name is Millie. They won't come here. It would look too suspicious. They only visit where there is family. I don't think they would ever pay for a hotel. And I have no reason to go home. So I guess, yes, I'm safe here." Admitting to feeling out of harm's way was a helpful release.

"Time will bring you and your family back together. Have patience. It will work out."

"I hope you're right."

"Everyone carries a weight. That's why we need each other."

"What's your weight?" Lilly asked, curiously.

"I had to leave California, friends, and the ocean. But since we've met, that's becoming the past."

"I feel the same way. I enjoy being with you. I haven't had a real girlfriend since fifth grade. Her parents moved and I've never trusted girls since."

"I'm the first girl you trusted since fifth grade! Wow!" Ann smiled.

That's what Lilly loved about Ann—her optimism, her lighthearted point of view, and how easy she was to believe in. Ann wasn't complicated.

THREE ISN'T A CROWD

"Ann, give it some more thought, for me, please? We could be roommates and still have your house to hang out in on the weekends, with the added benefit of your mom's cooking!" Lilly used her most convincing voice to try to get Ann to return to college.

"It would be fun, Lilly, but I don't want to go back to school. I'll be happier in a two-year program."

"Can't you do that on a college campus?" Lilly pressed on.

"My program is only offered at the community college. We're still going to be with one another, just not as often."

"I know," Lilly gave in. "I dread thinking about moving into a hamster cage after being free all summer. Thoughts of starting over again make me anxious and nervous and then I drink more. See how important it is that we live together?" It was her final hopeful shot.

"Change is inevitable," Ann said in her down-to-earth voice. "That's why I'm here today. To help you pack up your things."

"Do you always have to be so rational? Don't you think that I've had enough adjusting to do for a lifetime, or at least for a few years?"

"This is a fresh start for you! Look at it that way. Maybe the man of your dreams will happen to live in your dorm."

"Oh, for sure, look how successful I've been with the boys this summer!"

"You had a date every weekend."

"That's all they were…dates, free drinks, and sex."

"Knock off the 'poor me' attitude. You can't fall in love again until you stop loving *him*," Ann reminded Lilly. Lilly tuned her out and held up an old toaster. "So what do you think, take the toaster or not?"

"Not, leave it for Anthony."

Ann looked around the apartment. "I don't think it's going to take a day to get you packed. More like an hour!"

"Hey, I came here with a suitcase and a backpack," Lilly teased. "There has to be enough clothes and stuff now for at least *one* added garbage bag, like my bedding!" Lilly pointed out her comforter and pillows. "I bought them with my first paycheck!"

"Wow, that'll take all of three minutes to pack," wisecracked Ann.

"So how much space do you think I'll need in the dorm?" inquired Lilly, looking at her simple belongings.

"I'd say about three drawers and you'd be crazy not to ask for half of the closet. After all, you're paying for it."

"True, but what if my roommate needs more space than me?"

"Be smart, Lilly, you *share* the room. Cut it right down the middle and as you get to know one another, make changes."

"That makes sense; it's just not the way I think."

"For you it's always how the other one feels. Now it's time to pay attention to what Lilly feels."

"Like that will ever happen. I have the word 'sucker' stamped on my forehead. Everyone else comes first."

"Wait, don't say another word!" Ann interrupted, looking mysterious.

"What is it?" Lilly whispered.

"I need a Kleenex. Your sob stories are too emotional."

Lilly threw the Kleenex box at Ann and asked, "Smarty pants, do you want a beer?"

"Sure."

Lilly went to the kitchen and returned with two cold bottles of brew. They sat on her bed, looking around and thinking of farewells to make to the humble bedroom.

"Lilly, are you going to take those statues to the dorm?" Ann pointed at the Virgin Mary and the little nun.

Lilly's heart sank. "This is what I mean about making changes. My roommate will think I'm some kind of religious freak, which is not the case. Those two statues have been my protection since I was eight. I would never leave them or Dad's prayer book. That's me in a nutshell: a nun, a saint, and a bunch of hopeful words."

There was a quiet pause and then Ann slammed back, "Definitely not the nun or the saint."

"Smartass." Lilly loved Ann's wisecracks.

"You haven't told me much about your roommate—how come?"

"What's there to say except that I'm nervous about living with a stranger."

"You're in college now. Everyone feels abandoned and scared to some degree."

"Maybe so, her name is Trudy and she's from somewhere near Detroit."

"She's a city girl. This should be interesting."

"Hey, I'm working on being less country." Lilly looked down at her engineer boots, hip-hugger jeans, and a tied shirt revealing her belly button.

"I like you just as you are and so will Trudy. There's no need to change."

"Will you come with me on move-in day? I think it's going to be hard seeing kids and families together."

Ann wore a concerned look. "I wish I could, but I have to work until five thirty."

Lilly hid her disappointment and changed the subject. "This was one of my best summers. We had a ball, didn't we?"

"We did. I'm happy you came over and waited on me that morning. Think of how lonely we would have both been, living here and knowing no one. My whole family is happy that you came into our lives."

"And I'm equally happy that I'm part of your family. I really mean that, Ann."

"Oh, don't get mushy! You're only moving to the dorms, not another town!"

Lilly laughed at her own drama and made a toast. "Here's to change!"

※

A few days later Lilly sat on the grassy knoll overlooking her dorm. She watched the farewells between parents and their teen-aged children. It was a hard reminder of how broken she and her parents had become. Since she left home there had been little communication and no interest in visiting.

She even turned LeRoy away when he found out where she was and came to visit. He offered to enroll in college if she would give him a chance. However, Lilly's choices were now all about staying alive for herself and that, in itself, was a difficult mission. There was no room for anyone else but a girlfriend in her life.

After a few hours of self-torture, she wiped her tear-stained face, grabbed her belongings, and walked down the hill to her room, which would be her new home.

She knocked on the door. Trudy answered. They faced one another with nothing to say. Lilly did a quick study. *She's downright gorgeous. Look how she flashes those big brown eyes and tosses her long, thick, to-die-for hair, and there's not one pound of extra weight on that petite and shapely body. She dresses in fashion and smells like a bouquet of tropical flowers. How could the college put two such different people together?*

Trudy also did a quick study: *Oh my, a tad bit overweight, and she obviously doesn't know a thing about fashion, or makeup for that matter. Look at her boring hair. She needs a style and those engineer boots have to go. Is she a hippie or a country girl or both? She has potential, a lot of potential, but definitely needs refinement. This is a mismatch of personalities if I've ever seen one!*

The room shrank inward a few feet more. Lilly broke the silence.

"Hi, I'm Lilly." She held out her hand in a peace offering.

"I'm Trudy." They shook hands. "Come on in." Trudy grabbed the suitcase. "Where's the rest?"

"That's it; I travel light." Lilly felt a little embarrassed as she followed Trudy.

"I gave you the top three drawers as you asked. They're not very deep, but the closet is big. I think I went over half, but if you need the space"—she paused and looked at Lilly's one suitcase—"just push my clothes over."

Lilly glanced around the small, cell-like room, which connected to another through a shared bathroom. The only view to her beloved outside world was a window next to a built-in desk, which Trudy had taken. She clenched her teeth, forcing her mouth shut. The outdoors was her balance, her grounding force, and how dare this city girl just *take* the desk without asking or flipping a coin?

Trudy followed Lilly's glare. "Oh, the desk," she said flippantly, "I didn't think you would mind if I took the window side. It's cool to have a tree that close. Something I wouldn't have in the city."

"I love looking out the window too. Maybe next semester we can switch," Lilly suggested, getting no response from Trudy. She started unpacking statues first, to avoid damaging them. She moved three perfume bottles on the top of the dresser to make room.

Trudy jumped out of her chair and pushed Lilly's hand away so swiftly the statues nearly fell to the floor. In a surprisingly loud voice she yelled, "Don't ever touch my belongings without permission!"

Lilly stepped back, thinking, *this is exactly why I can't live with most girls. They're overly possessive and touchy.* "Whoa," said Lilly. "There's only one dresser top, and I need a safe place to put my statues. That's all; I don't want your perfume. I don't wear perfume."

"Are you a religious freak or what?" Trudy asked.

The expression on her face entertained Lilly. It said everything and then some.

"No, I'm not a religious freak. I didn't want to leave them behind for someone to break or throw away. They go back to my First Communion."

Trudy looked suspiciously at Lilly. "Well then, put them up there, but don't touch my belongings. I'll move them myself, just ask."

This is going well, Lilly thought doubtfully.

"Oh, our RA stopped in, and we're having a meeting in the television room in twenty minutes. It's *mandatory*."

"I'll hurry." Lilly let out a frustrated sigh.

"Do you want to go together?"

Lilly stopped her organizing. "Sure, that's a good idea. I can hardly wait for the lecture." She hadn't had many rules all summer, only the ones she and Anthony made together and he tried to enforce.

When they entered the meeting room, Trudy went right up to the front seat. Lilly stopped and hovered back by the door. When the RA wasn't looking, she ducked out to call Ann to invite her over, and then stretched out on her bed for an anxiety break.

An hour later she heard the door open. "Trudy, is that you?"

"Aren't we supposed to always lock our door?" she inquired.

"Yes, we are, but since I was in here I didn't think it mattered. But you're right; we should keep it locked all the time. I'll make sure I do that," Lilly promised.

"I saw you sneak out."

"Sorry, but I'm not good with rules. Was there anything that I absolutely had to know?"

"Not really, everything she said is in the handout."

"I hope you don't mind, but I invited a friend to come over and meet you after dinner. She and her family moved here from California."

"Sure, the more the merrier, and there's nothing to do tonight anyway."

Lilly could hear the displeasure in Trudy's voice, but she didn't worry. There was nothing not to like about Ann.

It was the right move. They shared conversations about growing up, high school, family, and going to college. Lilly felt hopeful as the icy edge between her and Trudy appeared to be melting.

Another girlfriend bond began.

KEEP YOUR HANDS OFF

Lilly's head filled with confusion after reading the first five midterm questions of her Psych 101 class. *What is this?* She asked herself. *The questions make no sense. Did I walk into the wrong class or the wrong hour?* She looked around at the other students. *They seem to be okay.* She bravely raised her hand.

The professor approached and whispered in her ear, "Do you have a question?"

She whispered back, "Yes, is this the right test, because none of this material is in the text or from the handouts."

The professor stood up and looked down at her. Quietly, he answered, "I'm not familiar with your face."

"This is Psych 101 and you're Professor Samuel, right?"

"Yes, I am. Have you attended my lectures?"

"I attended a few but chose to opt out. It was an option, right?" Lilly's heart was beating to a different, less confident drum.

"Oh, yes, it still is an option. Attendance isn't mandatory, but eighty percent of the test is from class lectures." He patted her on the back. "I wish you well."

Lilly sat speechless. She should have known better. Nothing that easy came without a hitch. She prayed for a lucky C.

Instead, she received a D. It was the first failing grade in her life. There was only one test left for the semester, and she had to score an A on it to pass the class with a C.

"I am so pissed off at myself—I will never miss a class again, even if both of my legs and arms are broken," she scolded herself as she stormed back to her dorm. "I should have taken twelve credits and not fifteen; not in my first semester and with a work schedule. A lesson learned. Damn, I'm so pissed off!"

Back in her room she found Trudy perplexingly irritable too, blaming it on a chemistry test that had gone very badly. The silence drove Lilly mad, making it impossible to sit still.

"Lilly, can you please stop pacing around? I am trying to study, and you're picking up this and straightening out that. It's driving me nuts!" Trudy exploded.

"I'm cleaning up as I always do after supper. It's a habit!" Lilly answered, picking up one of the perfume bottles and dusting under it.

Trudy shoved her chair back. "I thought I told you never to touch my things again!"

Lilly stood confused. She always dusted the dresser top, moving things around, "What's your problem with those perfume bottles anyway?"

"It's none of your business! You are so annoying, always doing something, like a caged animal!"

"I'm irritating and you're the perfect roommate? That's a joke!" Lilly had been holding back her impatience with Trudy; now it felt good to let it go.

"What do you mean by that? Spit it out!" Trudy walked closer to Lilly.

"I think you're a spoiled little city girl who has everything in life she wants."

"Is that right? Who got the top three drawers of the dresser?" Trudy walked over and opened one drawer after another, taking items from each and throwing them on the floor. "How does it feel to have me touching your things? Look, now you have plenty to pick up!"

Lilly walked to the closet, grabbed some of Trudy's blouses, and threw them on the floor in retaliation.

"That's it!" Trudy picked up an empty pop can and threw it at Lilly's head.

Lilly ducked. She was shocked and tongue-tied. In her entire life, not once had a girl—or anyone else for that matter—thrown anything at her other than a fist. She picked up the pop can and threw it back, hitting Trudy in the head.

Trudy looked equally shocked. She picked up a book and slung it at Lilly. Lilly opened one of Trudy's drawers and threw the belongings all over the room.

The fight continued until the closet and every drawer were empty. Then they moved to one another's mattresses, throwing linens, blankets, and pillows on the floor, against the wall and at each other. The room looked like a small war zone.

They abruptly stopped, hearing the sound of a loud whistle. First they looked at one another and then at the door where the RA stood. "I take it you're both feeling better?" she inquired with a stern voice.

Trudy and Lilly looked around the room, observing the destruction.

Lilly began to laugh. It started as a small *Oh no, look at what we did* chuckle, and then it grew into uncontrollable laughter. It was the first time either of them had been in a fight. Trudy started to laugh too.

The whistle blew again. "I don't see any humor in this behavior and neither should the two of you. You both have one hour to get this room back into shape before I inspect for damages and hand out fines."

By this point, both girls were on the floor, holding their stomachs and trying not to look at one another. If they did, the laughter would start up again. They watched the RA leave.

Lilly sat up first. "Did you hear her? She said the word 'fine.' We should get going. I'll take one side and you the other?"

They raced to collect underwear, socks, books, hair rollers, pens, and pencils—the entire room was out of place. They didn't care now what drawer held whose belongings or which side of the closet the clothes belonged, or who touched what. All that mattered was to get the room back together and to do that, they had to work as a team.

"Do you know why I'm so touchy about the perfume bottles?" Trudy asked, holding one in her hand. Lilly shook her head no, as she pulled the mattresses back onto the beds.

"I have a semi-boyfriend back home, and each bottle represents a special occasion that we spent together, such as prom and the senior ball."

Oh my God! Where are my statutes! Lilly suddenly remembered them. She slowly turned around. For the first time that evening, there was dead silence in the room.

There lay her broken faith. Trudy carefully picked up Mother Mary's head and studied it.

"It's a clean break. We could easily glue it back on. I'm so sorry, Lilly." She held the pieces in her hands while her big brown eyes filled with remorse.

Lilly saw the incident in a picture frame. The image of Trudy holding Mother Mary's head was too much, and once again, she burst into laughter.

"You're not mad at me?" Trudy asked, bewildered.

"No, I don't have an ounce of anger right now, only exhaustion. We'll glue it on and put my nun's chalkboard back together at the same time. I am learning that what's broken can be fixed. It never looks the same, but close enough."

The two worked as one, checking the room for damage. Money was tight and neither of them wanted to waste weekend cash on chipped wood and dented frames.

They passed the inspection.

"Do you girls want to move into different rooms?" asked the RA.

Trudy and Lilly read each other's faces. "No," they said in unison.

The RA shrugged but warned, "This behavior is not allowed. If it happens again, you are both out of here."

"It won't happen again. I promise," Lilly said, crossing her heart.

"What about you, Trudy?" the RA asked.

"Never again!" Trudy crossed her heart too, trying not to crack up.

After the RA left, the girls sat down at their desks.

Trudy spoke first. "How did this start?"

"I touched a perfume bottle and was making too much noise for you to concentrate on chemistry."

"That's my toughest class. College sucks. I miss home." She returned the question to Lilly: "What are you so angry about?"

Lilly paused. *How do I answer that? It goes back to being four years old.*

"Do you have classes tomorrow morning?" asked Lilly.

"Not until one. Why?"

"How about we go out for a few beers? Then I'll tell you my side."

They grabbed their coats and went off to a bar Lilly had frequented during the summer months.

※

"So you never told your parents and you're still not going to? That's insane!" Trudy couldn't grasp the idea that fear could have such an iron clad hold over someone, especially when that someone was the strong-willed, determined Lilly that she had gotten to know.

"I don't expect you or anyone to understand. I want them to, but how could they without going through it themselves?"

"Lilly, they aren't your secrets. They are his, and he wants you to stay quiet. That's wrong. He needs to go to jail, and you need to tell your folks."

"What if it kills them, or what if they don't believe me? I can't take that risk."

"But you're taking that risk right now, sitting here, and telling me."

"I know, and it scares the shit out of me that Millie and Frank will come and hurt you or Ann or your families. My godparents are dangerous people. If I never go home again in order to feel safe, I won't. That's how terrified I am."

"You're trying to build a new life for yourself, but you need help. You've been through too much to try to get through it alone."

Lilly poured another glass of beer. "People are supposed to fix their own problems."

"But this *isn't your problem*! Why can't you see that?" Trudy sat back against the wooden booth, disgruntled.

Lilly teared up. "I don't know. When it comes to him and Millie I can't think straight. They are in my head with threats. It's a complicated mess and I understand if you don't want to room with me. Heck, I don't know if I could room with myself!" She braced for the negative answer that was sure to follow.

Trudy turned up her animated facial expressions. "Oh, hell no! Who else on campus has such a mysterious roommate as me? For sure I'm staying!"

Lilly had one of her voiceless moments, this one created from overwhelming joy.

FLYING COWS AND MUSICAL NOTES

Lilly and Trudy did everything together: studying, eating, laundry, cleaning, and partying. They listened and laughed. They filled the void of homesickness with one another's company. They shared clothing; Lilly dressed up, while Trudy dressed down. And occasionally Trudy shared her collection of perfume. On the weekends, Ann joined them. They were the Three Musketeers, bonded in friendship and laughter as they visited bars and explored the city.

For Lilly, the world was once again alive and big. She wanted to place time in a bubble, keeping everything exactly as it was. She had found love again, a different kind—the kind between best friends—and that was fine with her.

Then Ann fell in love, followed by Trudy. It put a dent in their Three Musketeer evenings, leaving a mopey Lilly.

As their first year wound down, Trudy and Lilly met up, as usual, for the dorm dinner. "Isn't life strange?" Lilly mused. "I'm the one who's looking for love and you and Ann found it. Next you'll both be getting married and I'll be alone again. Abandoned and left to dry my own tears."

"Oh, cry me a river, Lilly. You talk like it's the end of the world."

"It kind of is, Trudy. No one is going to replace what the three of us have."

"True, but new people come along."

"It won't be the same."

"Stop being so pessimistic; we still have the rest of the semester!" Lilly gasped. "You're not coming back next year?"

Trudy hesitated. "Sure I am. I didn't study this hard so I could drop out!"

"I don't believe you." Lilly had her suspicions.

"Don't be ridiculous! Tell me about this Stu guy." Trudy leaned in, getting Lilly's full attention. "He's in one of my music classes and mentioned your name. What's that all about?"

"It was a blind date and we hit it off, that's all."

"You like him?"

Lilly blushed. "I do. He knows how to handle me…most of the time."

"Wow, that's impressive, someone who can handle you!"

"I'm not difficult to handle," Lilly protested.

"No, not at all. Last week you watered the heads of all the balding men in the bar with beer and they kicked us out, remember?"

"Oh, that. Well, I was really drunk and thought it might help their hair grow back." Lilly flashed an innocent grin.

"And what about the time we thought we lost you? There you were, crawling on the floor, biting ankles!"

Lilly let out a big sigh. "Come on, those aren't difficult situations, just silly ones."

"Lilly, when someone dares you, you accept without thinking about the dangers."

"But that's changing. I don't want to be that person anymore. Stu keeps me on an even keel, except for the other night."

"What happened?"

"We toked up and I had a bad trip. Went running out of his dorm room and down the hall, and once I got outside, I ran all the way to Ann's house. I thought his room was on fire and I was going to burn to death. Then I saw Frank laughing at me and holding my melting doll. I thought I was going to die! I couldn't breathe!"

"You were hyperventilating and that was your head playing games with you about the past. It wasn't real. You should have told Stu you felt uneasy."

"I felt fine in the beginning. It's not like the first time I ever smoked weed." Lilly gave Trudy a questionable look. "His band is playing next week at the club, want to go?"

"Sure, I've wanted to hear his music and to tell him to stop playing that stupid Beatles song you like at six in the morning."

"You're just jealous that I have my own personal DJ!" Lilly paused. "It seems surreal to be finishing up our first year. Doesn't it?"

"It does! And it went by so fast!"

"I need to start looking for a place to rent this summer."

"You're really not going home?" Trudy asked in surprise.

"No, this is home and it's where I have a good paying job."

"Can't you rent Anthony's place now that he's graduated?"

"I would have to find two more roomies. For the short time I have, I think it would be cheaper and easier to find a single room. Also, I'm actually getting a promotion at work. I will be your hostess with the mostest!" Lilly teased with a sexy pose. "What about your plans?"

"I can't wait to get home and beyond that point I have no idea," replied Trudy.

"Can I come and visit, or will you be too busy with your lover boy from high school?"

Trudy warmly smiled. "I would absolutely love that, and Stu doesn't live far from me. We could visit him and have a double date."

"No can do! He's a counselor at a private camp of some sort, and then he's vacationing in the Keys. His parents have a home there."

"Nice life! Hey, are you going out with me and Ann tomorrow night?" Trudy asked.

"No, I don't think so," Lilly answered. "I'm so drained. Everything is an effort lately. I took tomorrow off at the resort and figured I'd lie around all weekend and power up for major studying."

Trudy looked at Lilly with concern. She was never sick or too tired to socialize. "You are so hard on yourself, taking eighteen credits, trying to keep an academic scholarship, walking five miles to work, waitressing for six hours, partying, and studying! It's too much. You need to slow down, girl. That's why you're tired."

"I'll try to, *Mom,* and studying shouldn't have been last!" she teased back.

The next evening, Lilly lounged in her pajamas and visited with Trudy, who was busy getting ready to meet up with Ann.

"Have a good time, but don't wake me when you come home unless you need to. I'm going to take a long shower and crash."

"Sure you don't want to go? It's never the same without you!"

"I'm sure. Tell Ann I'll call her this weekend."

Trudy fluffed her hair and grabbed a sweater. "See you later, alligator, and lock the door behind me." Trudy dashed out, leaving her scent behind. Lilly crawled down from her bunk, locked the door, showered, and crawled back into bed. Sleeping deeply, she was pulled out of a dream state. She awakened befuddled and in a mental haze. She looked around the room. It was alive.

Why is Trudy's pink cow floating near the ceiling? Lilly asked herself, disoriented.

"What time is it, what day is it, where is Trudy?" she said aloud, looking down at the floor. "Something isn't right. I need to get up!" However, when she dangled her legs off the bed, she saw the floor sink downward and the room grew into a giant gymnasium with her at the ceiling.

Whoa. She pulled her legs back up. *I'll kill myself if I try to get down. What's happening? What are those black shapes floating in the air? They look like musical notes.* She reached out to grab one, but her hand went right through it. *This isn't real,* she told herself.

An intense pain pounded in her head. *Something awful is happening to my brain.* She heard heartbeats in her ears and felt them behind her eyes. *I'm scared. I need help. Where are you, Trudy?*

In the early morning hours Lilly heard the door unlock. She tried to call out to Trudy, but she had little voice. Whatever was wrong had worsened. Trudy tiptoed to her bed and grabbed her pajamas.

Lilly moaned her name, spooking Trudy.

"Stop screwing around! You nearly scared me to death." No response.

"Lilly, get up, I'll tell you about tonight." No reaction.

Trudy climbed up and looked into a pair of dull, glazed eyes. "For heaven's sake, what did you take?"

"Trudy," Lilly tried to reach out for her friend.

"Lilly, what pills did you take? This is not funny!"

"No pills," Lilly answered in barely a whisper.

"Come on, let's get you down." Trudy reached out for Lilly's arm, but Lilly pulled it away, shrinking tighter into the wall at the thought of how far down the floor was.

"What's wrong? You are freaking me out! Give me your arm, and I'll help you." Trudy noticed beads of sweat on Lilly's face and touched her forehead.

"You're burning up! I need to get you to the infirmary. You have to help me. Are you listening, Lilly? You have to get up!"

Lilly gathered her strength and Trudy wasted no time helping her down. She threw a sweatshirt over Lilly and led her out of the dorm. It was a dark spring night with a light mist in the air. Lilly began to shake.

"Oh no you don't! Not now, Lilly Francis! Use your legs and keep walking!"

"I can't walk. I'm too tired and cold. Put me down and go get help," Lilly faintly pleaded.

"No way am I leaving you alone." Trudy placed her arm around Lilly's waist. "Here we go. You can do this," she cheered Lilly on, carrying most of the weight herself.

They were near their destination when Lilly's legs buckled. Again, Trudy scolded. "You can't pass out here. We're about fifty steps away. Lilly, Lilly…" Trudy wasn't getting an answer. She began dragging Lilly along the sidewalk, trying to keep her semiconscious with talk.

"Trudy, don't let me die," Lilly said faintly, fading in and out.

Trudy used her loudest and most commanding voice: "No one dies of a fever anymore. You got that?"

The doors were a welcome sight. Trudy propped Lilly against the wall and rang the after-hours emergency bell. A male orderly arrived and lunged forward to catch Lilly's unconscious body.

A BARREL OF MONKEYS

Listlessly, Lilly opened her eyes. *Where am I?* She looked around the room, observing the pale-yellow cinder block walls and white linoleum floor. Above her head and to the sides were two bags of clear liquid dripping into tubes that led to her arms. The sight of the needles poking under her skin sickened her. She looked away, toward the window.

There on the ledge was a stuffed pink pig. *Ann and Trudy must have bought me that. Only they know how much I love pigs.* Her attempt to smile came to a quick stop as a shooting pain took hold. Instinctively she swallowed and felt a scratchy, almost chalk like throat. *Damn, that hurts.* She put her lips together, keeping them motionless, and took several deep breaths.

A male nurse and a female doctor entered, walking up to her bedside. The doctor directed her attention to Lilly and said sternly, "Hello there, welcome back to the living." She ruffled through a thick pile of papers on a clipboard. She reminded Lilly of a military officer preparing to lay it on one of her failing cadets.

"Can you hear me?" She nearly shouted. Lilly gently nodded yes.

"Good. Here is a pen and a tablet. It's going to be difficult to talk for another week, so if you have questions, write them down." The nurse handed her the writing materials.

"Your diagnosis is infectious mononucleosis with severe strep throat. The swelling of your liver and spleen is significant. They are beyond the protection of the rib cage, which means you will be on limited activity for six months. Your liver will also need to heal, so no alcohol or street drugs. If you do, it'll send you right back here with possibly irreversible liver damage. Do you understand?"

Lilly nodded yes.

"Good. You are lucky your liver wasn't punctured on the walk to the clinic! That fever would not come down. You may remember the ice bath. It helped, and you fought hard to stay with us. Right now we have you quarantined because you are contagious, and the only visitors allowed are family. Questions?" She lowered her clipboard, waiting for Lilly's response.

Lilly closed her eyes, understanding the gist of the message. *I'm fucked and not going anywhere soon.* She was mad and scared and had a question that needed an answer. She picked up the pen and paper, wrote it down, and handed it off to the nurse.

The doctor read it out loud. "How long have I been sleeping?" She took her glasses off and let them dangle from her neck on a beaded strap. "You have been sleeping for two weeks. We have kept you in a semi-coma to aid in your healing. Your vitals were extremely weak when your roommate brought you in. I don't think you realize how close you were to leaving us."

Two weeks, that cannot be possible. People don't sleep for two weeks!

Lilly panicked and wrote her next question. *What about school?*

"There are some choices for you, but we don't want you to worry excessively about school at this point. Instead, put your energy into healing. By the way, your father and brother have been here several times to sit with you. Nice family."

Lilly wrote out one last question: "Did my mother come?"

The doctor put her glasses back on. "I've spoken with her on the phone. She's very knowledgeable in medicine, and I'm looking forward to meeting her."

The doctor walked out as briskly as she came in, leaving the nurse behind.

Overwhelmed, Lilly looked up at the ceiling and thought, *This is impossible! I remember Trudy helping me down from my bed. I remember musical notes floating in the air and going to the infirmary in the middle of the night and a metal tub with cold water. Now I learn that I have missed two weeks of school, and at the end of a semester!*

The pain and dry crusty feeling in her throat wouldn't let up for a minute. She picked up her tablet and pen to ask another question of the male nurse.

"Why does my throat feel like it's made of cardboard?" She scribbled in her notebook.

The nurse answered, "The scabbing and chalky feeling you have is from the sores of strep."

Lilly wrote, "Are those sores on my lips too?"

"Yes. You still have a severe case of bacterial strep. We have you on a liquid diet for a few more days, and then you will be able to eat soft foods. Don't worry; I'm going to help you. Each day will improve now that you're done with intensive care. It's time! Are you ready for me to clean up those scabby sores?"

Lilly scrawled out another note: "I must look like shit."

The nurse smiled. "I've seen worse—not by far, but there has been worse."

Wiseass, thought Lilly.

"Tell me if I'm hurting you. I've been cleaning and scraping while you slept, so today is the first day I'll know how much pain I'm actually causing you."

Great, it hurts without being touched. Lilly laid her head back into the pillow and prepared for more excruciating pain.

"Keep breathing and open as wide as you can."

Lilly clenched her fists. Not only was the cleaning agonizing, it was downright grotesque. The nurse attempted to keep her mind off his work with senseless chatter. "You know what the doctor says about college kids? The only difference between monkeys and them is that a monkey knows when to go to bed and college kids don't. I love that saying!" He laughed and looked for a faint grin from his patient. There was none.

He and that doctor probably told Dad that I was partying too much and that's why I got sick, but it's not the entire truth. I study my ass off, I work twenty to thirty hours a week, and I keep an academic scholarship. I am not only a party girl. I have responsibilities too! Lilly was downright angry, a familiar sign that she was turning the corner to wellness.

Daily highlights were being able to stay awake for an hour and drinking chocolate malts. The worst were the repeated cleanings. With nothing to do but heal, her self-pity grew into a daily internal negative speech at each awakening. She missed Trudy and Ann but they weren't allowed to visit. And then one morning, as she opened her eyes, she saw Vincent sitting in a chair next to her bed. She hadn't seen him since Christmas. He looked worried and sad. Two feelings she knew well.

With a labored breath she asked, "Where are Mom and Eva?"

He took her hand, "Mom had to work, and she didn't want Eva exposed to the infection."

Mom not getting off work is garbage. She didn't want to come because I embarrassed her. Instead, she sent Dad.

Lilly turned her head, hiding the tear that needed to fall.

"Your mother wanted to come, she really did, Lilly," Vincent tried to reassure her. "When we come to take you home, she and Eva will be here. I promise you." Vincent squeezed her hand.

The hate she felt for him a year ago was fading. When she went to Trudy's house for Easter, he sent her money. When she stayed on campus for spring break to work, he called. It was never much, but it helped, and he took the time to let her know he was there. That meant a lot to her.

In a gentle voice Vincent continued, "I don't want to upset you any more than you are, but we need to talk about school."

Lilly let out a sigh of relief. "Do I have to retake all of my classes?"

"No, that's the good news. You sure learned how to gain your professors' respect! They said you were their top class participant, setting off many good debates. That took me by surprise—in high school you were shy and hated talking in front of the class."

Lilly half-smiled, "College changed me. So did leaving home." She scratched out with a hoarse voice.

"I can see that, but I can also see the curious little Lilly I knew long ago."

I am not in the mood to reminisce and get cozy, not yet. There are still many bridges for us to cross, she thought and returned to her major worry, school.

"Did the professors say anything else?"

"They were all concerned about you and are willing to work something out upon your dismissal. Some said you could record your answers instead of writing them out. Others suggested a modified test, with more time allowed."

At least I didn't hear that I have to take any classes over. I can be a sophomore next year. Lilly offered up a pathetic, sickly grin. "Did you say you were taking me home?"

"As soon as we can. Once home you're going to need another six weeks to fully recover."

The idea of returning home horrified her. She liked no Frank or Millie, no stress of physical punishment, no reminders of Blake, and she loved her job.

"Work. They promoted me. They need me. I can't lose this job."

"Lilly, be sensible. You won't be able to work this summer. I have already spoken with your advisor. She's looking into a work-study on campus for next year. The resort is too far and too many hours."

Lilly pulled away in thought. *I am not going to give up my job. I can work at the resort on weekends and have a work-study too. I don't want to go home; not yet.*

"Let's not worry about money and work. Your only directive is to get better. Oh…" Vincent stopped, reached into his pocket, and pulled out an envelope. "I have a letter here from a guy named Stu." He handed it to her. "Is he a friend?"

"Yes," she said. "Put it on the nightstand. I'll read it later."

"Is there anything you need before I get back on the road?"

"No, the nurse is great."

He leaned over and kissed her forehead. "The next time I visit I'll be able to take you home. That will be a happy day."

For you, thought Lilly, dreading the idea of returning to nightmare memories. She understood she had limitations and help was necessary, but she wanted to receive it somewhere else, like at Ann's house.

With Vincent gone, loneliness once again settled in. She reached for the envelope. Inside were a cassette tape and a letter.

> Hey Lilly,
>
> I finished my finals early and left for the Keys to get a week of sunshine before camp. The college insisted I take a mono test. I aced it, as I usually do with tests. I made you this tape at the studio. Miss waking you up on the radio with your favorite songs and hope this will bring a smile. I know how much you love my raspy voice.
>
> Have your home address. Will write. Here is mine. Miss you. See you in the fall.
>
> Luv, Stu

Lilly looked at the tape with fondness and hummed a line of "Lonely Days." She closed her eyes and went back to more pleasant times with Stu, Ann, and Trudy.

※

"Rise and shine!" The nurse pulled her curtains open. "Today is the big day! You are getting out of this joint and I have to admit that it won't be the same without you. Never gave us a boring day, Miss Lilly."

Lilly smirked and replied, "How about you come home with me? I don't think I can live without your malts. They're the world's best!"

"You'll be moving up to liver and onions! Mmm, I bet you can hardly wait."

"Are you kidding me?"

"No, it will help rebuild your blood," he responded, busying himself with her vitals.

"Tell me I can stay another few days."

He sat down on the chair.

"Tell me why you wouldn't want to go home and be pampered."

Lilly looked away, avoiding the truth. "I'm independent. Having others take care of me is not my forte and sitting around is my least favorite pastime. However, that's all I'm capable of doing."

"Every week you can do more and more. In two months you'll be almost back to normal."

"Why almost?"

"Some people never feel quite as energetic after having this combination of infections."

"That's not going to be me. I'll make sure of it. By the way, what am I going to wear home? Do I have any of my clothes here?"

"Your parents left some in the closet. How about you shower and get dressed?"

"Fine." Lilly dragged her feet across the room, not feeling any familiar bounce in her steps. *Maybe I won't ever be the same.* Lilly looked at her reflection in the mirror. *I think I look a little blue. Actually, I look like the walking dead.* She pulled the skin down from under her eyes, making a monster face. *Eva is never going to go to college if she thinks this is how everyone looks after one year.*

For the most part, it has been a good year, as good as I could make it and next year will be even better. Always look for tomorrow! Keep moving forward! Ride on the river's current.

From the mirror, she saw her sister peeking at her. Lilly spun around to grab a hug from Eva.

"Hi, munchkin, I missed you! Let me see." Lilly stood back, studying her little sister, who wasn't little anymore. "You are looking good, Miss Eva! Have a boyfriend yet?"

Eva blushed. "No! Not yet, but almost!"

"Hi, dear." Gwen stepped forward with open arms.

Lilly hesitated. She wasn't sure if she wanted Gwen to touch her. She had learned to live without a mother's love and felt no need for it to return. She managed a weak emotionless hug and then shifted her attention to Vincent. "Hi, Dad. How was the drive?"

"It's a great day! You will enjoy the spring forests on the ride home. The new leaves smell so fresh! And the creeks have little rapids from the snowmelt."

"I haven't been outside for nearly a month."

"What did you do all this time?" Eva asked with concern.

"I slept, that's about it. Oh, and I built that pyramid." Lilly pointed to her windowsill, which displayed a tall pyramid built of tiny pill cups.

"That's cool. Who gave you the pig?" asked Eva.

"My girlfriends," informed Lilly, filling with pride.

"Well, Lilly, let's go over the rules from the doctor…" Gwen was ready to fulfill her nursing job.

Lilly chanted along in her head: *Limited exercise, ten minutes a day for a few weeks, absolutely no alcohol or street drugs, no sexual intercourse, and no crowds of people until the liver is once again in the safety of my rib cage. Last, but not least, is the directive of ten hours of sleep per night with a time of rest in the afternoon.*

"I'm impressed, Mom, you've got that down pat!"

Gwen smiled. "You know how much I love taking care of sick people."

"Yes, I do. You were a great nurse when I was a kid."

"Do you remember when you had the German measles and *then*, a few months later, you had scarlet fever? You missed a month of school!"

"And here I am, nineteen, just as sick and missed another month of school." Lilly looked around the room and at her family. "It's time to get out of here."

※

What could have been a fun-filled summer turned into boring days of counting cars and lumber trucks as they passed by her house. On a good day, she counted up to seven. Time crawled as Lilly regained strength while living the country life once again.

She had a few fallbacks; one was seeking out Blake and the other was hooking up with an ex-classmate who was more like a young Frank than the boy she remembered in school. However, phone calls with Ann and letters from Trudy helped refuel her happiness. Yet, the hunger to return to her safer and more exciting home at college was unquenchable.

Mail was once again the most exciting time of the day. It was a connection to the rest of the world, other than the nightly news. That day, Lilly received a letter. From the smell of it, she guessed it was from Trudy.

"'Don't you love her?" she asked Vincent. "She's such a girly-girl! Look, she even kissed a seal with her red lipstick!"

"You should take some hints from her," Gwen piped in.

"Sure Mom, maybe this year." Lilly said whatever she thought her mother wanted to hear, which was now easier to do knowing her real home was back at Black Rock.

About sixty seconds into reading, Lilly stopped, tore Trudy's letter to shreds, threw it on the floor, and stomped on it. "I hate you!" she screamed and ran out the door.

Gwen looked at Vincent. "What was that about?"

"I don't know, but I'll talk to her when she comes back. Whatever it was, she needs time right now."

Still weak from the illness, she collapsed in exhaustion onto the prickly dry grass of the field. Looking up at the sky, she yelled at God.

"Why do you hate me so much? What have I done to make you so angry with me? How many pieces of my heart are you going to break?" she cried out to the sky. "Tell me!"

There was no answer, and she had little faith there ever would be. She laid, doing nothing but feeling the sadness of her tears until the sound of Vincent's footsteps crunching through the dry weeds awakened her to the present.

"You don't need to be here," she said.

Vincent sat down next to her. "How about telling me what was in the letter?" he asked.

"Trudy isn't coming back to school. She's in love and wants to stay close to home. She enrolled at the community college. Then she had enough nerve to say she wants to stay friends and keep in touch! Why can't my world ever stay the same?" Lilly kept her eyes on the large cumulus clouds.

Vincent listened empathetically and then slowly replied. "Trudy found happiness and wanted to share that with you."

"But she's a big part of *my* happiness too."

"You love her as a friend."

"I do. She's my very best friend. Now she's gone, like everyone else. People love me and leave me. I hate her like I hate them!"

"Lilly, hate isn't in your blood or your heart. Is a good friendship worth losing over something she has no control over, like falling in love?"

"But she could have said something earlier rather than wait until a couple of weeks before school."

"Put yourself in her shoes. It was probably as hard for her to write as it was for you to read."

Lilly thought about her father's words. "That's probably true."

"It's not the end of your friendship. Why don't you write back to her and plan on a visit during your first break?"

"You and Mom won't care if I don't come home for Thanksgiving?"

"We understand."

"What about a roommate? Who is the college going to shove in my room with such short notice? The thought of starting over *again* without her kills me."

"I'll call the college if you want."

"No, I'll deal with it myself."

"You don't have to always choose the most difficult path. Let me help this time."

"Thanks, but no thanks. I have had worse predicaments to deal with. It hurts, that's all. Everything will be different. I have to start over again and Anthony won't be around to lean on."

"You still have Ann and her family."

"Yeah, right," Lilly mumbled, knowing that Ann and her family were important to her and still there, but not as a replacement for Trudy. The world had only one so special.

"It's been tough getting back to normal and now more challenges! Does life ever get easy?" Lilly asked.

Vincent put his arm around her shoulders.

1986 – SESSION ELEVEN – SORROWFUL ACCEPTANCE

"Tell me about the day you opened the letter from Trudy."

Lilly let out a sigh, stood up, and walked over to the couch. She lay down and closed her eyes, returning to the scene. "I can see myself standing in the kitchen, near the dining room, and ripping the letter to shreds. Then I watched the paper float down to the floor and stomped on the pieces. Next, I ran out of the house."

"Explain the emotions that you were feeling."

"I felt livid. She abandoned me. She knew she wasn't coming back and she lied! She knew before school was out that she wasn't coming back."

"That's a fact you knew for sure."

Lilly squirmed in her chair. "No, not exactly, but it doesn't matter. I can't hate Trudy. I couldn't feel that way toward her. It was the fact that she was going to mess up my new tidy world."

"Along with feeling abandoned again and having to face change."

"Yes. I lost control and focus of how I was going to survive. My snow globe cracked, letting the water drip out slowly, destroying the wonderment of our bubble."

"When the globe cracked, you felt your dreams for the future run dry. That had to be frightening."

"Yes, doomsday arrived...again. Not wanting to share Trudy may have been childish, but losing her was a major shake-up in my life. I didn't want to start over with a roommate and I was tired—so tired—of a hard life."

"Your friendship with Ann and Trudy gave you a new life."

"They gave my world a big dose of hope. I depended on them and when they fell in love and moved on with their lives...Well, it was devastating."

"Trauma victims are more likely to be depressed and feel self-failure if their world begins to change."

"Really! I could write a book on that. Change freaks me out because I need to keep a balance of control. Without that feeling, life is scary and returns back to Frank and unpleasant times with Dad and Mom. Change creates chaos and chaos creates fear and fear is paralyzing."

"Yet, you faced your fear in opening up to Ann."

"I was so scared and tense, but also proud of myself even though the words were hard to find. To let go of my quiet fears and shameful secrets is hard—how do I put Frank's actions into words? How do I describe the shame it left? How can anyone tell someone else about emotional death?"

"How did you?"

"I told her only what I had to for her to get the idea. But when I was done, I freaked out for weeks that Frank was going to find her family and hurt them."

"Then the fear vanished."

"It did. I felt this unbelievable sense of safety. Nothing could harm me. I was invincible. Reality was taking root inside of me. Frank set me up for failure and I wasn't going to give it to him. I was finding myself again. I was feeling strong."

"You were feeling rational and then you met Trudy, developing another friendship you could open up with."

"At first our friendship wasn't as smooth as it was with Ann. Trudy and I had to live together, share our space, and neither of us wanted to do that."

"You didn't want to share?"

"Not at first. I had worked hard for what I owned and some items were sentimental. Trudy felt the same way about her belongings."

"Tell me what items were sentimental to you."

"My statutes."

"You took the statutes from your First Communion with you."

"Yes, and the black prayer book Mom gave me to keep the nightmares away when I was little."

"Out of all the items a kid brings to college, those were the three most important to you."

"They symbolized my faith, hope, and love. They reminded me of my fears and sadness, and that I got through those dark days. Therefore, I could do it again if I had to. They were my sounding boards. They hold my secret life; in fact, I still have them in my bedroom. They're all I have of my youth. Mom was the opposite of a hoarder. She pitched our toys out as soon as we outgrew them. That's why I took the statues with me, if I hadn't they'd be gone like everything else that belonged to me."

"You show little emotion about your lost reminders of youth."

"That's the tough side of me. The emotion is there, but not having souvenirs of my childhood are far from an important issue."

"You and Trudy settled your differences."

"In the oddest way, but yes, we grew to have deep respect for one another. We were very close. Rarely did we do anything without the other. We laughed more than anything else and we loved being friends."

"That was healing."

"Having friends was something I hadn't experienced before Trudy and Ann. They were my guardian angels of the time. I was full of self-failure and that stopped with Ann and Trudy. They helped me reconnect with my femininity. They listened without judgment. They are happy memories and I will always hold them close to my heart."

"What other memories from the past are happy for you?"

"Everything I did with Anthony growing up and living on the river, but remembering Black Rock is the best. It was the beginning of a new me, a new world! Life was going to be what I made of it. The lake, the evergreens, the cliffs, rocks...it was the most beautiful place in the world to my eyes."

"The outdoors is an important place for you to feel grounded. Do you ever go back?" questioned Dr. Bricks.

"Almost every year for a few days. It's like an addiction and I need my fix."

"It's centering for you."

"It's where I found myself. It was the beginning of my journey to independence. I had success and failures, but I owned them. If I messed up, there was no one to blame but me. If I accomplished an achievement, I rewarded myself. Going back is a reminder of how and why I am still here. It's always a grateful visit."

"I'm happy to hear that you stay connected with that part of your life."

"Sometimes I return to where I grew up. It's a melancholy feeling with a bittersweet sting. It's not the fight song of Black Rock."

"Meaning?"

"The regrets make me cry, the happy times make me laugh, the paths I walked with Frank make my stomach churn and overall, I want to mourn for my little girl. I don't get those mixed emotions in Black Rock."

"You felt more secure in Black Rock."

"I had a job to be free of my mom and dad. Working made me feel like an adult. It gave me people skills. I was proud of my paychecks. I was a hard worker and the manager noticed. That helped me move up the ladder."

"You became quite ill at the end of the second semester."

"That was a scary time." Lilly fidgeted in her chair, it was hard to talk about. "As a kid, I had scarlet fever, many cases of tonsillitis, whooping cough, the mumps, and German measles, but never was I that sick!"

"How did it change you?"

"It slowed me down and brought my parents back into my life. Those were the positives."

"What were the negatives?"

"I felt that all the adults saw me as a messed-up party girl and I wasn't. I truly felt that life was coming together for me! Getting sick sent me backwards, in my opinion. My self-esteem slipped. I didn't have Ann or Trudy by my side. I had to return to the country and its memories. At home I was sick often. A sign of weakness."

"Why do you say that?"

"My fifth-grade teacher told me I would never live to graduate from high school because of a chronic cough that turned out to be asthma. Millie said I was a lot like her and she was always sick, carrying around a suitcase of pills. Guess I heard messages that I was frail and sickly ever since I was a youngster."

"A poorer development of the immune and nervous systems due to childhood trauma has been getting more attention in research."

"Thank you, Frank and Millie. When they said they would be in my life forever, it was true. That often makes me wonder more about who I was meant to be from the beginning."

The room filled with a sorrowful silence. Then Lilly concluded, "But we will never know. I'm starting to accept that."

"As you continue to heal, you may surprise yourself with discoveries showing how your core self is returning."

"I'm ready: physically, mentally and emotionally."

HESITANTLY SUSPICIOUS

In her first semester as a sophomore, she absorbed herself in her schooling so as not to reach out to alcohol or a joint. Without Trudy, she could feel her stability wobbling and the feeling of abandonment began to dwell in her mind. She didn't feel confident and in control; it was the opposite, falling into a more fragile state of mind. Her new roommate, Kenzy, was more of a casual friend. Not one she could feel comfortable talking and sharing the past with. Gracie, on the other hand, was plain old weird. For Lilly, the Saturday morning phone call from Vincent was a lifeline.

"Hi, Lilly, this is Dad. How's everything going with your roommates?"

"I'm so tired! Gracie reads into the early morning hours with a bed lamp that shines into my face. Kenzy and I are kind of getting along, but it's lonely. I miss Trudy. Thank God for Ann and her family for taking me in on the weekends. If I don't get more sleep soon, I'll have to drop the semester. I'm that tired."

"I understand you want to handle this yourself, but sometimes a parent can make things happen faster. I called the housing department, and they currently have a room open in your dorm."

Lilly felt a rush of hope. "Really, Dad?"

"However, there's one problem. You would be living alone."

"What? Did you say I would get a room all to myself? For how long?" Lilly's hope turned to elation.

"No roommate until next semester and then you'll have to find one or pay the extra fee."

Lilly squealed with joy. "Yes, my own room! How did you make that happen? The campus is overcrowded."

"They said your medical note waived the extra cost and allowed them to set you up in a single."

"Dad, you're a miracle worker. Thank you so much." Lilly released a long sigh of relief.

"You had the papers filled out and that helped the process move faster. All you need to do now is talk to your RA for a move-in date."

"I can't believe it! I can sleep all night."

"Hopefully they'll let you move in this weekend and then get some rest." The news was exactly what Lilly needed to hear.

"What do you think, Ann?" Lilly danced around her new dorm room, enjoying the space, and plopped down on her bed. "I can't believe I have a room to myself. This is going to be wonderful!"

"I worry about you being alone."

"Oh, don't be silly! I am doing well. Frank has been out of my life going on year three and I have no boyfriend to break my heart. This is it, Ann. I'm turning the corner, away from the streets of hell."

"You are, Lilly. It was a near-death experience, but hey, you're making a positive from it."

"That's right, and it's only going to get better by avoiding the three B's—boys, bars, and beer—and focusing on my major instead."

Ann smiled at Lilly's upbeat, go-get-them attitude, but she wondered if that was what Lilly felt deep down inside; or was she hiding something? It was hard to tell with Lilly.

With her health once again strong, Lilly decided to go home for a visit. She wanted badly to canoe the river before the leaves fell and to see Eva, who was turning thirteen.

She put up a notice for a ride on the community bulletin board and shortly received a call from a girl who lived in a nearby town and needed help with gas money.

"This is a big step for me," she told herself as she packed. "All I have to do is get through the weekend without a fight or driving around looking for lost love. I have to park my butt and stay put."

She didn't doubt her decision after arriving and seeing Eva's growth. It was all the affirmation she needed. "Eva!" Lilly gave her a big hug and squeeze. "Look at you! Braces!"

Eva bowed her head in shyness.

"No, they look great! You look cuter and older! Don't hide your smiles!"

"You really think so?" Eva asked with pride.

"Absolutely! Hey, Mom, Dad, how come she got braces and I didn't?" Lilly asked, pointing to her snaggletooth.

"We couldn't afford you *and* Anthony *and* Eva," replied a worried-looking Vincent.

"Come on, Dad, I'm just fooling with you. When I get my first job I'll have it fixed. Actually, I see it as my beauty mark." She gave them both a hug.

"I've made one of your favorite suppers," Gwen said, leading Lilly to the kitchen.

"Which is…?" Lilly always stumbled with that word, favorite.

"Fresh walleye!"

Lilly smiled: after brook trout, walleye was high on her list. She began to chat with Gwen. "Eva is growing up. Seems like yesterday when I was in middle school. Any news about Anthony or Joan?"

"Joan is doing fine, busy with the kids. Anthony loves his teaching job and is still dating the girl he met in college."

"I can see those two getting married," responded Lilly. "I have that feeling."

"Speaking of marriage—did Anthony tell you about your cousin Dawn?"

"She's still dating Roger, his friend from high school, right?"

"Yes, and they're getting married this spring. She wants you to be a bridesmaid. What should I tell her mother? Wouldn't it be fun? There hasn't been a wedding in our family for years! And you and Anthony can walk down the aisle together!" She sounded almost giddy.

"Let me think about it, Mom. It could be right around finals. That wouldn't work."

"Oh no, it's early spring, closer to your break! We can do the first fitting of your dress when you come home for Christmas. I'm so excited!" said Gwen.

"I can see that! Anything else, Mom? How's your job?" Lilly could barely cope with the small talk as memories of weddings past were coming to the forefront of her mind.

"Work is work; you know how that is. I am up at four and home by five. I meant to ask, you're not drinking, are you? Remember what the doctor said about alcohol and your liver."

"No, Mom, nothing but water, tea, and coffee. The semester has been tough without Trudy."

"Your health is important, more important than friends and parties. Remember that!"

"I will!"

"And let me know what your decision is about being a bridesmaid before you leave."

"Sure thing. I'll think it over. Everything looks and smells delicious. I cannot wait to eat! Dorm food is awful this year."

"Well, sit down! I made more than enough!"

There were benefits to visiting, but alone in her bedroom, her thoughts wandered to the past, as she battled with the decision to be a bridesmaid or not.

Of course they will be at the wedding and I don't want to be near that pervert freak and manipulative Millie. Thinking about them makes my heart beat like war drums. That's a good reason for not standing up as a bridesmaid.

Family weddings are never good. And I won't survive another attack, not at this age. If he ever touches me again, or drugs me so I can't defend myself, I think I would crack up. So what do I do? Disappoint mom when we are finally talking to one another peacefully or start another family argument and fight?

She picked up the phone.

"Hey, Ann, I have a question. Can you talk?"

"You always ask me that. I would tell you if I couldn't," she jokingly replied.

"My cousin wants me to stand up for her wedding this spring. I know Frank and Millie will be there, but I feel I cannot bail out on Dawn, not on her special day, and it means a lot to Mom. The last thing I need is to start a family feud."

"Well, a wedding is only one day, not even twenty-four hours, and then you'll be back at school."

"True. However, that is at least fourteen hours of constant vigilance, and I haven't needed to do that since I left home. I'm out of practice."

"But you're older and wiser than you were at seventeen."

"He only needs a moment and a plan made with Millie. I haven't been too successful at outsmarting him and I've tried many times."

"You have to be the wiser one or..."

"Or what? That's the answer I'm looking for!"

"Tell your dad."

"And ruin Dawn's wedding day? Never!"

"Then say no. Your mother and Dawn will get over it."

"Causing a family scene right now wouldn't be good for me."

"Lilly, be careful. I worry about you going back into that entire wedding family scenario. For once, do what you know is right for you."

Lilly answered bravely, "I feel stuck. I do not want to let Mom down, or my cousin, but I don't think I could take another attack. Then again, I am nineteen. Would he be that gutsy to go after an adult female?"

"I don't know, but I'll support you in any decision you make."

Sunday morning, Lilly went to church with the family and came home for brunch before her ride picked her up. "Have you decided?" asked Gwen.

Lilly looked away and then at her mother's happy face. "Yeah, sure, I'll be a bridesmaid. It'll be fun to be with them on their wedding day."

"You and Anthony are in the same wedding party, how exciting!" Gwen clasped her hands in joy.

On the ride back and during her unpacking, all Lilly did was rethink her decision. So much so, that it became obsessive. In the weeks and months that followed she turned into a recluse. The complete opposite of her normal campus life. She walked to classes alone and studied alone. The only other students on campus who seemed to be as lonely as her were the Vietnam vets.

The number of young men wearing fatigues had increased. The news said the war was ending, but by the looks of the young men she saw on campus, she knew the war would never be over for them. Lilly could see into their uncomprehending eyes and feel the edginess of their body language. They were older than their age, much like her.

She knew the challenge of trying to forget horror while letting go of guilt. She understood sharing days and nights of bad dreams and triggers. She knew how their secrets ruled their lives, and how no one wanted to listen to their horror. Lilly didn't wear the uniform, but she had lived decades of fighting a war against one evil enemy. She and the vets shared being oddities of society.

Then random panic attacks began as the wedding drew near. Her gut told her not to go. But her heart told her to keep trying to be part of the family.

She was back at war with herself and the worlds she lived in.

※

Lilly took a deep breath and let it out. *The ceremony is over. Now I have the wedding pictures to deal with. I am in a group and the photographer has no resemblance to Frank. Afterward, we go to the reception. That is where I need to remember what Ann said, "Don't drink, and stay by people all night. Never be alone." I can do that, only four hours to go.*

Frank watched Lilly as he lit his cigar standing on the church steps with Millie on his arm. "Such a beautiful woman she turned out to be. Don't you think so?" remarked Millie. "Hmmm, still a cute country charmer! Does she have a boyfriend?"

"Not that I know of and according to Gwen she hasn't been serious since her high school crush. That young man broke her heart. I tried to tell Gwen to put a stop to it. Then there was that fight with Vincent. We were almost her parents. It was so close. I still feel a pit in my stomach from losing her."

"She'll come back to us."

"I don't know how you can say that. She's independent and rarely comes home. Thank goodness we still have other nieces to love. Come; let's go to the reception early. I want to see everyone walk in, check out what they're wearing, and how they've changed. This is such fun!" Millie said with excitement.

Out of the corner of her eye, Lilly examined her godparents.

He still wears his favorite color: brown, and he went bald! Oh, it's ugly and creepy how the top of his head shines like his shoes. Then he has those few hairs combed over it. Gross! He appears to be enjoying a life of gluttony with the inner tube around his middle. Millie doesn't look too bad for a dying woman. Overdressed, if you ask me. Still playing the role of the uptown girl. Oh, they disgust me!

※

At the reception, her vigilance returned as sharp as ever, checking out each exit: the bathrooms, windows, corners, even table arrangements. *I know how Frank works. He will make it look like he is drinking heavily, when he's not. Instead he is buying drinks for all the young mothers and fathers so they don't watch their children. Then he starts to prowl. Looking for his victim.*

"Lilly, honey," Gwen addressed her. "Come and visit with us."

Lilly looked to see who was at her parents' table. It was *them*, Millie and Frank. "I'm going to go and hang out with Anthony."

Gwen took her arm. "Oh, come on. Just for a few minutes and then you can do whatever you want." Frank began to shake the coins in his pocket. He laughed as he explained how it became a nervous habit. *That's a lie,* thought Lilly. *It's his sound. He's ready to play his stalking game.*

Stay cool and level headed. His tricks will not work on me anymore. In four hours I'll be home and tomorrow…back at school, back in my safe world.

The one I made. Now it's time to find *Anthony.*

"Well, this has been interesting, Mom and Dad, but I need to join the wedding party."

Frank's eye twitched.

"That's fine, dear," replied Gwen. "Go and have fun."

"Thanks, Mom. I will."

Lilly walked away, feeling Frank's eyes watching her every step. She found a corner to stand where she could watch *him* and reclaim her composure.

This was not going to be one of his usual family weddings. Not with her eyes on his every move.

When the band took a break, she ordered a beer, just one. When she turned back around, there was no Frank. Anxiously, she skimmed the room. He was nowhere. Terror took its proper place.

Maybe he is in the bathroom. She watched the men's door for a few minutes and no Frank. *Where is Dad? He could be having a drink with Dad.* She saw Vincent dancing with her aunt. Then the worst possible thought came over her. *Oh my God, Eva, where is Eva?* Pure panic overcame her. She was no longer cool-headed and focused. She was a maddening mess.

Her legs weakened, making her feel a loss of control and throwing her off balance. She looked as if she were drunk. *I only had one beer, but it feels like I had twenty. It's the panic taking over me. I have to keep it together and find Eva.*

She stopped and leaned against a wall, searching for her sister. *There she is! I see her! She is dancing with her cousins.* Lilly closed her eyes in relief. *Everything is going to be fine if my head would stop spinning! I feel like I did the night Trudy took me to the infirmary. Maybe it is some kind of relapse from my nerves. I am going to pass out if I don't get some fresh air.*

Taking one uneasy step at a time she made it to the door and stepped outside. Anthony was in the distance, joking with a group of his friends. *That's what I need, to hang out with the guys for a while. They are a fun group and Frank won't go near me. He is afraid of young men. They're strong and would take him out in a second.*

She held onto the railing and stepped down, calling out Anthony's name. To her surprise, she had no voice, just a hoarse rasp of air left her mouth.

At the bottom step she saw Frank lurking in the shadows of the building's corner, watching her lose self-control.

"No!" Lilly mumbled. "This isn't a relapse. He drugged my beer. He must have paid the bartender. That was the only chance he had." She tried to kick off her heels and make a run for Anthony.

She was out of time. Frank pounced, placing his white handkerchief over her mouth. Half dragging her to his car, he opened the door to the back seat and pushed her in.

❖

The smell of bacon woke her from her sleep. In one movement she sat up, frightened and angry. She was coming out of a horrible bad dream—and then she saw the pink dress on her bedroom floor.

"That fucking bastard, I'm going to fucking kill him!" She walked over to the limp dress and kicked it across the room. She remembered his strong hold on her before they reached the car. Her legs were useless as well as her screams. Did she want to remember any more? She did, but it wasn't there. Her mind was a void except for the memory of a car and Frank and her dress falling over her face as she fell into the backseat of the car.

She had no headache or remnants of a hangover.

Back and forth she paced in her bedroom. *What did he do?* She grabbed her robe, pulled it tight around her body, and walked downstairs to find Anthony.

"Good morning, sleepyhead." Gwen greeted her too cheerily. "You sure enjoyed yourself at the wedding last night, but I have to admit I was worried you were dancing too much. It hasn't even been a year since your illness."

Lilly grabbed a slice of crisp bacon. "Mom, I don't have any more restrictions. Where's Anthony?"

"He's still sleeping in the guest room. Go wake him up and tell him breakfast is ready."

I feel dirty and sleazy, like a whore. I worked hard to get rid of that trashy feeling and now...it's right back. Why did I ever think I had a chance at normal?

Sitting on the edge of the guest bed, she shook her brother lightly.

"Anthony, wake up!" She could smell the booze as he groaned and rolled over. "I'm telling you to wake up, now!" She nudged him harder.

He opened his eyes. "What is your problem?" he asked hoarsely.

"What's *my* problem? Let's start with who drove me home?"

"Not me!" he snapped back, putting the pillow over his head. "I was too drunk to drive. I think Willy gave you a ride. You are going to break that guy's heart one of these days. You flirted with him all night while you two danced."

Lilly let up on her brother and put her hand to her head. "Willy? Oh my dear Lord. I haven't seen him in years."

Anthony lifted the pillow. "By the way, what were you on last night? You were flying all over the place."

She jumped off the bed, ready to slug him. "Nothing! By the way, breakfast is ready." She threw the extra pillow at his face and stomped out. *How dare he accuse me of being on drugs! I was...what was I...raped? How do I know? Photographed...another "I-don't-know."*

Lily threw on some old jeans and a shirt and headed down to the river, pushing the canoe off into the cold waters. As she paddled she tried to let the night go. *What happened is in the past, but what really did happen? I am right back to where I was when I left home. What will I tell Ann? I think I remember hearing him tell me I owed it to them. What could I possibly owe them? Being grateful that I am still alive?*

<hr />

"Your ride is here," Vincent said, slipping her an extra ten for gas.

"Thanks, Dad." She bowed her head, not wanting to look him in the eyes. She was ashamed to be his daughter. "Are you okay? You look anxious."

"I'm fine, just tired again. Cannot wait to get back to the privacy of my room. It was worth every extra penny I saved."

"Glad that worked out well for you. Have a safe trip back. Be careful and know I love you."

Lilly looked carefully at his face. His eyes were peaceful, like those she remembered as a child. She choked out a faint, "I love you more." She had failed them and herself. She wasn't as strong as she thought, or as wise. She was still a captive of Frank.

The hate and anger she felt stewed within her the entire four hours back to college and by the time she reached the dorm, her rebellious horns of her secret life had returned.

The phone rang. It was Ann. "How did the wedding go?"

"Like you said, only twenty-four hours and I made it!"

"Yes, I knew you would be safe! I was a wreck yesterday thinking about you! Do you want to have supper and tell me about it?"

"Thanks, but I'm tired and I have a ton of leftovers from home. Think I will crash early. Say hi to your mom and dad for me, okay?"

"Will do! See you this week, maybe Thursday?"

"Sounds great, I will see you then! Thanks for calling!"

Now she was back to lying, even to Ann, who she had never told a fib to. The humiliation of being a victim at her age, with a pervert she knew from the past, was eating her alive. She could not cope with the disgrace and repulsion.

I need something to help me forget and move on. I need some golden ale! Maybe one good drunk would flush out the toxins of Frank.

AN UNKNOWN SOLDIER

"Hi, I'm Lilly from down the hall," she introduced herself to the party host.

"Hi, Lilly, I'm happy you came. Help yourself to the booze. Beer is over there; wine is in the bucket. Up on the desk shelf is hard liquor." He pointed out each item.

That bottle of vodka looks mighty fine, Lilly mused, walking over to the shelf and snatching it up.

"Would you like a cup for that?" a young man asked.

Lilly hadn't seen him before and wasn't in any mood for a pickup line. In fact, the sight of every male sickened her.

She took a good swig from the bottle and made a sour face as she explained: "Only the first few drinks are harsh. After that, it's a smooth pathway down."

"Do you mind if I join you?"

Lilly took a long, hard look at him. He had to be a freshman and with that poor pickup line, not too wise either. "Yes, I do mind." She guzzled again and left him standing alone.

She recognized a few faces, but no one she could lean on and spill her guts to. *I wish I knew where Kenzy was,* she thought. *With all this free liquor and pot we could make a good time, but damn that girl. She disappears like a magician, never leaving a clue*

Lilly found a beanbag chair stuffed into a corner, plopped down, and fed her self-pity with each drink until there were only a few swallows left.

Loosely carrying the bottle, she got up and staggered back to her room.

She felt as if she were being watched; an all too familiar feeling. She turned around and slurred out loudly, "You piece of shit!" Thinking she was talking to Frank. "Like hell you can always see me! If you're out there, then come on! Finish me off. Get it over with!"

She swayed, waiting to hear the jingling coins and the stench of his sickening cigar. However, the hallway was empty and silent.

"Well then, fuck you! Fuck me! Hell, fuck this whole damn world." She raised her vodka bottle, finishing off the last swig and bounced off the walls into her room. Within minutes she passed out into oblivion upon her bed.

Quietly, the young man from the party stepped through her open door and moved directly toward Lilly's bed. He looked down at her with concern. "Are you alright?" He nudged her seemingly lifeless body.

She groaned in pain.

"Do you need help?"

She batted her eyes open. "My stomach hurts," she whispered. Her breathing was shallow and erratic.

Again, the young student awakened her and this time she could see the silhouette of three others. They were talking. Their voices sounded worried as they paced like nervous hyenas.

"I think we should call the ambulance," suggested one.

Lilly heard him. *No, don't call anyone. Just leave me alone. Let me go.* She spoke only in thought, unable to talk. "Maybe we should call security."

"Are you nuts? We're responsible for bringing the liquor to the party. We'll be dead!"

The young man who had followed her joined in. "If we don't do something, *she* will be dead. And that can fall on us too."

"We're out of here," said his friends, leaving him alone to carry the burden of making a decision.

The pain in Lilly's abdomen sharpened, awakening her to semi-consciousness. *I don't want to die* ran through her head. *I need help. Someone has to help me.* She tried talking to the shadow that stood over her, but all that came out was a groan of excruciating pain.

"I'm going to get you help. Hang in there," the young man whispered in her ear and then ran up to the fourth floor where a vet lived.

She hadn't let go of the world yet, but the exit door was near and her resistance had become paper-thin. A deep penetrating coldness grew within, causing her to shake uncontrollably.

The vet crawled behind her. He lifted her head and rolled her body to its side. The movement caused her to vomit. She felt a finger in her mouth, triggering a gag, and vomited again. Then he raised her head with an extra pillow and pulled the comforter over her body. She tried to roll onto her back, but he persistently kept her on her side.

Stop moving me! It hurts and makes me sick. Leave me alone! She wanted to tell him in her drifting state of mind.

He rolled her to her other side. It brought on one last big heave and then consciousness.

Through blurry eyes she saw a man wearing military fatigues and holding what looked like a gallon of milk. Lilly was now aware of her surroundings, but too weak to talk. She was intent on falling back to sleep and he was determined to keep her awake.

"Here, I want you to take a few sips of milk," he said, picking up her head to help her drink.

"No, I can't," she said with a weak voice. "My stomach hurts!"

"Take very small sips, very slowly." He assisted, controlling how much she swallowed.

It made her gag and vomit, causing pain that was more unbearable. In time Lilly regained enough strength to sit up while holding her stomach contents in.

Lilly placed both hands on the edge of the bed. "Whoa, the room is spinning way too fast!" The man rushed over just to guide her body back down onto the bed.

"Hey." He lightly wiped her face with a cold washcloth. "What's your name?"

"Lilly."

"Lilly, I'm going to help you get up and then we're going to walk," he said, holding onto her arm.

"No, no, no," was her drunken response. "I don't have legs. How can I walk?"

"With my help." He wrapped the comforter over her and let her weight fall on him as he pulled her up. "Okay, Lilly, we're going to walk around your room and then out into the hallway."

"I don't want to. It makes me sick and dizzy."

"It doesn't matter what you want. It's what you're going to do."

Who is this guy? The fighting anger that kept her alive so many times before briefly returned. *Who does he think he is, ordering me around?*

She managed to half walk on her own, while he dragged the rest. "What happened?" Lilly asked in confusion.

"What happened?" he said, oozing sarcasm. "You poisoned yourself by drinking a bottle of vodka. That's what happened." Lilly said nothing. She remembered wanting to be free from her life, but she hadn't set out to poison herself.

"Don't keep your vomit down; if you feel the need, let it come up. It's flushing out your insides."

"But it makes everything hurt more."

"That's the reality of being stupid."

"I'm not stupid," she growled.

"You can't convince me of that. Keep walking."

"I don't want to talk."

"Fine, keep walking."

They walked for what seemed like hours before he took her back to the room. "Now what?" she asked, hanging on to his strong shoulders.

"You, young lady, are going to take a shower."

"Oh no," Lilly said, pulling back. "I can't stand up on my own. No shower, please, I'm begging you."

The veteran had already turned the water on. "Here you go!" In one sweeping movement, he picked her up and set her down on the floor of the shower directly in the stream of tepid water.

The beads pounded against Lilly's face, head, and body. "Turn it off! Now! It's beating me up!" she screamed, hands over her head and face in protection.

"It's going to help you."

"Then turn down the pressure," she ordered.

He didn't move. He sat on the floor, watching her.

"Go away; I don't like people watching me," Lilly shouted through her hands. He sat motionless and quiet, watching.

"I hate you, I hate everybody, get me out of this goddamn shower!" She rolled onto her knees, thinking she could crawl out on her own.

"You're pathetic," he said, with little empathy, as he helped her dry off and wrapped her in her robe.

The movement caused another vomiting jag, but this time Lilly made it to the toilet on her own, noticing the stranger was not as eager to help. "Who *are* you?" She looked up at him from the bathroom floor. There was something unusual in his eyes. They were irate and callous, yet soft and trusting.

With the help of the walls, she pulled herself up and walked to the sink to brush her teeth.

"I know you're a veteran." She squeezed the toothpaste out onto her brush, a simple task that she found surprisingly difficult. "Will you say something and stop watching me! It's freaking me out!"

He stood up and moved behind her. Lilly watched in the mirror. She put her toothbrush down, ready to defend herself. In a quick second, he grabbed a handful of her hair, smashed her face into the mirror, and screamed into her ear, "What the hell were you thinking? Those boys could easily be looking at a murder charge, kicked out of college and in prison because of some drunken college girl who didn't like her mommy and daddy."

The last words ricocheted through Lilly's poisoned brain.

"You don't know me or anything about my life. Who do you think you are?" she shot back at him with her teeth clenched. *"Go. To. Hell!"*

He wouldn't let up. Using the counter, Lilly tried to push off. He slammed her again, into the mirror.

"Look at yourself, look!" he commanded as his powerful hands maneuvered her head. There was nothing for her to do but to stare at her reflection.

Lilly closed her eyes to escape the face in the mirror.

*"*Look!" he shouted. "Open your fucking eyes and look at yourself."

"No! Get away! You're hurting me!" she yelled, trying to push herself free.

"I'll leave when you take a good look at yourself."

Cautiously, Lilly opened her eyes. She hated looking at herself. Frank was always lurking right behind, laughing, chewing his stub cigar, and reminding her of the lesser person she was. She spat at the mirror and hissed, "She's a piece of shit. She's ugly. And I *really* hate her!"

"You hate her enough to kill her? Because that is what you're doing. What can be so bad that you want to die because of it?" he sneered.

"I don't know!" Lilly's voice dropped. "Not anymore. I don't know anything. Just let me go. Please?" Her voice cracked as tears began to slide between her and the mirror. "I'll be alright," she begged, letting her muscles weaken.

"No, you're not alright. You nearly killed yourself. What were you thinking?" She sensed compassion in his tone as he guided her depleted body down to the floor. The two sat with their backs against the cold cinder block wall.

"I *wasn't* thinking, I was feeling. And what does it matter to you?" She choked out the words. "And why do you want to know when no one else does?"

"I carried many men off the field, dead at age twenty, some younger, and not one of them wanted to die. Then I come home to this! I cannot imagine what could be that bad. I need to know." He sensed that if she could see herself, and her problem, she would make it. He had been in her shoes.

"Like you said, I wasn't happy with my mommy-and-daddy world. That's what you want to hear, right? So go be a hero somewhere else and leave me alone," Lilly mocked.

"You are one spoiled little bitch; you know that? Whatever it is that you're running from, the run is over. You keep acting this way and there will be no more you." He stood up to leave.

"No, wait! Hear me out. Everybody thinks I am somebody I'm not and for sure I am not a spoiled little bitch. I didn't fight in *your* war, but I have one of my own that won't end. It just won't!"

He looked down at Lilly. "What kind of war would a girl like you have to fight?"

She returned a belligerent look. "Rape, pornography, fear of dying or seeing someone I love die. It started when I was a little and it hasn't ended. A week ago he drugged me, and I don't know what he did. I can't tell anyone, because I have no memory. What is there to tell? After he threw me in the car and sat on top of me I blacked out." Lilly wiped her face on the sleeve of her robe. "You know what I saw in the mirror? I saw the ugly mess he made of me, and the lies; there are so many lies. I don't know how I can live with myself anymore. I have failed at everything. I've lost all hope."

He returned to sitting by her side. Lilly curled up in a defensive ball, waiting for a blow to the head or a kick to the stomach. He observed her reaction. "You've taken a beating before too, haven't you?"

Lilly nodded yes.

He put his arm around her shoulders and they sat, neither of them speaking, but reliving their own personal battles on the cold, damp floor. Lilly felt safe with him next to her. She placed her head on his chest and cried. She cried for every year she lived as he stroked her hair.

"What you see in that mirror isn't what others see. You are a beautiful girl and smart. When you look into a mirror, you need to see who is looking back at you and not who is behind you. You have had to be brave to get through this. And you have to get tough again to pull yourself up and tell your parents what you told me."

"It's not easy. You practically killed me before I opened up."

"True. If you can't tell anyone, then stay clear of the people who hurt you."

"Even if it means I have to leave my family?"

"If that's what it takes to keep safe, yes."

Lilly shook her head. "I can't. I don't do well being alone. Tonight is a good example of that."

"Listen, I wouldn't walk into a minefield just because I thought I should be on the other side. I would go around it to keep my men and me safe. The enemy doesn't control you or your moves. You make your own plan and plots. Don't plot yourself right into a dangerous or deadly path."

"Every plot I made failed."

"You'll come up with another. Don't stop trying. I saw the fight in you. You're not his prisoner, not now, not ever." Lilly looked into his haunting eyes, believing and trusting his words.

"Find yourself a good man and lay off drinking for a while, promise me that?"

"I promise." She meant those two words. They came from deep within.

"No smoking cigs or weed either. Your liver is going to need a rest. Water, drink plenty of water."

"I will drink a ton of water…won't smoke anything…cross my heart."

He walked toward the door with his backpack in hand.

"At least tell me your name before you leave!" she shouted.

There was no answer, only the quiet seal of her security door.

※

"Where is this guy?" Lilly asked herself. She had searched the dorms for two weeks. "I want to thank him and tell him I'm keeping my promises, but no one seems to have any info about where he is! The kids at the party are mum, not wanting to get into trouble."

He was nowhere and Lilly couldn't let him go. Like his eyes, his words stayed with her. She kept true to her promise.

Taking solace in the lake and the wind, she sat on a black rock that was a safe distance from the waves' strong grip. Looking out over the endless blue horizon, she couldn't let go of what she'd realized when the soldier held her face in the mirror. *I never wanted to look deeply at myself. I couldn't, because Frank was always behind me, snickering and belittling me. I only saw what he wanted me to see. I wasn't able to see the truth. That's different now. Frank is not going to be haunting me in my reflection. Now I struggle with a new question... who am I? Who is that girl looking back at me? How did we become so distant?*

IN THE REAL WORLD

"Dad, I have to get out of these dorms next year. The food isn't healthy and it's not as safe as you and Mom think. There are parties and drugs everywhere and I don't want to be near any of it. Being a junior, I can live off campus, cook my own meals, and have quiet nights to sleep and study."

"Apartments are expensive."

"I found some new rental units a mile off campus. Will you look at them with me?" Lilly pleaded. Since the night of her near-death experience, she had buried her energy even deeper in her studies and work schedule to avoid the temptations of dorm life.

"I don't know if that's the best idea, Lilly." Vincent hesitated. "Dorm life gives us a feeling that you're protected. Living in an apartment would be more dangerous."

Oh, really, thought Lilly, *now he is going to worry about my safety? If he only knew!* "Do the math, Dad. It will *save* us money. It is cheaper than what the college is charging, especially if I share the apartment with three roommates, and it is safer! They have an intercom system and locked entry door. Come on, please, Dad?"

"How are you going to get around for groceries and laundry?"

"Maybe I could use Anthony's old car?" She crossed her fingers, knowing she was throwing out a lot for her dad to consider.

"Nope, that's definitely not a subject we're going to venture into."

"Okay, I understand. I can walk. I walk everywhere now and have for two years. Ann will help me out in emergencies. And I promise to take care of the apartment as if it were my home. No matter when you come to visit, it will be spotless."

"Let me talk to your mother. Maybe—and I'm saying maybe—we'll consider it."

Lilly twirled her hair. It was difficult not to allow the emotions of what had happened to her at the wedding and then at the dorm come into their conversation. She cleared her throat and asked the next big question.

"I also want to ask you about work. I need to save money if I want an apartment."

"No, Lilly, you're not staying up here for the summer."

"Agree! I cannot afford it. So, I was wondering if I could come home and work at the resort's sister property. It's about forty-five minutes from our house."

Vincent didn't respond. Lilly wondered if his face looked anything like hers, shocked that she was agreeing to live at home. "You *want* to come home for the summer?"

"Yes, Dad."

"That's a great idea! It would save you a few months' rent. And then we could talk about using Anthony's old car."

Lilly bit her lower lip to keep from screaming with joy. "That would be awesome! Do you think Mom will be okay with the plan?"

"I'm sure she will and Eva will love to have you home too."

"There's one more thing." Lilly carefully pushed out the rest of her sentence. "I can't live with the rules you had for me at seventeen. I'm soon to be twenty and I've been living on my own for two years."

"I understand. We'll come to an agreement. And Mom and I will look at the apartments when we come to pick you up at the end of the semester."

She sighed with satisfaction. *Fingers still crossed*—she scanned the room—*I will never live in a dorm again. I am so ready to put this life away and be independent: cooking, cleaning, and grocery shopping. That's the life I understand and feel secure in.*

Two weeks after school ended, her parents agreed to cosign for the apartment. The owner had tough rules to follow, which pleased her parents, and the pricing was workable as long as four girls shared it.

Lilly was bursting at the seams. Not only was she able to move off campus, she had met a young man who was home for summer break from a private college not too far from Black Rock. He was polite, funny, and treated her as if she were the only girl in the world.

Her independence had grown strong and she had stayed true to the promise she made to her unknown soldier. She was growing up in reality.

1986 – SESSION TWELVE – THEN AND NOW

"Face it, people don't want to hear the dark side of my past. When the subject comes up, it's 'let's not go there' time."

"How does that make you feel?"

"Frustrated, perplexed, and lonely."

"You mention feeling misunderstood often."

"That's because people make it obvious they don't want to hear about it; avoiding a difficult conversation. They don't know how hard it is to work at being normal, trying to fit in with the rest of the world, when you've been traumatized and know you're different."

"This all takes time. You have kept everything in for so long and now you want to tell everyone. There will come a time when it balances out."

"Maybe so. I have made big steps with Mom and Dad and I never thought that was going to happen, but it has, and I am grateful. Also, I am able to focus my thoughts on the present more consistently. Now that I look at it, I am much better off now than I was as a teen."

"Those were formative years for you."

"And confusing; being torn between friendships, lovers, drinking, work, home, and college. If I screwed up, I was going to let myself down, not anyone else. This was my 'me' era. I reached out to parties, sex, and everything else. Then came the wedding."

"Tell me about that day."

"I was so ashamed after that day. Its memory wouldn't get out of my head, so I decided to drink until I blacked out from alcohol poisoning. If it wasn't for my war hero, I would have died that night from being stupid."

"He saved your life."

"Yes, and in many ways. He made me see a Lilly who was good, caring, and full of life, not the one hiding behind humiliation and guilt, wanting to die, and be defeated. He tapped into an emotion that was nearly gone."

"Tell me about that emotion."

"Willpower—that last attack at the wedding shattered me. It was degrading and humiliating beyond words. It stripped me of my self-control and determination to survive. That's why I nearly drank myself to death."

"When you were young, it was too dangerous for Frank to be public with you because a youngster is quite unpredictable. The day at the beach was an age where you were becoming aware of your physical being, and he knew that. *You* came out of the water more deeply humiliated and damaged, ensuring silence. *He* came out of the water with more control and dominance."

Lilly added, "And he needed to do that again, which is why he attacked me that night. He hadn't been able to get close to me for a few years. I was secure and happy in the new world I had built. He enjoyed shattering my happiness and sending me back to feeling victimized and helpless."

"It parallels his past actions."

"He didn't want me to succeed, so he brought me down, and it worked because at age nineteen I was completely aware of my body, sexually and physically. It was mine. He knew the embarrassment would be destructive and devastating."

"Of course he did. And he knew he wouldn't be able to overpower you, so he disabled you." Dr. Bricks slowly added, "You had no way of knowing what Frank was up to at the reception."

"You're wrong. I knew he was dangerous. I knew I was putting myself in harm's way."

"That's like saying I know there's a hail storm coming and I want to protect every leaf and flower in my yard."

"That's impossible," Lilly responded. "Frank *is* a hailstorm, and no one can predict what damage he is going to do. If being a bridesmaid hadn't been so important to Mom, I wouldn't have accepted. I knew there was danger involved, but I thought I was ahead of his game. I was quite confident that I would never be his victim again."

"This wasn't an easy decision for you. Do you blame your mother?"

Lilly's face reflected deep concern. "I did what I thought would make her happy, so I cannot blame her any more than I can blame myself."

"People do things for those they love, even when they know it's not the best decision."

Lilly looked away from Dr. Bricks and contemplated his words.

Then she replied, "You're right. At any age we can make a bad decision, however, the shame that it can cause may be harmful." Lilly paused, thinking to herself, and then turned to Dr. Bricks. "If the shame goes away, will the anger of that night leave too?"

"Very possible, since shame leads to anger."

"I'm pissed off enough to kill him. I clearly remember the stalking of that wedding night. It is an evil and nerve-wracking act to do to someone. I hate it. I hate stalking with all of my body. It was his foreplay," she angrily stated, clenching her fists. "There should be a lot more information out there about stalking."

"You're correct. Stalking hasn't been researched to any great length until recently, and we are only now beginning to understand its effects."

"It crushed my strength of mind."

"Stalking can do that since it's a display of dominance to gain control."

"And here we are, back to the word 'control' and how it can change a person when overused." She closed her eyes. "The coins, the cigar, his whistle…I can still feel the fear they created in me. I hid to protect myself, thinking I would outsmart him. But I seldom did."

"I can't imagine the terror and helplessness you felt that night."

"It was pure fear. How he watched me. It's haunting."

"Understandably," he replied. "However, it's possible to overcome and manage the effects."

"I don't see how. The fear makes me shake. I want to scream. I want to squeeze his fat neck and watch him choke on cigar juice. Once I get the feeling that someone is watching, I cannot think rationally. It's nearly impossible to do daily life activities and it stems from Frank's stalking."

"It left a negative reaction."

Lilly began to feel the present slipping away. She dug herself into her surroundings, hoping to stay in the here and now. "This is why I can't talk about it. Stalking is a major trigger. I feel like I'm moving backward to twelve and six and then three…I don't know *how* to talk about it, so I avoid it."

"The words will come as you feel safer and protected. For now, ground yourself with the room. Be aware of your breathing. Feel the tension in your muscles and send your breath there to release it." They took several breaths together.

Lilly closed her eyes, and whispered, "Scared. Hide. Quiet. He's coming; I know he is."

"How do you know he's coming?"

"I can hear him."

"What do you hear?"

"I hear the coins in his pocket and I hear him whistling. I hear his shoes. Oh no, he is close; really, *really* close. He's going to find me!" She gasped for air. "I want to throw up," she said, holding back her gags.

"It's safe for you to vomit."

"No, I can't throw up; he'll make me eat it." She took several big swallows.

"Lilly, how old are you?"

"Six."

"Where are you?"

"I'm in the bushes under Anthony's bedroom window. I see him coming. I can smell his cigar. There is nowhere for me to go."

"Lilly, I want you to take a deep breath and come back to my office, where you are safe."

"Shh, I can't talk. I can't breathe. That is how he finds me. He hears me breathing."

"Lilly, you aren't under the bushes. You are in my office. We are having therapy." Dr. Bricks allowed Lilly time to process. Her breathing grew less labored, and she appeared to be coming back to the present. "That's good. I want you to wiggle your toes and fingers," he said. "Feel them attached to you."

She wiggled her fingers and toes, then suddenly dug her feet into the couch cushions as she twisted and turned, as if she were fighting someone off.

Dr. Bricks moved his chair closer to her. "This is Dr. Bricks. I am going to place a stress ball in your hands. Squeeze it with all of your strength. Feel that power within you." There was a pause followed by his comforting words, "I am right here."

Lilly whispered, "Uncle Frank is going to hurt me. He always hurts me after he finds me. I can't move. Why can't I move?" The stress ball rolled out of her hand and onto the floor, her body falling limp and filled with terror.

"You can move, Lilly. Your feet and toes, arms, and fingers have been moving. You have moved your head from side to side. Your uncle is not here. He cannot hurt you."

"Tell him to take his hand off my mouth. I want to scream, but I can't. He's too strong."

"You can scream. He has gone, and his hand is no longer over your mouth. You have the power to scream."

Lilly screamed and screamed until she exhausted herself. Her arms fell to her sides, and her breathing began to regulate itself. "I'm safe," she repeated the words she had heard from Dr. Bricks.

"You are in the present where you are safe. You are Lilly: a mother, a wife, and a teacher. Feel the coolness of your breath as you breathe in and its warmth as it leaves."

Several minutes later Lilly sat up and looked around the room. Then she rested her eyes on Dr. Bricks. "I feel drained. What happened?"

"You were reliving a past experience; in this case, stalking."

Lilly began to pull herself together, still feeling foggy. "It was so real, as if I were watching television. I could clearly see myself in my white shirt and blue capris. The grass wasn't green yet, but the ice had left the river. It was spring. The bushes had just budded with their leaves. I heard the coins jingle and " Lilly realized she had completely lost control; the very reason why she avoided reliving the past.

Embarrassed, she flushed and asked, "Did I do anything embarrassing?"

"No, you didn't. You did important and courageous work. Your inner child felt safe to release this memory. You were ready to listen and protect her. There is nothing stupid about that. The willpower the soldier saw in you is still there. It has never left."

"I kept my promise to him. I'm taking better care of myself." Silence filled the moment of reflection. "But here we are. A decade later and I'm still having flashbacks and reacting to triggers."

"But now you're aware of them and they're losing control over you."

"Awareness is the beginning of change, isn't it?"

"We can't change what we're not aware of or willing to accept."

"The only part of me that was constant was my goal not to succumb to Frank's words of my worthlessness and being like him. I was going to be a *good* person. Just the opposite of *him*."

Dr. Bricks leaned in, looking directly at Lilly. "That's why we focus on *you* and not Frank."

I am the focus, Lilly said to herself and shyly smiled. "I don't allow that to happen too often."

"It feels a little awkward for you to be the center of attention?"

"That's stating it lightly. I think of myself going to therapy for my family, especially Owen and Mick, but deep down inside, I know I'm here for myself. That's not easy to admit but I'm not one for secrets and lies. Not anymore; that was then; this is now. I even quit drinking. I quit cold turkey, thanks to an allergic reaction. Life has a funny way of working things out for me."

Lilly relaxed, listening to the falling waters outside his window. She was exhausted, a good exhaustion, as from a hard day of work.

HALLELUJAH

Lilly moved to the edge of her chair. "I've been giving this great thought." She paused, knowing that the next sentence was going to blow her college advisor away. "It's important for me to student teach in Ledo."

"Really..." Her advisor sat back in surprise. "Tell me your reasoning."

"It's a large city and the student population is more diverse. The curriculum is advanced and I would like to learn from it. Plus, the special-needs program is four times larger than any other placements." Lilly eagerly waited for a positive response.

"You do understand that Ledo is four hundred miles away and we only place four students there—those who are confident and able to stand on their own two feet, listen to their supervisors, and be responsible representatives of our school. These student teachers do not receive much assistance."

"That's why one of those students has to be me!" Lilly flashed a confident grin. "I've been working at the resort since I was eighteen and have advanced to dining room manager. I know responsibility and I respect my superiors. Plus, I've been a leader in my education classes."

The advisor looked over a large list of names. "The fall semester is filling in quickly; however, we do have two openings left for Ledo. You can apply immediately, and Lilly, don't be too hopeful."

"Thank you. I am the right candidate. I will make the college proud." Lilly walked out with the confidence of a lion. Two weeks later she received the good news; she was going to Ledo.

Bursting with pride, she had to call someone and the person closest to her was her boyfriend, the young man she met during her summer at home. "Sam, I have great news! The college accepted my application for Ledo! Isn't that great?"

"Wow! That's exciting," he said flatly.

"Do you know what an honor this is? Students who practice in Ledo never leave. They get hired!" She spoke rapidly, filled with excitement and pride.

"I like what we have now. Ledo is four hundred miles away."

"Really, Sam, I thought you would be happy for me! And proud." The joy in her heart was sinking.

"I am! But you'll be starting a new life without me. I have another year of school left, while you'll be looking for a permanent job. Those are some big differences and changes."

"You're afraid I'll cheat on you, is that it?" she asked somberly.

"You'll be in a big city. You're cute and single—yeah, it worries me." Sam tried his best to never see her sad, but this time he couldn't find a hint of humor in the situation.

There was silence, then Lilly continued, "If it would make you feel better, why don't we commit to one another? You know, get engaged, but not married; I am not ready for that step yet."

Lilly was tired of playing games. She wasn't going to waste time with someone who didn't see her in his life forever. She was ready to settle down, take the next step, and she thought he felt the same. She had had far too many longtime relationships without a commitment.

Sam remained quiet, while she pulled her heart away for protection.

Waves belong on the water and not in my life, she believed. *I am exhausted swimming against them, and I don't want to take on the slightest ripple for student teaching. My head has to be clear and focused, Sam is afraid that he is going to lose me, and I'm afraid that he's using me.* They spent Christmas apart, giving one another time to think.

Gwen, Vincent, Eva and Lilly gathered around the tree.

"With Anthony getting married and your student teaching position coming up, we couldn't afford much for Christmas. However, we hope you'll understand and find this gift helpful." Gwen handed Lilly a small weightless box.

"You and Dad have helped me enough by finding the studio apartment in Ledo," Lilly replied. She slowly opened the box, finding a sealed envelope. Inside the envelope was a key—a car key. "Is this what I think it is?" she asked, holding it up and breaking a gigantic smile.

Vincent laughed. "Yes, it is. Let's go out to the garage."

That was when Lilly met the Blue Goose, a 1967 Plymouth Fury.

"Oh my God, Dad, I can't believe it! Thank you so much!" She wrapped her arms tightly around his shoulders.

"What do you think?" he asked when she let go, rubbing the kink out of his neck.

Lilly was at a loss for words. She didn't like to drive, but it was a necessity of student teaching and she had been looking at used cars, but not anything quite like this—huge and blue.

"I think you found the biggest and brightest car that exists, and I love it!" She opened the door and sat behind the wheel.

"You know how much your father worries about you driving and now that you're going to be in the city we wanted to make sure that you were safe," Gwen said happily. "That explains the size and color."

"You have no idea how grateful I am." Lilly fought back tears.

"Tomorrow we'll help you pack the car," added Gwen. "Are you sure you don't want Dad and I to follow you and help you move in?"

"Not this time, Mom. I'll be fine. I have twenty-five students waiting to meet me and hopefully I can help change just one of those lives. And: no…more…college classes!" She squished Eva with a big hug.

Later that day, Lilly dressed up warm and walked through the field, down to the river.

"Hey, here we are!" she said to the icy stretch. "You're all frozen and white, but I know the water moves beneath you. So here I am, leaving again and this time to the city. I may not come back. There could be a job there for me."

"I'm in a good place and I'll be safe. If Frank and Millie come around, you have to protect Eva for me. Maybe you could drown him." She smiled to herself. "Although we will be miles apart, know that you're a part of me and I thank you for holding me up in the worst of times."

She stood in the quietness of a winter day, looking over the vast sheet of snow and ice. It felt cold and eerie, as if Mother Nature knew she wouldn't be back.

With her car packed and all good-byes said, she pulled out of their gravel driveway, up the small hill she remembered all too well, and headed south to the highway and Ledo. She let her hair down, turned up the radio, and drove without fear in the protection of her Blue Goose.

FOREVER IN MY HEART

"It's over! Three months of being a student teacher and I loved it, but I am so happy to be back home at Black Rock! In one week, I will graduate. That gives me a little time to pack up the apartment. Are you going to be around? Or does the hubby have you nailed down doing laundry and housework?" she asked Ann.

"Hi, Lilly! No, I'm not nailed down!" Ann chuckled.

"Lovebirds!" Lilly teased. "Can we get together? There is so much to catch up on: stories about my students, Sam, and life in the city. And did you hear that Trudy is tying the knot?"

"I did. That is going to be a big wedding! Can't wait to see you— where do you want to meet?"

"What about the breakwater at the park? I love it there. Hate to think that I'll be leaving it."

"Are you for sure not staying here?"

"There's a job in Ledo that's looking good, but if it falls through, I'll try further south. Teaching jobs in the north are far and few. Leaving Black Rock isn't going to be easy. It will always be my first home, the one I built by myself, but it's time to move on. My college days are over."

"It was one heck of a ride, wasn't it?"

Lilly grinned as she thought back to some of their best times together. "It sure was," she answered, and shifted her distracted thinking back to making plans. "How about I pick you up in the Blue Goose tomorrow morning?"

"That will work!"

"Then it's set. See you around ten!"

After hanging up, Lilly glanced over the apartment looking for damages and determined it was mostly in need of a deep cleaning to insure a full refund of Vincent's security deposit.

I remember how excited I was when Dad co signed this lease. She reflected. *I was thrilled to get off campus but this way of life has lost its thrill too. I'm happier in the city.*

Waking bright and early, she drove to the resort for breakfast and to say her good-byes to the many employees she had grown close to over the years.

It wasn't easy, but not as painful as it was going to be to say goodbye to Ann.

They drove out to the breakwater and nestled into their familiar perches.

"Something about this lake still tempts me," Lilly said, watching and listening to the powerful waves.

"She's beautiful and taunting, but remember what your brother said?" reminded Ann.

Lilly smiled. "Like it was yesterday. 'Don't give in to its temptations.' And I never did."

Ann looked at Lilly in surprise and asked, "You wanted to?"

Lilly nodded, "More often than I care to admit."

Stillness fell in the comfort and understanding of their friendship. In time, Ann spoke up. "How are you going to be happy without a river or a lake to guide you?"

"That's a good question. I've thought about it, and at the moment, I don't have an answer."

"Are you scared? You always hated changes."

"That's the thing: change *has* always frightened me and made me regress back to unguarded times, but not now. I feel I can keep myself safe and help others at the same time."

"Do you miss your students?" asked Ann.

"My students are little therapists that keep me in the present, because that's where they are and where they need *me* to be. There's no time to daydream when you're teaching." Lilly hesitated. "Can I ask your opinion on something?"

"Shoot!"

"Mom and Dad are throwing me a graduation party and I do not want Frank and Millie there. What should I do?"

"It's your party. You're an adult. I think you should invite whoever you want."

"Mom will carry on and on, asking why this person or that person isn't invited."

Ann faced her. "What do you *want* to tell her?"

"That I only want friends and relatives that live nearby. Just once I wish she could do that for me."

"Then that's what you say."

Lilly looked at Ann. *She has always been a clear-headed thinker, pulling me up from many weaknesses. That's my Ann; beautiful, smart, and honest.*

God, I am going to miss her. She takes the complexity out of life like no one I know.

"I am going to miss you, Ann. Can we stay in touch?"

"Of course! Maybe I can get away and visit you in the city."

"I would love that. So let's not say 'good-bye.' Let's stick with, 'See you soon.'"

ADULTHOOD

1976-1986

COMPLETELY UNEXPECTED

Two weeks after graduation, Lilly landed her teaching position in Ledo and went out to celebrate with her new roommate, Janus. "We'll have two pitchers, one for her"—Lilly pointed to Janus—"and one for me!"

"Celebrating?" inquired the waiter. "Yes, we are," Lilly proudly answered.

They sat back, relaxing after a hot and humid day of moving into their duplex.

"I never believed I would see the day where I felt I was living like royalty. We have a garage, a yard, and a huge living area, not to mention we each have our own bathrooms! It's a big step up from the corner of my brother's living room, the dorm cell, an apartment with four girls, and my studio."

Janus added, "And a paycheck every two weeks,"

"Fifteen thousand dollars—no more suppers of chicken noodle soup, soda crackers, and Tab. Good riddance to that lifestyle! And my loan will pay itself off after five years, because I'm working in a low- income school." Lilly was elated.

On their second pitcher, a man pushed his body between them, getting too close to Lilly's face for her own comfort. She pulled back.

"Hi! I'm Mick," he introduced himself. "The bartender is a friend of mine. He said he heard the two of you talking about teaching and going to college in Black Rock. I'm a teacher, and I also graduated from there."

"Sure you did," Lilly said with skepticism.

He had a big grin, a little like a joker. "I graduated in '69 and have been teaching art here ever since."

"And you came to our table to offer us advice?" teased Lilly.

"Absolutely! For starters, not all children are going to love you. There's always going to be personality conflicts."

"That's good to know." Lilly gave Janus a shifty look.

"Where did you grow up?" questioned Janus.

"I grew up in a town north of here called Greenberg. Have you heard of it?"

Janus and Lilly shared more glances of superstition. There were too many similarities between them and this man called "Mick."

"I have," said Lilly. "It's near the ski mountain."

"That's right! Do you ski?" he asked.

"No, never."

Feeling like a third wheel, Janus interrupted, "Hey, think I'll head back home. Lilly, do you want a ride?"

I do and I don't, Lilly thought. *Since Sam, I haven't looked at another man with interest. So how do I explain that this Mick character is drawing me in? He's nothing like any boyfriend from my past. Maybe too honest? Maybe too old? I don't know, but I'm completely intrigued by him. His smile, his corny pickup lines, his wild hippie fringed leather vest and long out-of- control hair.*

"I'll take you home," Mick offered.

Janus looked at Lilly, clearly suggesting she leave now and with her.

However, Lilly didn't want to. Her gut told her differently. "I'll have Mick drop me off."

"Are you sure?" Janus asked one more time, looking concerned.

"I'm sure. I'll see you in the morning!"

Lilly reflected on her decision as she watched Janus step out the door. *I'm going to trust a stranger to take me home, after we've both been drinking more than we should have. I don't trust so easily. What is going on in my head?*

"I can't believe we grew up near one another," said Mick.

"That is strange—though I would have been eleven when you were seventeen." Lilly chuckled. They found no shortage of common ground and talked for another hour until it was near midnight.

"How about finishing up this pitcher and coming over to my apartment to see my art?" Mick suggested. Lilly shook her head in disbelief. "That is the worst pickup line ever!"

Mick laughed, "I've never been good with pickup lines, but I really am an artist and I would like to show you my work. Do you like art?"

"I love art," she paused, thinking of his invitation. *We've been talking for only a few hours, but it feels like I've known him for years! Am I taking a risk here? I'm usually good at character reading. What does my gut say?* She closed her eyes, focusing on her inner feelings, and then answered, "Sure, for an hour, and then I need to get home. I'm waitressing at the country club until school starts and need to be there by ten in the morning."

He led her through the parking lot to his car, which wasn't a car. It was a van. *Vans are for perverts to kidnap and rape young girls,* she thought. "This is your *car*?" she asked cautiously.

"Yes, it's a short wheelbase van. I'm converting the inside. Check it out." He opened the two side doors to display a luxurious interior of wood, carpet, and copper.

"Wow, you're doing some great work here. Who did the copper inlays?"

"That's my work!" he proudly replied. "Look at the back of the van. I painted the mural."

Lilly walked to the back cautiously. The mural was there, just as he stated. It was art done to perfection. "That's amazing, Mick. How did you do it?" She gently touched the metal surface of the paint.

"It's called airbrushing."

"How long have you been doing art?"

"Since I was seven." He walked to the passenger door and opened it for Lilly.

"Impressive!" She stepped up on the running board and settled into a soft captain's chair. "I've haven't ridden in anything like this." She looked around at all the lit buttons for the stereo system. "You did all this wiring?"

"With some help from a friend," and he closed the door.

She could feel a fear of the unknown resurfacing. *Okay, Lilly, keep your eyes open and pay attention to his driving, the roads, and landmarks. Keep yourself safe.*

He pulled up alongside a sidewalk. "This is home." He pointed to an old Victorian house painted white with burgundy trim. "I rent the first floor."

"Nice." Lilly scanned the environment. There were two floors above him. There was a front door and most likely a back door. The windows were long and low to the ground. The building was not made of cement, which meant the walls could share sounds. Vigilant, she stepped out and followed Mick to the front entrance. It was another piece of art, displaying the crafts of woodworking and stained glass. He opened it, allowing her to enter first.

"Would you like a glass of wine or a can of pop?"

"I'll take the pop, thank you." *He seems nice enough*, she thought to herself as she walked slowly down the narrow hallway toward the living room, observing the art and posters that were everywhere. *He really is an artist—a good sign that my gut is right.*

"You know art is in the eye of the beholder. Come here, I'll show you some other pieces." They went through the apartment for hours as if it were a gallery.

Finally, Lilly began to feel light-headed from fatigue. "What time is it?" she asked, covering a yawn. "It's nearly four!"

"Oh, wow! I didn't realize it was that late. I need to get home!" She tightened her muscles, thinking this would be the final test.

"Sure, sorry that I carried on for so long," he answered as he began to tidy up, putting the glasses in the sink and the chips and snacks away. She was impressed. *I've only dated high school or college guys and never realized how different the working, single man can be.*

"It's pretty cool out. Do you want a jacket or sweater?"

Lilly continued to be captivated. "No, thank you. I'll be fine."

As he drove her to her apartment they continued to talk. It was the same feeling she had had with Blake; there was always something to share and discuss.

"Here we are." He turned off the engine and turned toward Lilly with that come-on look. "Can I see you again?" Lilly didn't know what to say.

Seeing her indecision, Mick took a gamble. He moved in closer and kissed her tenderly, allowing her the room to engage or pull back. She nervously pulled back. She had enjoyed the kiss and wanted a repeat, but it was too soon after Sam.

"Can I have your phone number?" He handed her a business card and pen.

She nervously held the pen and wondered, *Should I or shouldn't I? I like him and I want to get to know him, but...* She took a deep breath and scribbled down her number.

Handing the card back, she thanked him and quickly exited.

He called several times. They played tennis, went out for lunch, and eventually he invited her to his apartment for dinner. It was the

Fourth of July, the Bicentennial: a huge celebration, but she and Mick chose to make their own fireworks.

The next morning, they took a walk along the industrial river that flowed through the center of the city.

"I feel as if we've been waiting for each other our entire lives and all the other relationships we've had led to this one," Lilly said to Mick.

"I feel the same way. We fit each other."

CANDLELIGHT

There was only Mick. The past was exactly that and there wasn't enough time in the day for them to be together.

Nine months later, she snuggled up to him in their apartment. "I was thinking we should get married." She turned to face him. "Would you marry me?" She slid it in low and fast, like a stealth bomber, waiting for his reaction.

Mick paused. "Yes, I'll marry you."

Lilly sat up, rather shocked. "I'm not kidding. I'm serious. I don't need two years to figure out if I'm in love or not. I could have married you three weeks after we met. That's how I felt then and now. I don't need a long relationship."

He wholeheartedly replied, looking deep into her eyes, "Neither do I! And I told my uncle, just a month after we met, that I had finally found the right girl."

"So you're saying yes?" she asked in pleasant surprise.

"Yes, Lilly, I will marry you!"

Love has never been this easy, she thought. *He's toying with me. There's only one way to see if he's serious about this.*

Slyly, she continued, "If you really mean it, then call your mother and tell her we're getting married."

Mick picked up the phone and dialed as Lilly's jaw dropped.

"Hi, Mom, is Dad there?"

Lilly could hear her reply. "Yes, I'll get him."

"I want to talk to both of you."

"Okay, hang on. Tony!" she called out. "Tony, hurry up and get over here. Mick needs to talk to both of us!"

"Hi, son, what's up?"

"I wanted you and Mom to be the first to know. Lilly and I are getting married." An Italian celebration of words and joy poured out of the phone.

"When are you two tying the knot? Your mother wants to know," asked Mick's father. "Lilly, when do we want to get married?" Mick asked his thunderstruck fiancée.

"I have no idea. I proposed to you a few minutes ago. I think we'll have to talk about a date." Stunned, she scrunched her face in bewilderment. Mick's mother grabbed the phone. "Mick, I'm looking at the country club's calendar for next year. Here, August eighth is open."

"Lilly? What about August eighth at the country club?"

Still in shock, not knowing what to say or do, she simply answered, "Sure! August eighth will be perfect."

They planned to marry in Mick's town, at his church, with a late afternoon candlelight ceremony. Lilly kept the promise she made to herself so many years ago, on her First Communion day. She would never wear a white dress again. Instead, she chose a fitted ivory dress embroidered with crocheted lace that gracefully draped her thin womanly frame. It was not the chiffon dress of her mother's choosing. It was Lilly's pick.

She stayed vigilant to include no connections to her past, which went well until it came to the rings and the guest list. Both were triggers that relit her anxiety. She had to tell Mick about the secret world she grew up in, and to do that, she had to trust him.

As they watched television, she looked up at him and asked, "Can I share a secret with you?" Mick muted the volume.

"I've told only two people about this and they promised to keep it just as it is, a secret. Will you promise too? It cannot leave this room." She did not hide her apprehension.

"What's up? Why so nervous?"

"You haven't promised that you'll keep the secret between us."

"Of course I will!"

Lilly studied his face for sincerity. It was there, but with her batting zero for most of her life with love, she proceeded cautiously. "I'm afraid that after I tell you, you won't want to marry me."

"I love you, Lilly. Nothing can take that away. Come on! Sit up. Tell me about this secret."

"It's about my godparents, Frank and Millie."

"I remember meeting them; big city gangster-like!"

"That's them. They have some sick underground connection to porno and drugs."

"What are you saying?"

"That Frank used me for his pornography and then some." Lilly turned her head away so Mick could not see the shame in her face. Mick grew quiet.

Lilly's heart raced and her eyes throbbed with nerves. "It makes me sick and I want to puke. He didn't stop until I was nearly twenty. I've made it a point to avoid being anywhere near him and Millie, but now Mom and Dad insist on inviting them to our wedding."

"That explains the tension between you and your mother. Millie's her sister, right?"

"Yes, Millie is her manipulating, *evil* sister."

"Millie knows about Frank?" Mick asked in surprise.

"Millie helps Frank and manipulates Mom to get to me." Still fearful that Mick would reject her, Lilly felt compelled to continue, "I had to tell you. I don't want any secrets between us. What should I do?" Lilly stood up and began to pace. "Telling family secrets before the wedding would take the day away from us and it would become a nightmare for both of our families."

"Lilly." Mick stood up and reached out for her hands. Holding them, he continued, "I don't care about your uncle and aunt. I only care about you and us. Nothing you say or do will change that. You said Frank hasn't touched you in four years. Right?"

"That's right, and I don't think he would try at our wedding because too many people are watching the bride. Also, he'd be in unfamiliar territory."

"Yes! It's in your town and at your parents' country club."

"Is this why you didn't want to get married in your hometown?" he asked.

"Yes, I know that making him uncomfortable will make me safer." "Then let's keep it as it is. Let your parents invite them. You'll be safe at the wedding, as well as everyone else. I'm not afraid of Frank and neither should you be. For now, we'll keep it a secret, and I assure you that other eyes will be watching him all night. I have many friends. Like you said, Frank is on our turf and we can make it very uncomfortable for him. Trust me."

Trust him. I trusted him, and that's how we came to be. That was such a difficult word for me until he came into my life. Lilly took a deep breath as he wrapped her in his arms. "What about the rings?"

Mick whispered in her ear, "Is this another secret?"

"Not really, but it's tied together. I have this thing about rings. It's partially because of Frank and partially because of you-know-who."

"Blake?"

"Yes, rings aren't the symbol I once thought they were."

"How would you like to handle it?"

"Can we look at bands instead of diamonds?"

"We'll go to the jewelry store and you can pick out whatever makes you happy and feels comfortable. You don't have to wear it again. We know we'll be married without wearing a ring."

"I love you, Mick—more than you'll ever know. Can we write our own vows too?" Mick grinned. He loved her free will.

"We'll write our vows."

It was a beautiful candlelight ceremony and fun-filled reception. Frank and Millie spent most of their night in a corner, not feeling a part of the crowd, which was mostly Mick's family and friends. Lilly's gut feeling to have the wedding out of town proved to be the right decision for all.

CODE BLUE

"Can't I stay pregnant?" Lilly asked the nurse who was pushing her wheelchair. "I'm finally feeling good. I could stay pregnant for the rest of my life! I just want to go back home!"

"That's not how your baby feels."

Oh, brother, thought Lilly. *This entire pregnancy was tough, except for the last trimester. That's how long it took me to accept my body's changes and feel some control. Now that's all about to change again and I'm not ready for it! For five years Mick and I were so busy having fun, I forgot about Frank. However, since I became pregnant he's returned, sneaking around in my head at the strangest moments, and I've told no one.*

"Here we are! You can start unpacking and I'll be back soon." The nurse left.

Lilly reluctantly put her things away as she tried to tell Mick what was worrying her. "Mick, can you please mute that television! I need to talk to you."

Mick quickly turned it off.

"I'm worried and afraid I'm not ready to be a mom."

"Honey, you're the readiest mom I've ever met. Think about tomorrow when you'll be holding our son."

"Will you stop that? We don't know if it's a girl or a boy. All nine months you've been telling everyone we're having a boy! We don't even have a girl's name picked out!"

"Don't need to. I know it's a boy." He smirked.

The nurse returned. "So what do you think you're having, a boy or a girl?"

"Oh, really!" Lilly rolled her eyes. "We were just talking about that. Mick knows it's a boy."

"What about you?" asked the nurse.

"I really didn't want a girl, so a boy would be nice."

"Why on earth wouldn't you want a baby girl?"

The nurse's questions made Lilly feel edgy. "It's a long family story," she answered, and her tone convinced the nurse to drop the subject.

If they only knew all the triggers I've been battling with lately. Again, Frank's words ring true...he'll always be with me during the most important times of life. The sick bastard. I should have told the doctor, but I'm too embarrassed, and it's complex. I need to use my tools and get a hold of it. This would be a good time to start!

Breathe, she reminded herself. *Get out of my head! Go away! You're nothing to me anymore,* she snarled at the flashbacks on the screen of her thoughts.

"How are you doing?" asked the nurse.

"Okay," Lilly lied.

"Let me know if I can help."

Lilly nodded as the images of a baby wrapped in a clown-covered blanket, in a casket, raced through her head. She drank some water, swallowing hard, hoping to drown the partial memory. It didn't work. In her gut she felt that something horrible was going to happen.

"I need to walk," she told the nurse.

"I'm sorry, sweetie, but your water broke and the doctor ordered no walking."

"Can I walk to the bathroom and back?" Lilly asked in desperation.

"Sure, let me help you."

"No, I can do this myself," Lilly replied. She inched her way to the bathroom, *I need alone time. The more commotion around me, the more flashbacks I have.*

"Lilly?" called the nurse. "How are you doing?"

Can't she go away? Lilly asked herself. *I'm losing control here. I feel like I've run a marathon.* Sweat beaded on her forehead. "I'm just about finished," Lilly called out, wiping her face with a towel.

She shuffled her way back to the bed, rubbing both hands across her lower back and nervously watching the nurse set up a machine next to the bed. "What are you doing?" Lilly asked, even more vigilant.

"I'm setting up the monitors. This is all normal. It helps us watch the vitals of you and your baby. It also helps monitor your contractions. Not to worry. You're right where you should be."

Easy for her to say. She's not the one in labor. She's not having flashes of her childhood. I don't trust her. I wish my doctor were here.

"How far apart are my contractions?" Lilly asked, feeling another wrapping around her like a python.

"It's different for every woman, but at the moment yours are five minutes apart." She pointed to the screen. "You can see the baby's heartbeat."

Lilly watched it. "Why did it drop lower? Is the baby okay?"

"That's a common drop once labor begins, especially if it's a boy. I think your husband may be right." Lilly cracked a smile.

"What will you name him?" asked the nurse.

"Owen Jon. They're names from Mick's family tree."

"Owen Jon Marzone. I like that! I can hear a teacher calling out his name," the nurse replied.

Lilly laughed. "I completely agree!"

Twelve hours later, Lilly found herself closer to the edge of losing it. She no longer had images. She was in her past and present at the same time—both leaving her with different kinds of pain and too much to cope with.

The hospital room was setting her off, the beeping of the machines, the pain, and she couldn't control any of it. Her body was on its own mission, with or without her. Too much like the memories with Frank.

"Where's my doctor?" Lilly asked angrily of the newly arrived morning nurse. "I haven't seen a doctor since I was admitted last night!"

"He should be in soon. We kept in contact with him throughout the night."

"Does he know I'm not moving along very fast?"

"I'll check exactly what the communication has been and be right back."

As soon as the nurse left, Lilly turned to Mick. "Go to the nurses' station and talk to someone," she pleaded. "I don't feel good about this. Something is wrong, Mick. I can sense it."

Mick returned with the doctor. "I called at midnight and the nurse said you were doing well and moving along normally. I called again at four and received the same message. It was just minutes ago that I was informed you weren't having an easy go," explained her doctor. "I want to suggest you have a spinal. I know you wanted this to be a natural birth, but you're very anxious and one part of you is battling the other."

Lilly knew exactly what the battle was. Her body was trying to protect itself, which it didn't have to do. "I don't know if I can keep going! If the spinal will help, then do it," she agreed. The powerful force of fear had taken over.

"Doctor, the baby is in fetal distress!" a nurse called out a few hours later in the delivery room.

"Lilly, we're going to use forceps and we have to make a few small cuts. The baby is coming shoulder first. All I need is one more strong push. Can you do that for me?"

Lilly gave him a thumbs-up. She held onto the words "one last push" as the room fell into an eerie silence filled with anticipation.

Then the strangest feeling came over her. All the signs of labor disappeared. There were no contractions, no anything. "I'm not having contractions." She grabbed the nurse's hand. "There is nothing to push with."

"You can do it, Lilly! At the count of three, bear down and push as hard and long as you can. One, two, three!" Everyone in the room was helping her push, cheering her on, and finally she heard the doctor say, "I've got him!"

Mick leaned over and whispered in Lilly's ear, "It's a boy."

Minutes later Lilly held her son. "So we meet, my precious Owen."

He turned toward her and she was sure he recognized her voice from all the stories she had read to him and conversations they shared. She looked him over. He had flawless ears, a sturdy neck, and powerful legs. "He's strong!" remarked Lilly.

"Sure is! I'll take him now." A nurse swept him away.

"Okay, Lilly, one more push for the afterbirth and your job is over," the doctor said in waiting. That push never came. Lilly started to hemorrhage.

"She's crashing; blood pressure is falling." Lilly reached out for Mick.

"Get him and the baby out! Code Blue!" shouted the doctor.

The nurse closest to Lilly stood over her and yelled, "Stay with us."

Lilly wanted to leave, to drift away to a place where she didn't feel anxiety or pain, but the team wouldn't allow her.

One nurse straddled her and began pushing on her abdomen, trying to do the job of the contractions that no longer existed. Another was poking at the veins in her arm, failing to find a good one, while yet another was giving her light slaps on her cheeks to keep her awake.

"She's crashing!"

"Get that pit juice in her now!" yelled the doctor. "Or I'll come over there and do it myself!"

"Her veins are collapsing."

Lilly drifted in and out of a blissful internal peace. She felt a temptation to go with the nothingness, to stop fighting her personal war for the last time, but she couldn't retreat without her baby and Mick. They needed her and she needed them.

The warrior within her returned, and soon afterward her blood pressure improved, and the internal bleeding stopped. She regained consciousness. "Where's Mick and our baby?"

"They're together; both are fine." Lilly closed her eyes in thankfulness.

"You gave us one heck of a scare!" said the doctor, holding her hand. "You'll need a blood transfusion, maybe two, and that will help you feel better. We're going to keep you here for the week, limited visits, and plenty of rest. You'll be fine." He patted her shoulder. "You're a strong one. You did a great job!"

"Thank you, Doctor."

However, by the end of the week, her nerves hadn't settled. In fact, Lilly couldn't get a grip on them. They fired constantly. Once more, she found herself uncertain and afraid of the moment she was living in.

"Why am I still feeling light-headed and dizzy?" she asked Mick.

"You need more rest. Your body went through trauma. It will take time to heal. The doctor said this is all normal and you're going to be fine," he said encouragingly.

"I still think something is wrong. I feel scared inside. My heart and my thoughts are racing. How am I going to take care of a baby feeling this way?"

"It'll be easier when we get home. You never liked hospitals and doctors' offices. Home will help with the nerves."

"I hope so, Mick, because I don't feel right."

She did feel better at home, but her heart continued to pound harder and faster than normal, and she tired easily. Holding Owen in her arms and rocking him was the only form of comfort in her day. And she knew that it wasn't normal. *I cannot spend the day like a baby; rocking, cuddling, eating, and sleeping, but it's all I feel I can do. There's a heaviness weighing on me. I'm not sure of who or what I am. I am definitely not the mother Owen needs. Poor little guy. He's getting love, but needs so much more. What on God's earth is wrong with me?*

A few weeks later, as Lilly began to change Owen's diaper, she stood back and asked herself, "Is it safe to touch his bare bottom? Does that make me a pervert? Am I becoming like Frank?" Her mind replayed the sight of herself experiencing her godfather's wandering hands. Frank had once again crept back into her head with a grasping, paralyzing fear.

That night, she knelt beside her bed and prayed, "I'm trying to be strong, but I'm afraid and I don't feel well. Get Frank out of my head. The memories make me feel helpless and doubtful as a mother. Before I had Owen I could bury Frank, but now he's always somewhere in my head. I can't live this way!"

She laid her head down on the mattress and wept.

1986 – SESSION THIRTEEN – ENDURING

"My anxiety shot through the roof when I was pregnant. I went back to being sickly and weak, like Millie."

"It was hard to cope with the unexpected problems of labor and pregnancy."

"The physical and emotional changes spun out of control and I didn't know how to stop them. My worst emotions resurfaced, such as fear, panic, and anxiety. I felt doomed. Either Owen or I wouldn't make it. That message was embedded in my brain."

"The normal changes in your body acted like a trigger."

"That's how I see it now, but not back then. Before pregnancy, life was great. I was confident in work and marriage. We had bought a home and were fixing it up. I had a yard with flower gardens. We had friends and fun weekends. I was living a dream and that changed by the second month of pregnancy, and it didn't go away. I still wake up hyper vigilant, looking for safety, escape routes, and visible dangers. My heart pounds and I sweat like I just ran a marathon. That kind of life is what brought me here." Lilly's face reddened.

"You are describing common traits of childhood trauma that can return after giving birth," Dr. Bricks explained.

"It seems unbelievable that the abuse led to this." Lilly said.

"Dr. Bricks sat quietly, watching the scared, unprotected child who dwelled within Lilly. "I sense you are troubled with a thought."

"I am. Why can't I rationalize and explain all that has happened to me? Even with therapy I can't digest it."

"It's a lot to digest, Lilly. You have symptoms of post-traumatic stress and general anxiety. This came about not because you were sickly or weak, but rather because of what your body had to go through to survive. It's like the aftermath of an earthquake. With that said, you are way past the cleaning up stage; you are moving into taking care of final details."

"You said 'symptoms.' What symptoms?" Lilly asked in a moment of denial.

"Behaviors such as the lasting negative belief system you hold about yourself and your inability to stay present."

"Both of those are improving! I catch myself quickly if I begin to zone out and it is easier to restate negatives to positives. But you said 'symptoms,' plural."

Dr. Bricks held back shortly, and then continued, "Feeling alienated and misunderstood; the hyper vigilance, and disassociation. Each one of those has an explanation that connects with your life in the past, as well as the present."

"My burdens," Lilly wore a concerned look. "People say it is all Frank's fault, but I am the one who has to learn how to live with what he did. He was the creator and I am the carrier. I have the label of being mentally ill because of him. When I hear the word ill, I see a gravely sick, bedridden, dying person. It's a negative and unkind image and it makes me feel *worse!* That's not me. I'm a fighter. I'm a soldier of special forces who has been in a mighty long battle."

"I said nothing about being ill. PTSD affects one's mental health, similar to the way a lack of insulin affects one's physical health."

Lilly released a loud sigh of frustration. "That's a stretch! No one sees mental illness like that. I was born into this world a happy, normal person, and that part of me still exists. But the traumas I endured paint such a different picture."

"You've been working hard at succeeding and lessening the effects of trauma as you return to the original you."

She considered the doctor's words. "I have improved from the day I walked in. I am definitely more grounded and going back to revisit the assaults, while thinking as a rational adult, has answered many questions that were holding me back."

"Accepting what happened to you as real and that it no longer needs separation from the present is critical in healing."

"I failed to stay present in labor." Lilly drew her knees up to her chest. "Frank nearly won that time. I almost did die. There were too many triggers firing at one time. I lost control."

"As you know, changes can have a greater effect on people with PTSD."

"They don't all go into panic and disassociate, do they?"

"No, not all, but your sense of fear during pregnancy heightened, which isn't unusual for people with a trauma disorder. How would you help someone going through the same feelings during a pregnancy?"

"I would tell them to be open and honest with their doctor and if the doctor doesn't address it, find a different one. If I would have only done that," Lilly spoke firmly.

Dr. Bricks sat back, allowing her time to process.

"And because I told no one about my problems and fears, I blew them out of proportion, which I often do." She was visibly angry with herself.

"That's a trained response that needs more retraining. The body never forgets—there is truth in that statement. But the reaction *can* be altered."

Lilly nodded in agreement. "Now I tell doctors and when they look at me as if I am over-reacting to some trivial matter in my life, I leave. Being able to recognize my problems is progress."

Dr. Bricks looked at Lilly with pride. "You have come far and I think it's time for us to discuss returning to work."

Lilly looked surprised. "Really?"

"I believe you have gathered enough tools to help you reconnect with a healthy balance between home and work. Besides, it is a great opportunity to practice what you have learned and what still needs to be addressed."

"I'm scared to go back, worried that I'll fail at my job and let the kids down."

"Lilly, you are ready to use your new tools to make you an even better teacher and I am here if you need me. I am not abandoning you. That's important to remember."

"So are you saying you will see me once a month?" Her heart raced with excitement to be on her own shadowed with the fear of messing up.

"How about bi-weekly appointments and *then* we will move to monthly when you're ready. How does that sound?"

"That sounds good." She dropped her shoulders and took a deep breath. "I can handle every other week. It's going to be a challenge, but I'll never know what else is pulling me down until I get back out there in the real world. Moving forward is the only path I know."

Dr. Bricks smiled warmly. "I believe you are going to have many more good days than bad. And remember that I'm here for you, as well as your parents, Owen, and Mick. You aren't alone. You have a network of people who care and know your concerns."

"There's a comfort in knowing that. The kind I felt with Ann and Trudy." Lilly sat quietly. "I still can't help but wonder how different I would be today if Mom and Dad chose different godparents."

"Maybe you became a better person than you would have been."

"That's an interesting way to look at it! Maybe I would have been a brat and not cared much about others. I could have grown up selfish and a narcissist. How awful would that be?"

"You are definitely not that person," Dr. Bricks chuckled. "Tell me Lilly, what years did you feel the most like your real self?"

"That's easy, the mid-teens and then the mid-twenties."

"Are you really that different today from those years?"

"I think I am because I worry more and don't feel the freedom I had back then. Those were years when I experienced new happy feelings, however, I have a lot of life ahead of me and who knows what other emotions are out there. So I guess I have to wait and see. Like you said, 'I'm under construction!'"

NO MORE HIDING

"How do you feel about your parents' decision to move close to us?" asked Mick as he began eating his dinner.

"I'm excited! It'll be great for Owen. And I actually want to see more of Mom and Dad."

"Does their move mean Frank and Millie may come back into our lives?"

Lilly set her fork down. "I didn't think about that. I know Mom still talks to Millie and sometimes they get together in Florida. Mick, they can't step foot in our house. Not ever."

"Have you talked with Dr. Bricks about this?"

"We've talked about how I sheltered Owen from my side of the family *because* of Frank and Millie." She inhaled deeply and let the cool air slowly escape.

"How about we finish this conversation later and enjoy our dinner." Lilly picked up her fork and returned to her meal. Mick followed suit.

It had been a long time since she allowed any talk of her godparents and when she heard Frank's name the muscles in her body tensed and a streak of fear ran through her.

As she washed the dinner dishes, her thinking went into overdrive. *Avoiding family events because Frank still frightens me and he can't be trusted means that I'm still* their *prisoner. I think I'm doing what's best for Owen and me, but am I? Stop thinking negatively! Mom and Dad are moving to be closer. Stay focused on that. It's a happy thought. I want to be near them. I want Owen to know his grandparents.*

In the following weeks, she visited her parents' new home, making sure it would be move-in ready for them. She baked and froze a few meals, as Mick kept up the lawn and shrubbery. Finally, the big day arrived.

"Mom, I'm so happy you're here and in walking distance from us!" She gave a big welcoming hug. "And look at Owen and Grandpa. Aren't they two old souls?" They both watched from the kitchen window as Vincent showed his grandson a worm.

"He wants to take him fishing at the children's pond," informed Gwen.

"Owen will love that!"

Gwen smiled. "Can you stay for a cup of tea and fresh bread? It just came out of the oven."

"How can I say no to that? I have about twenty minutes, and then I have to get back to work."

"How about going shopping this Saturday and having lunch together?" suggested Gwen.

Lilly didn't think for long, "That would be fun! What time?"

"Let's leave here at ten. Grandpa will watch Owen so Mick doesn't have to change his work schedule."

Lilly buttered her warm bread. "Mick will appreciate that, as will I!"

"Just wondering Lilly, why haven't you returned the RSVP card from your cousin's wedding? It's coming up soon," inquired Gwen. "We've been so busy. Let me talk to Mick. I promise I'll send in the response this week."

Lilly avoided eye contact, as she thought about the lie she just made. *Ever since I received that invitation flashbacks have returned. That's why I haven't responded. But I cannot avoid family forever, nor do I want to.*

Lilly found herself back to feeling as if she were nineteen, making up excuses while being pulled between what she wanted to do and what she should do.

✳

Later, Mick tried to soothe her worries. "Lilly, you're not avoiding your family if you don't go. You're keeping yourself and Owen safe. That's a big difference."

"But I made up excuses for years before I met you. Then Frank and my past seemed to disappear until we had Owen. Now I protect him like a mama bear. Hardly anyone has seen our beautiful son. If I can't enjoy my family, then Frank still owns me."

"A few years after our wedding we saw Millie and Frank for two hours and you ran to the bathroom to vomit. I took you home. Remember?"

"Yes." Lilly sighed, remembering the sight of Frank and the smell of his cigar, which made her violently ill for days. "I did get sick and haven't seen them since. Yet, why shouldn't Owen have fun with cousins his age and enjoy big family celebrations with my side? Mom and Dad aren't happy about it, and neither am I."

"I think we're on the right path by staying away," Mick replied sternly.

"But it's not right to keep Owen from part of his traditions. I have two perverted relatives, and all the others are wonderful people who I want him to know. We keep *your* traditions and that makes me miss mine even more."

"We aren't exposed to *them* when we're with my family."

"There has to be a way, just this one time. I don't want to miss the wedding. Their family has been good to us and Mom and Dad." They moved around the kitchen, as if in a familiar dance, as they prepared dinner.

"You've been beating yourself up about this, overthinking again."

"Yes, guilty as charged. It is bothering me. I feel like Frank still has control over me and I don't want that. I want to be able to face him and still keep myself and my family safe."

"You believe you can do that."

"Safety is standing up to him. Not running away or staying in hiding."

"Then tell your folks the truth!"

Lilly filled a kettle with water and placed it on the stove to boil. "I am going to tell them, right after the wedding."

"No, you're not. After the wedding there will be another excuse or something else will take priority."

"Fine, I'll send a gift and leave it at that!" She slammed the large spoon down.

"That's not exactly how I feel. I think we should go to the wedding, but not with Owen. You could leave him home with me and go with your sister," suggested Mick.

"I'm not going without you."

"We'll get a sitter for the shower and the wedding."

"That defeats the whole idea of family tradition for Owen. Why can't we make a plan to watch him in shifts at the shower so that he's never out of sight? And he still gets to enjoy the party and his cousins."

"But you've said that it only takes seconds for Frank to grab his victim."

"He likes to groom them first by watching and stalking. He hasn't had that chance with Owen. Owen doesn't even know who his great Uncle Frank is. Thank God!"

"Lilly, you don't really know who Frank is anymore either. It's been years."

Lilly sat quietly, remembering to breathe. It upset her to hear Mick's logic, but he was right. *Who is Frank now? What has he become?* She wondered and then rebounded.

"No, you're partially right and partially wrong. This is Frank we're talking about, and his lovely coconspirator, Millie. They may have changed, but Frank's patterns haven't. He always keenly observes and stalks first. Then he jingles the coins and keys in his pocket and lures little kids in with what he sees them liking: candy, money, a ride in a big fancy car. That will never change. That's who he is. And Millie, she's only concerned about saving her own soul and always will be."

Mick's concern was to see Lilly happy. "You're determined to go to the shower."

"You're mad! I can see it and hear it!"

"Of course I am. This isn't your normal way of thinking. You're usually overly cautious."

"I am thinking clearly. I just don't want Frank controlling what I can and cannot do. Together we can outsmart him." She paused, and then continued, "I'll stay with Owen upstairs, and you watch Frank downstairs. If he leaves the room, you follow him, and vice versa. If I need a break, Grandma will be there to help."

"She watched *you* when you were his age."

Lilly flushed beet-red. "That may be true, but Mom's different now. Her grandchildren are everything to her and she doesn't have other responsibilities. Her only job would be to watch Owen, *if* I needed her to."

"Guess it's set. Let Gwen know we're going to the shower with Owen, but *not* the wedding. We will get a babysitter for that. Agree?"

"Yes, thank you, Mick. It's going to work. Just wait and see."

"Lilly, we aren't going to do this whenever, or wherever there's a family event that includes your godparents."

"I know, Mick, one step at a time, with Owen being our number-one focus."

"Lilly, it's not only about Owen. It's about you, too. I worry about you seeing them and what it may do to you."

"I know it's been taking me a lifetime to tell, but I can feel it happening, more than ever before. And you know why?" Mick's heart ached as it was, and now there was more. "What is it?" he asked reluctantly.

"I don't know how to say this, but I'm going to try." She took in a deep breath and dropped her shoulders. "If I'm so afraid that Frank will go after Owen, what's stopping him from going after any of the other little children? Me being safe from him doesn't mean everyone else in the world is safe too! I have been so stupid not to realize this years ago! No child is safe near him. His trips to Florida? How many little girls did he abuse there? Then there's his 'business' in Chicago, and his travels North. What about my cousins and our neighbors? Have they been terrorized and abused too? I have to protect the children. We have nieces and nephews." Lilly fought back tears, walking over to Mick and burying her face in his shoulder.

He held her tight. "The sooner you come forward, the better for us and everyone else."

"Will you be there for me?"

"Always," he pulled her in closer.

EASY PICKINGS

The day of the shower, Lilly dressed Owen in a bright-red sweater so she could easily pick him out in a crowded room. "Aren't you excited to play with your cousins?"

"Is Grandpa going?" asked Owen.

"Yes, Grandpa and Grandma will be there and you cannot go anywhere without one of us. If you need to go to the bathroom, come and get me. Don't go with anyone else."

"Why?"

"Because only Mommy and Daddy, or Grandpa and Grandma, know how to care for you."

He's so curious and spontaneous, thought Lilly, and *he's only three. Listening to us hasn't been one of his strengths lately. It would be so easy for Frank to feed off a young mind and lead him right into his hands, like he did with me.* Lilly shivered thinking of how scared she must have been.

✺

"Mommy!" Owen pulled at her arm. "Can I go play over there?" He pointed to several children digging through a few boxes of toys. "Sure you can, share and play nice." She watched him join in and turned to Mick.

"Look at him. He's so excited!"

"I'm going to go join the guys. Is that okay?" Mick asked.

"Sure, say hi to Dad for me. Remember, both eyes watching at all times," she firmly reminded him.

As soon as he was out of sight Lilly scanned the room—exits, windows, steps, and hallways—and then she settled in at the kitchen table, next to her mother and overlooking the living room.

An hour passed, leaving Lilly thinking that soon they would eat and then she could bow out. Everything was going better than planned. Then Millie joined them, blocking Lilly's view.

"Hi dear, it's been so long since we've seen you and your family. I was watching Owen. He's special; such a good boy and cute as a bug." Millie leaned down and gave Lilly a peck on the cheek.

Gwen agreed, "He's smart too. You should hear him talk. He can argue and he's only three."

Thank God, now Mom will get Millie talking and that will free me up to keep watch.

"Lilly, could you please get your godmother a glass of water! I'm parched." Lilly looked at Owen, who was deep in play with another boy his age.

She walked a few steps to the sink. When she turned around Owen was gone. He wasn't playing with the blocks. He wasn't in the kitchen. He wasn't in the crowd of children playing with wrapping paper and bows.

Lilly's heart moved up to her throat. That's how clever they were. One little change in pattern was all Frank needed to make his move. He knew she couldn't remain in the kitchen chair forever and so he sent Millie to help move the plot forward.

Setting the glass on the cupboard, trying not to look like she'd witnessed a murder, Lilly frantically swept the upstairs of the house in search of Owen. "The only place I haven't looked is downstairs. I will kill Mick if he's not watching Frank!" she told herself as she ran down the set of steps. At the bottom, she turned the corner and saw Owen's red sweater in a narrow, dimly lit hall. He was laughing and running away from Frank, who was right behind in a game of chase.

"Owen!" she shouted in panic. "Stop right this minute!"

Owen turned and began to run toward her, but Frank swept him up in his arms.

"Put him down!" Lilly gritted her teeth and carefully began to plot out her every move. His hands had touched her son. All promises changed. No one could be more in the present than she was.

Frank sneered, his cigar hanging out of the corner of his mouth. "What will you do? What can you do? Try telling your mommy again?" He insulted her as if she were that little girl of long ago.

"If you don't put Owen down now, I will scream bloody murder so everyone hears and comes running. You'll be roadkill. So. Put. Him. Down!" she ordered in a slow, hateful voice as they glared eye to eye. For once, she felt no fear of his stare. Her thoughts were only for Owen's safety.

His thoughts were on Lilly, enticed by her feistiness. Wanting to play more into the game, he worked at weakening her motherly defense. "He's a cute little fella and so happy—reminds me a lot of you at this age." He tickled Owen's belly and Owen giggled.

The camera in Lilly's mind flashed. *That was one of his first touches, tickling.* For a brief second she looked down and out of the present.

"Memories, Lilly?" Frank quizzed her. "How about we make a deal? I'll put him down, never touch him again, and you come back to me." His yellow eyes bugged out with elation as he anxiously chewed the cigar.

Lilly, she awakened herself. *Stay in the present. Keep little Lilly behind you. Do not let her come forward.*

With her eyes on Frank's she inched her way closer.

"Never! You will *never* have him, and you will *never* have me. You made that promise about Eva, and remember how that turned out?" She was now close enough to smell his tobacco and whiskey-laced breath. "You are a liar." She stopped, a couple feet away.

He isn't going to win this war, she told herself and began to plot words to infuriate him. "Mick knows everything. I told him and everyone here will soon know too. Your days of feeding off our family are over; so is my promise to stay quiet."

The tense exchange frightened Owen and he reached out to his mother, trying to wiggle free. "Mommy, I don't want to play his game anymore."

"Honey, you don't ever have to play his game. Mommy's right here." She moved to take hold of her son.

Frank stepped back. "You told Mick!" he growled at her. "You crazy fool. I can snatch Owen anytime. I'm always watching, no matter where you are; you're never far. Neither is your son. He walks home after school with a neighbor friend, a little girl, and he plays in the yard on Saturday mornings. I've driven past your house many times without you noticing. It would be easy to snatch him, because you can't watch him every second."

Lilly's bravery faltered as she thought of an unprotected Owen. *I'm letting Frank get into my head. He's feeding me fear, and he's making sure I see that his hands are on Owen. I can't cave in. This is beyond his threats. This is about Owen's life.* She moved her anger into her feet, stood firm, and began to creep into *his* head for a change.

"When I tell the police everything you did to me you won't be wearing expensive suits ever again. More like an orange jumpsuit. And I've heard that child molesters are prisoners' favorite mates," Lilly snickered. "If you know what's good for you, put Owen down."

From the corner of her eye, she saw Mick. "Mick, he has Owen."

Mick ran toward Frank, ready to kill. Lilly stepped between them. "No, Mick, that's what he wants. He wants us to lose control." She stood strong. "For the last time," she warned. "Put Owen down *now.*"

Owen began to whimper.

Frank's eyes flickered back and forth, not knowing where to focus, and at that second Lilly lunged, grabbing Owen out of his hold and sending Frank backward into the wall.

With shaking hands and weak knees, she put Owen into Mick's arms.

"We were playing chase, Daddy. He was trying to catch me," Owen whined.

"Owen, you promised to stay close to Mommy and Grandma," scolded Mick.

Owen tugged at his pocket. "But look, Daddy!" He pulled out a silver dollar. "That man gave me this to play with him. He has more in his pocket. He made them jingle."

"You fat bastard!" Lilly plowed forward, smashing him harder into the wall, her hands around his neck. Mick put Owen down and rushed to protect Lilly, pulling her off Frank.

"You're crazy! A real mental case!" Frank spat a wad of cigar juice at her feet.

Vincent and several other men rushed out of the rec room and down the hall, toward the commotion. Vincent saw Mick holding a hysterical Lilly, while Owen stood terrorized.

Vincent swept his grandson up into his arms and looked at Lilly with bewilderment, "What's happening here?" he asked, glaring at Frank.

Frank spoke first. "Your daughter is nuts. I was playing a little game of hide-and-seek with Owen, that's all. And she attacked me." His voice was as calm as still water. He smoothed out his suit and moved his cigar to the other side of his mouth. "Go ahead and ask her yourself," he dared Vincent.

"Lilly, is that true?"

They were all watching her, not Frank, but her. In her mind, they already declared her a mental case.

"No, that's not the truth." She turned to Owen. "Give Mommy that coin. It doesn't belong to you, and we have to give it back."

She didn't want him to have anything of Frank's: no trigger, no money, and definitely no memory.

Reluctantly, Owen handed it over. She threw it at Frank's feet. "There's your damn money. Don't pull another trick like that again."

Frank laughed. "What did I tell you, guys? I played a little game of magic with Owen and she flipped out. What's the harm?" He held his arms out, acting totally confused and innocent.

"Grandpa, Mommy is mad," Owen said, looking at his grandfather's face.

Lilly pulled herself together. "Mommy is mad because that man tricked you to go downstairs with him."

"Jesus Christ," Frank interjected, "we were playing. Vincent, she's always had a hot temper, don't you agree? That big imagination of hers has always been a problem!"

"No, Frank, she's right. It was wrong to take Owen without her permission."

Mick stood shocked, numb, and unsure of what had happened; his only thought was to get the hell out of there.

With Owen safely buckled into his car seat, the reality of the afternoon hit Lilly and she began to shake. It was now safe to feel, and she was scared, a terrified little girl holding her breath behind the furnace, listening to the coins rattling and Frank's footsteps nearing. Seeing Owen tricked and lured into Frank's dark world was the force she needed to take the step she feared the most.

WAVES OF DESTRUCTION

"Are you ready to finish explaining yesterday to your parents?" Mick inquired the next morning.

Lilly put her pillow over her head. All night she had replayed the encounter with Frank, analyzing what she should have done differently. She muffled back to Mick, "To take it any further would have been wrong, with guests and family looking on. But I realized that the truth is going to turn our family upside down."

Mick dressed hastily.

"Where are you going? It's Sunday!" Lilly asked, dragging herself out of bed.

"To the shop. I have some work to finish," he said as he brushed his teeth. "It's always a matter of timing for you when it comes to Frank's secret. Or what everyone is going to think of you if you tell."

"It's not the timing," Lilly argued. "There is so much in my head. I don't know why I freeze solid every time I try. Maybe I still see this as my fault."

Mick looked up at her. "That's ridiculous. You've been through this in therapy many times." Frustrated and puzzled, he walked to the kitchen with Lilly following close behind.

"I don't expect you to understand. No one does unless it happens to them," she said sharply. He snatched his keys off the counter and left.

Lilly shuffled her way to the coffeepot and poured herself a cup, then sat by the kitchen table, looking out over their yard. "I wish my river and willow were there. Mick tries to understand me, but he can't possibly live in my head, not even for a day. He has no connection to a life of panic. But he's right. The reality of Frank going after Owen changes everything. I can't be Millie and look the other way. I can't be Mom and worry about gossip. What really scares me is the fear of how I'll handle the truth. I think it will kill me. I'll fall apart. I won't be able to be Owen's mother or Mick's wife, and what if Mom and Dad don't believe me? I'll lose everyone again. I will be exiled, not Frank. Is that irrational thinking or a reality?"

※

The same day, Vincent and Gwen were having their own conversation at the breakfast table.

"It was a lovely shower yesterday, until Lilly created a scene with little Owen right there!" Gwen buttered her toast.

"I saw her in the downstairs hallway. She was upset and so was Owen. Mick looked in shock. I think she's keeping secrets and I intend to find out what Frank was really up to," replied Vincent.

"There you are, falling back a few decades, joining my mother and her suspicion of Frank. Really Vincent; Lilly always has it out for Millie and Frank."

"Don't you ever wonder why she feels that way? She loves everybody else."

"It's because they're her godparents and Millie had a lot to say about her growing up. Lilly didn't like that. That's what I think."

Vincent shook his head. "I'm telling you, Gwen, there's something else going on with Lilly and I think she wants to tell us, but she's holding back, and so is Mick."

"If it's important, they'll let us know. Lilly can't keep a secret if her life depended on it, and we're not going to cause trouble in the family now. Whatever it is, it can wait until after the wedding, which is only three weeks away."

※

"We go, we eat, and we come home," Mick directed his comment at Lilly.

"That's what we all agreed to," Lilly said. "Right, Eva?" she asked her sister in the back seat of the car.

"I'm flying back early tomorrow, so I don't want to stay out too late. Kevin is working on a case and our neighbor is watching the children until I get home. I need to be rested," replied Eva.

"I'm so happy you're here. Nothing like sister time, even if it's only for a couple of days." Lilly meant every word. She had told Eva to leave the kids at home, without giving an explanation. Between her and Eva, words didn't always have to be said.

It was impossible to miss Frank as they walked into the reception hall. He sat in the center of the bar, facing the dance floor and main doors. He had a view of every woman, man, and child who walked in.

"Mick, there he is, sicko himself, raping every woman that comes through those doors with his eyes," Lilly whispered into his ear. "Don't look; do not give him pleasure. Hang on to my arm and avoid him completely."

Lilly scoped out the reception hall. To walk into a room and enjoy why she was there was something Lilly didn't know, even now in her thirties. For Lilly, fear entered first, then escape, followed by how she could protect herself.

She saw her parents at a table, talking to other relatives. Millie was standing by the wedding cake, looking over the guest book. She and Eva agreed that it was safe to look for the table with their name cards.

"Found them!" Eva called out.

Lilly joined her. "Look - Mick, Mom, Dad, Eva, and us! We are all sitting together with Uncle Dave and Aunt Dee. The dinner should be fun! And then we can go home."

"Lilly, Frank has been watching us since we got here. It's creepy," Eva whispered into Lilly's ear. "I've noticed," replied Lilly. "But as long as we stay together, there is not a damn thing he can do."

Mick joined them. "Look over there." Lilly pointed to a table tucked away from the rest of the room. "That's our cousin, Dawn, who married Anthony's friend when I was in college. Do you want to stop and say hello?"

"Don't they look worried? Maybe now isn't the time," said Mick.

"You're right, maybe after dinner." Lilly glanced back at them. She couldn't explain what she saw in their emotions, but it was strange, as if they were in mourning.

The three of them walked around the reception hall, talking to family and cousins they hadn't seen, until the wedding party arrived. At that time the guests were directed to their tables.

"That's weird," said Eva. "My name card is still here, along with Mom's and Dad's, but Mick and Lilly, your cards are gone. Someone else is sitting here. Never heard of them. Must be the groom's family." Eva looked at Lilly with suspicion.

"I thought we were sitting together," a surprised Gwen added as she joined them.

"We were, Mom!" Lilly answered. "Our name cards were here just a half hour ago."

Millie paraded her tall, lanky body across the dining room and stopped next to Mick, placing one hand on his shoulder. "*I thought* you and Lilly would be confused! I changed the seating so Uncle Frank and I could visit with the two of you during dinner. We have to apologize for Frank's ridiculous idea to play with Owen at the shower. We had no idea that would be so upsetting to you, Lilly, and I want to get to know this husband of yours better," she cooed as if she were twenty-one again.

Lilly assessed the scene. It was nauseating. *They are trying to rekindle their power first by going after Owen and now Mick. That won't happen. I can play their game too.*

She composed herself. "No worries," Lilly confidently replied. She gave her sister a nod to keep an eye on her and Eva nodded back. Then she and Mick followed Millie and sat down across from them.

Lilly stared at Frank's repulsiveness. *How can anyone eat with him? The mere thought of food gags me. Look how he keeps moving his tongue around his mouth and licking his lips, like a lizard. Moving the name cards was part of the stalking, his foreplay. Now he's working my nerves and drawing Mick's attention toward Millie, while he supplies us with one drink after another. I'm not falling for it.*

Repeating Dr. Bricks' words of advice, she said to herself. *This is now, that was then. I am confident and in control. I will not fall prey.* Her feet ached for escape, but she planted them firmly on the floor and tried her hardest to focus on the present.

She looked over the table settings. The servers had filled the water glasses before the guests were seated. *Millie or Frank could have slipped a drug in them, especially Mick's glass. He would be unable to take her and Eva home, or be too stoned to continue watching over them.*

Lilly dropped her napkin on the floor, and in bending to pick it up she *accidently* knocked over Mick's glass of water.

"Oh, I am so clumsy. I'm sorry, Mick. Did I get you wet?" She wiped up the mess and in doing so, purposely knocked her own glass over. "Must be my nerves," she mumbled as she flashed a bold look directly at Frank.

"What are *you* doing?" Mick snarled, irritated and confused.

They're already in his head, observed Lilly.

"She's been clumsy, since she was a little girl," Frank responded, looking back at Lilly.

Millie knew her job too. Feeling the tension, she upped her game. "You're a lucky man, Mick, to have a wife like Lilly," Millie gloated as she looked into his eyes, trying to find that feeling she had lost decades ago.

Lilly wanted to puke, watching Mick fall for their bullshit.

"It's time to freshen up these drinks. I'll be right back." Frank stood tall, appearing dominant and in control as he walked up to the bar and returned with a small tray of drinks and water glasses. "Here we are, one for you, Lilly, and another for Mick." He set the drinks down near their plates.

Lilly pushed hers off to the side, making sure he saw her refusal.

"Why, Lilly, you must at least try the drink. We discovered a special party mix in the city. You'll want another, I guarantee it!" boasted Millie. "It's like drinking dessert."

Lilly faked a smile. "I don't drink anymore. Here"—she slid it toward her aunt—"since you're so fond of it, you may as well have two. It shouldn't go to waste."

As usual, Millie drummed up a comeback in a matter of minutes. "Dear, would you walk me to the bathroom? You know my heart is weak and I often get dizzy spells. I would be grateful for you to hold my arm to steady me."

This is unbelievable! Do they really think I'm as vulnerable as I was at seventeen? The "I am so weak and helpless" routine and I had to carry her suitcases upstairs! The memory spun in Lilly's head. *I don't have to stress about being nice to them because of my parents, not anymore. I am an adult.*

She cattily replied, "You know, Aunt Millie, I don't have to visit the girl's room right now, but I can go and ask Mom to help you. She's right over there." Lilly pointed. "And I know she'd be glad to help." Millie changed the topic, glancing back at Mick.

"I can see that Lilly has found her voice being a mother and a wife," she stated.

Mick looked at Lilly, confused by the entire conversation, as Millie continued, "She's become quite determined and clever."

"I had no other choice from your teachings as my godparents," Lilly threw back at her and leaned over to Mick, giving him a kiss on his cheek and whispering in his ear, "Don't drink anything but coffee…drugs."

When the food arrived, conversation lessened, and Lilly was able to ask for two glasses of fresh water and two cups of coffee.

Millie continued to control the conversation with Mick about art, which they knew nothing of or had any interest in, but it provided time for Frank to work on Lilly's nerves with his constant stare.

Flashbacks fired, igniting one of her panic attacks.

Lilly stood up, excused herself from the table, and began to walk toward the bathroom. The floor felt like a wet sponge beneath her feet. Her nerves were overworked and overloaded. Getting to her destination felt like walking through a minefield, and when she got to the bathroom she reached out for the stability of the sink.

Eva walked in behind her. "You look like death, Lilly. What's going on?" She put her arm around her sister, acknowledging the fear they both had learned in their youth.

"I'm walking through the minefield and not around it."

"I don't get what you're saying," replied Eva.

"It's a saying from college, too complicated to explain now. Frank won't take his eyes off of me. He's stalking me visually, while Millie has Mick in her spell. Are you ready to go home? Because I have to."

"Yes. We both need to get out of here," Eva agreed. "I didn't bring the children because I was stressed that he would go after them. But I didn't think of you or me. I believed we're too old. But that's obviously not the truth."

"He'll never quit. As long as he can breathe and walk, we can't trust him. As soon as we believe *I'm* the target, he could turn and make it you. Neither of us is safe." Lilly spoke to Eva's reflection in the mirror. "When I get back to the table, I'll tell Mick that the babysitter called and needs help with Owen. Let's get out of here.

I'll make it quick at the table, not giving them time to rethink their plan. And then I'll come and get you."

Lilly intensely studied her reflection in the mirror, seeing her soldier behind her. *We're going home. Home is safe. I am not his victim. I am* stronger.

She stood tall. Together the sisters returned to their dinner. The news left Millie objecting and Frank nervous.

Lilly kept her head clear. "Can't predict a three-year-old's behavior, but we're needed at home. So, guess it's good-night." She pulled Mick up by the arm and led him over to her parents' table to pick up Eva.

"Why are you leaving so soon? That seems to be a habit of yours lately!" Gwen complained.

"It's Owen; he won't go to bed and he's being bossy with the sitter."

She noticed Vincent's quiet observation. "Eva, why don't you stay and ride back with us?" suggested Gwen.

"Thanks, Mom, but I would like to get a good night's sleep before going home."

It was uncomfortably quiet in the car. They each sat in their own world. One remembered trying to drink the memory of her cousin's wedding reception away with a bottle of vodka. One remembered being seven, sitting on the kitchen floor with her big sister who held a large knife, their backs against the door that led to the basement. They hoped that together they would be strong enough to keep Frank out if he came to attack them.

Then there was Mick. For the first time, he felt drawn into Frank and Millie's world without knowing how. It happened so quickly. It gave him a deeper understanding of Lilly's fearful world. If he had any doubts before this night, they were gone. Feeling the truth, not just hearing it, made him queasy. In a way, he felt victimized too, and he understood now how Vincent and Gwen had fallen prey. They easily pulled adults into their ring, especially with the use of alcohol. A child stood no chance.

"Will you take the sitter home?" Lilly asked. "Eva and I would like to have some time together."

"Sure. Give Owen a kiss good-night for me."

"I will. Love you, Mick. Drive safely." Lilly hugged him tight.

Eva and Lilly put Owen to bed and then sat down in the living room. They spoke of secrets, never shared.

THE RAW REALITY

In the days that followed, Lilly buried herself in cleaning everything, from the walls to the closets to the driveway and as she worked she planned how she was going to tell her parents about Frank and Millie.

The ring of the phone stopped her whirlwind thinking. "Hello," she answered.

"Hi, Lilly, it's Dawn. I saw you at the wedding and you looked upset."

"I thought *you* looked upset. That's strange how we felt the same thing about each other."

There was a pause and then Dawn continued, "I've been going to therapy, and my therapist wanted me to ask you a question." Lilly was surprised. Therapy in their family wasn't common.

"What is it?"

"Has Frank ever touched you in the wrong way?"

Time stopped.

Such a simple question, one she had waited to hear since childhood. One she could finally answer to explain her life. With the telephone pressed against her ear and her back to the wall, she froze.

What do I say, yes or no?

Both possibilities crossed her mind, and slowly, almost in a whisper, she answered, "Yes." She slid down to the floor, back three decades in time.

Dawn continued to talk, but Lilly was gone. Her two worlds collided. The phone fell from her hand, and its coiled cord dangled back and forth against the kitchen wall. No amount of time could have prepared her for this horrifying shock. Her memories were real. She wasn't alone. She never was crazy, or silly, or making up stories with her big imagination. Frank was real; her life was real; the pain she felt, and the stories she told to Dr. Bricks, all of it was real.

The promise of silence was broken. For thirty years she had feared this day.

Raw, fragile, and afraid, her body tensed, waiting for the deathblow that was sure to follow. Every threat Frank put into her head flooded her emotions.

She used her strongest and oldest survival skill: to float away.

❋

Gwen arrived with Owen. "Lilly, we're here! Where are you?" She walked into the kitchen and saw Lilly plastered against the kitchen wall, eyes glazed.

In a panic, Gwen reached for the dangling phone.

"Mommy!" Owen ran toward Lilly with arms wide open. Gwen swept him up. "Owen, your mommy isn't feeling well right now."

"Does she have a stomachache?"

"Yes, she has a stomachache. Why don't you get your building blocks out? Grandpa will come over and play with you." Owen took off to his bedroom.

Gwen put the phone back on the cradle for a few seconds and then dialed.

"Vincent, come over right away. Something happened to Lilly." Her voice shook with worry. She hung up and, softly and slowly, touched Lilly's face. "Lilly, honey, do you hear me? It's Mom."

Lilly's eyes refocused. "Mom?"

"Yes, Lilly, I'm right here."

"Where's Owen?" she whispered. The thought of her son helped her to hold on to the little bit of the present that she could feel. "He's fine; he's in his bedroom playing with his blocks. What happened?"

"I need some water," Lilly murmured. She rolled onto all fours and then carefully stood, feeling light-headed. "Here, let me help you to a chair, and I'll get the water. I think we should call an ambulance."

"No!" bolted out of Lilly's mouth.

Gwen jumped. She didn't want to upset an already upset daughter. "We'll wait until Dad comes. Let's stay calm." She noticed that Lilly's color and breathing were improving.

"I was so cold. That's the last thing I remember," a dazed Lilly commented. "It sounds like you went into shock. Do you recall what started this?"

"I received a phone call."

"From who? What did they say?"

"Dawn called."

"What did she say to upset you?"

"I'm still cold; maybe something hot would be better," mumbled Lilly.

"I'll make us some tea," suggested Gwen. "But I think we should take you to the hospital and have you checked out."

"That is *not* going to happen," Lilly replied. "I know why I passed out. Going to a doctor would only make it worse. Trust me!" Her boxes of secrets were opening relentlessly and what she needed the most was Mick.

"Can you call Mick and tell him to come home?" she asked. "Sure honey."

When Mick arrived, she clung onto him like a child to a mother.

"Lilly, tell us what happened," Mick asked, with his arm around her shoulders.

She looked into his face. "You already know."

"*I* have no idea what you two are talking about." Gwen paced nervously.

"Let them talk," Vincent told Gwen. "And sit down." Around the kitchen table, Lilly explained the unexplainable.

"I thought I was protecting the family. I believed that if I told the truth, something terrible would happen to us. Therefore, I kept quiet, as I was told to do. But then Dawn called today."

"Lilly, I don't understand what you're trying to say." A confused Gwen coaxed her further. "Who or what were you protecting us from?" Lilly looked at Mick, who nodded for her to continue.

"From Frank—and Millie."

"Oh, for heaven's sake, you have never liked them. Now what's the reason?" Gwen asked flippantly.

"Frank abused me sexually, and Millie helped him do that by getting me away from you and Dad's protection. They're not who you think they are. They lie. They are dirty, corrupt people."

Gwen sat back in a stupor. "How can you talk like that about your godparents? For heaven's sake, you've never given them a chance! What did Dawn put into your head?"

Lilly expected this reaction; after all, she was dropping a scandalous bomb about a beloved sister. "Dawn's seeing a doctor."

"What kind of doctor? Her mother never mentioned anything about a doctor at the wedding." Gwen's lips tightened.

"Dawn is seeing a psychologist and her mother was probably too embarrassed to tell you that it was because of Frank. He's a pedophile, a psychopath, and Millie is his right hand. It's the truth, Mom."

A painful silence filled the room.

"I don't believe you," Gwen finally said. "Why would you keep something like that a secret?"

"I felt trapped with nowhere to go, like Old Yeller in the movie, and he ended up being killed."

"Oh my God, that explains the nightmares! Lilly…" Vincent buried his face in his hands. Seeing him weaken tore at her heart and she felt a crushing blow of sadness deep within. This was the reality of telling. It was terrifying. It was awful.

"That's ridiculous, isn't it, Vincent?" Gwen asked, looking to her husband for agreement.

He ignored her and directed his attention toward Lilly. "How long has this been going on?" he asked.

Lilly felt shame heating her face. "Since I was three or four."

Vincent couldn't look at his daughter; he kept his head bowed. "Oh dear Lord, what have we done?"

"It's an accusation." Gwen was angry now. "You know what you're saying could put Frank in jail. Someone did that to him years ago. They said he touched their little girl. They arrested him and then released him after he passed a lie detector test. Millie was devastated with the neighborhood rumors. That's why they moved. Millie doesn't need to go through this again, especially from family!"

Vincent's eyes dug into Gwen's. "Why didn't you tell me this?"

"Millie asked me to keep it a secret; it wasn't anybody's business, and Frank was innocent."

Lilly asked, "Was the little girl around three or four? That's how old Owen is now and how old I was."

Vincent's fist hit the table. Everyone jumped. "I knew it! I've never trusted that man and should have listened to my gut! I was suspicious of Frank, and your mother was, too." Vincent looked at a shaken Gwen. "But I had no idea he was stealing our children. For crying out loud, I would have killed him with my bare hands!" Vincent rubbed the palm of his hand over his mouth. "Did he go after Owen at the shower?"

"Yes Dad, I should have been open about it then, but I put the wedding first."

"What did he do to you?" Gwen inquired with a skeptical tone.

I couldn't find the words thirty years ago. How do I find them now?

She closed her eyes, relaxed her shoulders, and slowly formed one thought at a time. "I remember that he took pictures of me to sell and we really didn't go for nature walks. Instead, he took me to the potato shed and camps Anthony and I made in the woods. When we went for rides in his car, it wasn't to ice cream shops."

"Oh my God." Gwen buried her face in tears.

I should have never told. I should have run away and disappeared. Mick and Owen would always miss me, but his family and mine would eventually replace me, thought Lilly. *If they thought I was dead, they would heal faster.*

Cautiously Lilly continued, "He changed my life. I couldn't even get through my pregnancy without being haunted by his threats. It's why I was defiant as a teen and why I didn't care if I lived or died after you sent me to college."

"This isn't happening. Vincent, what she's saying can't be true. Millie wouldn't let this happen to her niece and her godchild. This is all a made-up story between Lilly and Dawn," Gwen insisted.

"Mom, did you ever see one of his pictures of the so-called outdoors that he loved and photographed?" Lilly asked angrily.

"You're right," Vincent said. "We only saw one or two. And he brought those disgusting pornography magazines for me to share with the guys at work. I didn't think he was actually involved, moving beyond the pages. And the gifts…they were to earn my trust…and they did." His face reddened and the veins pulsed on his forehead. "Frank had a roaming eye with women, and once I caught him watching you too closely, Gwen. We nearly got in a fistfight."

"I just don't understand why you didn't tell us if it was that bad." Gwen's tears fell.

"I did, Mom, remember when I hid under the bed and I told you I didn't like Frank? You chimed in with Millie, agreeing that I was crazy and silly. I tried other times too, but you were too busy or didn't believe me. So I stopped trying by the time I was ten and you were sending me off to the city for a week every summer."

"Why didn't you tell *me*?" Vincent asked.

"Because I was embarrassed and ashamed. I believed it was my fault. I thought you would see me as a disgrace to the family and send me away. That's what Frank said would happen. I would go to his house or an insane asylum. He said it so often I believed him and then he threatened to kill both of you. I kept it to myself because that was the only way for me to survive without more loss."

"Maybe Frank could do something like that," Gwen added with teeth gritted, "but not Millie."

"Mom, I believe Millie grew up like you. She was happy and a loving person but city life and Frank changed her. She has secrets too."

"How do you know that?" Gwen accusingly inquired.

"Because she would cry to me about how sick she was because of Frank, and she bought me Frank's choice of undergarments when I was seventeen. She wanted me to wear them for him. She knew, Mom, she always knew, and she helped by creating chaos or falsehoods to get me away from you and Dad. She was a clever manipulative schemer."

"I am so sorry," Vincent said, still unable to look at Lilly.

"I was going to tell, even if Dawn didn't call. At the shower, Frank went after Owen because he wanted me back in his sick cult world. But I know he would take Owen too. He'd take both of us." Lilly held strong. "He can't be near our family ever again and neither can Millie. We have to protect our children and grandchildren. You understand that, don't you?"

"What about Joan and Eva?" asked Gwen.

"You'll need to ask them yourself, Mom. I can't speak for them." She paused. "There's something else I want to say." Lilly studied the faces of those she loved. She knew this was going to upset them further, especially Mick. "I'll be calling Dr. Bricks. I need more help. I don't feel safe with myself, or around others. I need alone time."

"Lilly, we can help each other without you going away," insisted Gwen.

"Honey, what about Owen and me? We need you," a worried Mick replied.

Vincent sat voiceless, in a world of his own revenge.

1986 – SESSION FOURTEEN – SAFE BEHIND LOCKED DOORS

"You know, I never dreamed that I would end up in a treatment center. I thought I was stronger and I had learned everything that was important with the sessions we had together." Lilly contemplated for a minute. "However, being here and going through the program has opened my eyes even more to the importance of staying in reality and thinking rationally, which was a lost trait for me as an abused child. I've come a long way, but there's still a bumpy road ahead." Lilly spoke with new awareness.

"Your understanding requires patience," replied Dr. Bricks.

"And that's not easy. It's time-consuming and costly, but here I am, going back home! Owen cannot wait! He misses his mother."

"And you miss your family, that's easy to see."

Lilly brushed her bangs out of her eyes. She was comfortable, relaxed, and secure in her decision to return home, but she still had a few questions. "What about Frank's past? Do you think someone taught him how to groom victims and become who he is?"

"What are your feelings about that?"

"I think he was a born psychopath."

"Anything is possible. Psychopaths have no guilt and justify their behavior as the fault of the victim. They have also been known to completely deny their behavior."

Lilly listened, thinking about Frank. "When I confronted him about the abuse, he called himself a teacher and pointed at me, saying I was a liar. He was calm and showed no remorse or guilt. He said he loved us 'girls' and was helping us to be good wives when we married—that he absolutely did nothing wrong."

"That had to be difficult to listen to."

"I wanted to shake him to death. It's a good thing I had Mick with me." Her face flushed. "He passed his guilt and shame onto his victims; just as you have always said."

Lilly's memories didn't scare her as often anymore, however, her need to understand them was much greater. "Tell me more about psychopaths."

"I am not saying Frank *was* a psychopath. I would have to evaluate him in order to do that. But from our time together and your journal, I see connections."

"Tell me what the connections are." She hungered for more information. "That isn't a part of my practice—to diagnose someone without seeing them."

"You're not diagnosing him. You are teaching me what a psychopath is. There's a difference."

Dr. Bricks proceeded cautiously. "It's a complex diagnosis and goes far beyond words or expressions.

She perched on the edge of her seat as if she were watching a thriller and the mystery was about to unravel.

"If your uncle was a psychopath, or sociopath, or a bit of both, he chose to be violent and aggressive with his victims, but he was also a pedophile. That put you in great harm. You knew he was dangerous and you protected yourself as much as you were able to. You endured his behavior. That makes you the victor."

"I hear those words often in our group activities and meetings, but something inside of me says, 'Slow down, Lilly, and be careful.' It's as if sometimes I don't want to accept getting better."

"The feeling or need to pull back from forward progress is normal. Your body is telling you to take time to process and reassess. It is a form of self-protection."

Lilly leaned forward, contemplating. "Frank had complete composure through it all. He raped me, then walked into our house and sat down at our kitchen table with Mom and Dad, laughing and talking as if nothing happened. He was not of this world. He was a mis-creation."

"That he was."

"I'm nothing like Frank, because I can *feel* and I have empathy and I know right from wrong. I can own up to my mistakes. I want to live a life of being his *antonym*."

"You already are. Where are you with your Mom and Dad?"

"Mom doesn't believe in psychology. She has her faith. The first parent night she didn't come. I was so hurt; I couldn't hide it from Dad. I don't know what he said to her, but the next week she came. That was a big step for both of them and it made me proud."

"They love you a great deal."

"I know they do, and I worry how this is affecting their health. Look at what it has done to mine!"

"Your parents can carry this."

"Maybe...Dad has worked so hard to gain my love back, and he has. All of his little gestures in college and afterward drew us closer. Mom and I are still a work in progress, but it's moving in the right direction. And I desperately want to return to my classroom. I miss the children. They are so grounding for me."

"You're ready, Lilly, to go out there and enjoy life."

"You know a nurse told me they locked the doors to keep the world out, not to keep us in. That made sense to me. This is a great staff and I'll miss them."

"You worked hard and we have a great deal of respect for you."

"Thank you." Lilly blushed. "I have your number in this folder, just in case."

"Don't feel shy about using it. How would you like to take a walk around the gardens?"

"Would I ever say no to that?"

The breeze was cool and every now and then, she sniffed out the scents of sage and lavender.

"Nature is not flawless," she mused. "Look at the weeds, the dead flower tips and the algae on the rocks. It is far from picture perfect and yet it's beautiful. I see myself in this garden. Sometimes weeds overtake the flower, as the past has overtaken me. We both need to have the weeds pulled out to make room for new healthier roots. My roots are established and growing again. I accept who I am. Living in that one compartment labeled 'Me' is a good thing. There is only one feeling that I don't have a handle on."

"And what may that be?"

"The fact that there is nothing I can do about Frank. He needs to pay."

"Lilly." Dr. Bricks stopped and directly addressed her. "There's nothing that can be done. The statute of limitations makes him a free man."

"Well that is just plain wrong. What about him going after Owen?"

"We can't prove his intentions, only what he actually did. He gave Owen a silver dollar to play chase. That would never stand up in court. There are no legal repercussions."

"I suffer, take a leave of absence from work, go to therapy, spend vacation money to pay for it, and he walks around smoking his cigar and doing what—abusing other children? We have to keep looking."

"Keeping *him* away from your children and grandchildren is an important and huge step."

"That's not enough."

"What would be 'enough'?"

"I'm not sure. Jail, but since that's not possible, I don't know!"

"Remember what has been said about healing: some things cannot be changed. We learn to accept them and move on."

"I get that. I know I can't change the law. Remember that you also said, 'anger can be used to make positive changes.' I'm going to get him, without doing anyone any harm except him and Millie. I don't know how, but the answer and the day will come."

She broke off a twig from the lavender bush. "You know I kept my promise to my war hero."

"He would be proud of your accomplishments, but he wouldn't want you to endanger yourself again by going anywhere near Frank."

Lilly flashed him a look of "I'm not stupid," and continued. "I wish I could have seen him again in different circumstances," she said smelling the leaves' sweet aroma.

"People come in and out of our lives for reasons we don't often understand until later. We can't always thank them personally, but we can live to be the better person they wanted us to become."

Lilly agreed, brushing the lavender leaves off into the wind.

A FORTRESS OF FORGIVENESS

Together, Lilly and Gwen began to clean up the dinner dishes. "How are you feeling, dear?"

"Mom, I'm doing great. Most days are happy ones. But there's still work to get to where I want to be."

"Your father and I are moving forward too. We've spoken with our priest a few times and each meeting helps."

"Good, keep doing it." Lilly had stopped the church routine but understood its importance to her parents. "So how was *your* day?"

"It started out just fine; I stripped the bed and started washing the blankets, pillows, and sheets, and then the phone rang."

"Who called?"

"It was Millie," Gwen replied softly.

Lilly stopped drying the dish in her hands. "You've got to be kidding."

"No, I'm not, and she was in rare form, too."

"What do you mean?" Lilly asked with great interest.

"First she began blaming you and Dawn for causing trouble in the family. She said you both made up the story about abuse. And then she started boasting about them becoming godparents again."

"Oh my God!" Lilly's mind raced. *Dawn and I cut off his supply of victims in our family, so now he's moving on to another family! They can't be godparents again. This is what I've been waiting for. This is the moment. This could be the one way to stop him.*

"Tell me everything you remember." Lilly sat down giving her mother complete attention.

"She said that she and Frank were sponsoring a young couple's baby at the church, and that the four of them have become friends."

Lilly envisioned the scenario; childless Millie whining about her lost years of no children or grandchildren and seeking out sympathy for her lonely aging life while she grieved about the family who abandoned her. And Frank standing near, eager to feed his appetite with an offering of their infant. It was appalling.

"That's unbelievable. I can only imagine how loud Millie was tooting her horn. I think she's trying to get back at you for exiling them. She wants *you* to feel bad. Don't fall for it," Lilly warned.

"I'm trying not to, but she was convincing. She bragged how they were finding a new family, a better family, one that adored both her and Frank. She did make me feel guilty."

"You know that's a lie. Right, Mom? Millie is manipulating the story for her own mental health." Lilly tried to keep her steam from blowing. She needed to stay calm and get more information.

"Did you happen to get the name of the people?"

"No, she didn't tell me *that,* but it's at their church this Sunday."

"I can't remember the church. What was its name?"

"It's Saint Theresa. You are not going there, are you? That wouldn't be wise," Gwen warned.

"Of course not, Mom, I don't have the time nor do I want to see the likes of them. Saint Theresa's, that's the church on Eighteenth Street, close to downtown, right?" Lilly did remember after all.

"Yes, that's the one. I can't stop thinking about that poor family. They have no idea what they're getting into. How could Millie use the church for their stepping-stone?" Gwen paused with a new awareness. "Lilly, that's what they did with us! They insisted on being your godparents. If I had listened to your father, it would have been Uncle David instead of Frank. It's going to start all over again! Is there anything we can do?"

Lilly wanted to stay and comfort her mother, but she burned to get home. She had a mission: to stop a baptism. "Mom, can you and Gramps watch Owen for a couple more hours? I need to stop at the store, and then I'd love to take a bath." What she really needed was time to put together a plan.

"Oh, of course! We'll help him with any schoolwork he has and read together."

"You two spoil us rotten! Love you." Lilly gave her mother a peck on the cheek and hurriedly left.

With sweaty palms, she headed for home, loaded with nervous energy and constantly thinking. *Can I actually report him? The law protects him more than me, however, there isn't a law against calling a priest. If there is, let Frank come forward with a slander charge. He would walk himself into a jail cell. I have nothing to lose. It's a win-win.*

His access to children must stop, and I can possibly make that come true, or at least make it more difficult for him. He isn't a patient man, and he likes to keep his pursuit orderly and timely. A disruption to his routine would anger him, and anger can open a door to error. The last few words made her smile. He had taught her well, and she was going to use his teachings against him.

She ran into the kitchen and dialed information for the telephone number of the church. She wrote it down on a yellow sticky note, walked to the rocking chair in the living room, and placed the note on the end table, next to the phone.

The house was quiet except for the ticking of their grandfather clock. She sat back, closed her eyes, and began to calm her muscles, then her mind.

Her heart settled in with the beats and rhythm of the pendulum. "I have to call. It is my duty," she told herself. "That little baby is not going to have a life like mine. I am not Millie. I will protect the child. I am stronger than fear. I have to be."

She glared at the phone and sticky note. "Frank hasn't suffered one single day." At that thought she could hear his humiliating laughter. It was a small remembrance of her past, but enough to start doubt.

The priest could be part of Frank's world. That would make matters worse. Instead of seeking out justice, I could be putting my family and myself in more danger. Church... What was it about the church? What did Mom say... How could Millie use the church to get into the family?

Lilly stayed with the past, recalling connections to her attacks. "Did Frank become a Catholic just to be my godfather? He needed that false sense of power and control, and it was an easy entry into the family. Did he use the church for his benefit? He twisted its teachings and used the confession to wash away his guilt. Oh my gosh, that's it!

"How could I be so blind? The Church is more than a religion to them. It is their fortress of forgiveness. It's their sanctuary where they can commit sins and be forgiven. Victims couldn't forgive, but a deity could. It's been in front of me for decades! Forgiveness from a victim would serve him and Millie no purpose but entertainment. That's it, the church.

"If a priest found out the truth behind them, they would be devastated and humiliated. Imagine the rumors that would get started! Millie will be shamed for the rest of her life, and Frank will have the lingering fear of the serpent's repercussions. Besides their money, the church is the second most important thing to them."

With no further hesitation, she dialed the numbers.

"Good afternoon. This is St. Theresa's Church," a woman pleasantly answered. "Can I help you?"

"Hello, this is Lilly Marzone. I'm inquiring about the baptism of a baby at your parish this coming Sunday. The godparents are Frank and Millie Monroe. Could I please speak with the priest who is going to perform the service?"

"That is Father Richard, and he's busy with a parish member at this time. Can I have him call you back?"

No, thought Lilly, *waiting won't work. My courage is strong now. That could change in an hour.* She stood in disarray with the phone in her hand, unable to speak into the receiver. *It has to be now.* She steadied her breathing.

"This is an emergency and I need to speak with any priest who is available."

"Stay on the phone. I'll be right back."

Lilly couldn't recall any other time that seemed so long and quiet. She paced, listening to her rapid breathing and the grandfather clock. "Hello, this is Father Thomas. How can I be of service to you?"

"My name is Lilly Marzone. I live in Ledo."

"I am familiar with the city. It is a strong, family-oriented community."

"Thank you, I agree. The reason I'm calling is a baptism that's taking place in your parish this Sunday."

"Are you family?" he inquired

"No, not to the couple, but I am a niece to the godparents, Millie and Frank Monroe. In fact, I too am their godchild." There was no room for chit-chat as Lilly's nerves were bundling inside of her.

"Oh yes. I have met both. How can I be of assistance?"

Lilly began to stammer, stumbling for words. "I'm calling because I was told that Frank and Millie were going to be godparents this weekend for a young couple's child in your parish."

"That's correct. It's part of a program we offer to bring people who have no family into our parish."

"Millie and Frank have a big family of brothers and sisters, nieces and nephews. But recently, they've been forbidden to attend any events where children are present."

"Why is that?"

"Frank and Millie used the title of godparents to get close to my family and especially me. They did not obey or respect the laws of the church. Millie lied to her sister, who is my mother, so Frank could be alone with me. He's a pedophile. He raped me, he assaulted me, he took pornographic pictures, and he used the teachings of the church against me to keep me silent and filled with guilt. My first memory of abuse is around age four, and recently he went after *my* three-year-old son. I'm now in my thirties. They are not the nice people you think they are, and this young couple is falling into their trap."

"Have you told anyone else about the abuse?"

"I have told my family, and there is a cousin who's in therapy too. The police in my hometown know, but the statute of limitations expired. I'm sure that my cousin, as well as my father and husband, would talk to you. I can give you their phone numbers. I also have a doctor who has been working with me for several years."

"No, that won't be necessary. Father Richard and I will look into the matter. We will meet with the parents and with Millie and Frank."

"Father, if I may, I would like to suggest that you speak with Frank separately, as well as Millie, and not have the parents present. Frank is very good with threats, and Millie is a well-seasoned manipulator."

"Thank you, Lilly. I will take your advice into consideration."

"Please, Father, I'm begging you not to allow this baby and its family to go through the hell my family and I have. I don't know if my life will ever be what God intended it to be, but I'm trying. I've always been trying. He'll ruin that family with no remorse. Do this for the baby."

"I am sorry for the ordeals you have endured. It took courage to call me. May God's blessings be with you and I promise that I will look into the matter. You have done a great deed, and it was right to inform us."

"Thank you, Father. I am going to pray that you'll do the right thing."

Lilly slowly hung up the phone. The abuse began in the church, and now the church was going to end it. She had opened up beyond her family and out into the world. *There was "no more secret."*

It was over. She looked up at the vast blue sky and breathed in its free will. She felt a sense of justice.

❋

Two weeks later Lilly and Gwen sat at the table. "I only wish I knew that the phone call worked."

"Here." Gwen slid over a folded piece of white paper. "What's this?"

"Open it and see for yourself."

Lilly opened the letter and instantly recognized Millie's handwriting.

She began reading aloud:

> My Dearest Lilly,
>
> It has been a while since we have spoken and I want you to know that I am disappointed in your behavior. Calling your uncle horrible names that will hurt him in the community was an uncalled-for decision. You should have talked with me first. Why would you tell a priest right before a baptism? Father Richard and Father Thomas called us into their office and confronted both of us regarding our actions with you as our godchild.
>
> We told them you always had a big imagination, but then he said another niece came forward and you had a doctor to verify your claims. I don't know what we did to make you hate us so much, that you

would destroy our lives in the community. Uncle Frank was nothing more but a loving teacher to you and all of his nieces and nephews. He helped you prepare for the real world. He never harmed any of you, and now the church has banished him from all functions that include children. Mary and Harold, the young couple we had become close to, filed a restraining order against us. This is your fault, Lilly. You were always thinking immoral thoughts and accusing Frank for them. Your behavior hurts me.

Now we must move, just as we did twenty years ago. You are like that little girl who lied to hurt others. Your Uncle Frank has always been innocent. Our new home will be in a wealthy suburb with more privacy. Too bad you and Owen won't be able to swim in its pool and play on the playgrounds. We would love to share what we have, but you've made that impossible. I feel for my little sister; she too must hurt deeply from your actions.

Sincerely,

Your Loving Godmother, Aunt Millie

Lilly folded the letter and slid it back to Gwen. "You can burn it. That's what I would do."

"But you wanted to know if your call made a difference. It did! You saved that family, and who knows how many others?"

"What does it matter, they found a new community with even more families for Frank to 'teach.' It infuriates the heck out of me."

"Lilly, this took courage. And a restraining order may mean he's in the system." Gwen put her hands comfortingly on her daughter's shoulders.

"Thank you, Mom. I did what I could, and it may slow Frank down, but I wish it were more."

"Think of your cousins, your nieces and nephews, and Owen."

Lilly dabbed the corners of her eyes. "They are free to think clearly and pursue dreams without fear. I love them all, Mom, I really do. It's the happiness in their lives that gives my life purpose."

"Honey, your purpose was to survive and help others. I'm proud of you."

The sound of silence was deafening. Lilly looked up at her mother. "Was my purpose here to survive? "

"I have no doubt," Gwen replied. "Why would *you?*"

Lilly looked away, into a distant time that only she knew of.

EPILOGUE

2016

"Lilly, that's a story to be shared," said her friend Mary Sue as they sat on the beach, soaking up the summer sun. "I would have never guessed that you had been through so much and it's hard for me to relate to. I've never had anything that traumatic, and to live with it for sixty years. I don't understand how you managed!"

Lilly wrapped herself up in a beach blanket, concentrating on an answer. "Look at the ocean," she suggested, pointing to water. "Do you ever see it stop moving?"

Mary watched. "No. It's always in motion."

"Exactly; that's how I've always seen life, even as a child. One day led to another. Each nightmare ended and a morning came. Every assault stopped, and my godparents would leave. I fought to reach the end, so I could begin anew."

"You knew how to do that as a child? It seems...far-fetched."

"Maybe I hold some kind of superpower," joked Lilly. "I really don't know. Except that in the quiet times with nature, I talked out loud to myself and answers appeared. It was the quieting of the mind, in my opinion."

"Do you still have flashbacks and triggers?"

"Yes, especially with sounds, smells and churches. Then there is heavy traffic, driving, and deep waters. Many memories and triggers will never go away. I accept that."

"How?"

"I don't feed them any more attention than I need to. I see them, acknowledge them, and let them go. I must move on. There's so much more to replace the past with. Just look around in the present!"

"Did your parents ever completely believe you?"

"Yes, Dad believed me that very day. We became friends, like old times. We shared many hours in the kitchen together, outdoor gardening, and Sunday football games. It took longer with Mom, but eventually she stood strong behind us children."

"Do you ever wish you hadn't told them?"

"No! Absolutely not! The truth is the hardest to say and to hear, but it is the only way to heal. I've learned it is easier, healthier, and smarter to reach out than to go silent. There's nothing embarrassing about seeking help. I feel it's healthy and necessary. Call me a wise old warrior, with lessons learned from a long-fought war. I have scars deep within. And each one represents 'silence'."

"I can't imagine how afraid you must have been. How do you forgive your parents?"

"It was easy with Dad. I was the apple of his eye when I was little. That love returned, and he worked hard to regain it. He even went to therapy with me, and we grieved together. But I'm not sure he forgave himself."

"You said he wanted to die before Frank. Did he?"

"He did. He passed twelve years after the day of truth, from cancer. That crushed me and it still hurts, I miss him so much. He changed his life, his temper, and how he became a man of only love and patience made him a hero in my eyes, and he did it mostly through prayer and self-determination. That's tough! I cannot imagine what Dad had in store for Frank's judgment day! But I know it was healing for him—not so for Frank!"

"I'm curious, how did Frank die?" Mary Sue drew the towel tighter around her body.

"Karma! Slowly and painfully, losing the mobility of his legs and then the disease progressed to his hands, leaving him completely helpless and dependent on others. That had to feel like an invasion of *HIS* body. Eventually it moved to the bones and organs, choking him of his own breath."

"Good! It sounds like a death he deserved."

"Yes, but it still bothers me that Frank never spent a day in jail. Not only for my assault, but for the assaults of the others that came to light. He never owned up to anything and stayed with his story that he wanted to teach us girls how to be good wives. He never did us any harm. Can you believe that? He took our childhoods away and changed our emotional and physical lives."

"There were others?"

"I think hundreds because of his use of the transit system in the city. We also had a big family with many little girls and boys."

"That just makes me shiver! What about Millie?"

"She passed away many years after Frank. She, too, never admitted to her role. She never told the truth to Mom. She continued to blame me for making the story up."

"She was a snake in the grass."

"Oh yes she was! But you want to hear something interesting?"

"Yes!" Mary Sue leaned in closer.

"When Millie died, she was buried far from Frank's grave, at *her* request. I told Mom that if Frank were as innocent as he claimed to be, she would have been right next to him in death, as she was in life. I see it as an admission that she always knew what a creep he was. That was Millie. Life was all about her and she never offered any help to the victims."

"You don't talk much about your mother."

"Oh, my dear Mom! Where do I begin?" Lilly asked, brushing her windblown hair from her face and looking up into the sky.

"Lilly, if this is hard, you don't have to say any more."

"No, talking helps I only wish I had this voice back then! Surprisingly, Mom and I became best friends. I never thought that would be possible."

"But it's wonderful! Tell me about that."

"Using the patience Dad taught me and being forgiving enough to make the first steps. After Dad passed away, I took Mom back to her homeland of Poland, where my grandmother was born. It was supposed to be their trip. I promised Dad I would make sure she went. Honestly, if you need bonding time with a parent, go to a foreign country with a language neither of you speak very well. We laughed from sunrise to sunset. We got tipsy drinking moonshine in the mountains. She was hysterically funny, and that night I saw myself in her. Mom was feisty, a little flirtatious, and not afraid of much. She enjoyed a dare. I always wondered where that came from because I do too! Mom and I connected during those days as if nothing had separated us since conception. She told me, 'I have more than a daughter, I have a best friend.' That meant the world to me."

"I wish I could have met your parents. When did she pass?"

"It'll be ten years this summer." Lilly looked out over the ocean. "Cancer took her too, but she fought it for four years and I never left her side. She passed on a Sunday morning, her favorite day of the week. Her children were with her. Mom was stronger than anyone I've known—an incredibly brave, intelligent woman! She worked until she was seventy-two!"

"I'm sorry, I made you cry."

"No, it's good for me. For years and years, I didn't allow myself to show this emotion. There's more behind the tears than her passing; they're more for the pain I feel realizing how much time we lost and how different our lives could have been. It's reality and it can't be changed. I tell myself to be grateful for the years we *did* have, but it's bittersweet."

"Even if your time together was shorter, it sounds like it was deeper, and more personal."

"It was very deep. No one could possibly understand the complexity of our relationship and journey. Now with both my parents gone, I have begun to feel unprotected and abandoned again. That's something I'm working on. Loss and change. There's been so much in my life. I guess there will always be something to improve on when one has a mental health issue."

"You are mentally healthier than many people I know."

"Thanks, but I still struggle with anxiety and panic attacks. I have a gigantic box full of tools I use to manage them. It's not easy living with anxiety, depression, and whatever else the medical world labels me as having, but my good days greatly outnumber the bad ones. Every year, I feel I'm getting closer to the 'normal' I chased in my younger days. I love being alive. I accept much of which I cannot change, but after trauma, life is always a journey."

"Are you sure you're comfortable on this island, so far away from Mick and your home?"

Lilly smiled slyly and answered, "Mary Sue, you know me for who I am today, not who I was sixty years ago. As I see myself in the moment, I want you to see me there, too."

"But you said, 'The past is a part of our present. We can't have one without the other.'"

"True. And speaking of that, do you want to hear what happened right before we left?" Lilly asked, with a mysterious tone. "Of course!"

"I went upstairs to get a suitcase from the small bedroom. When I walked into the room the air had a familiar smell, but I couldn't place it. I took another whiff. It was an odd scent, but not dangerous, like something burning, so I brushed it off and left. A few minutes later I found myself back, sniffing the air out of curiosity. I wanted to know what the scent was and why it was familiar. I stood in the center of the room and then walked toward the window. That was it! The smell of the warm summer attic, where we slept as a family in Millie's first house—the attic of several childhood assaults. When Frank knew I was going upstairs to get something from my suitcase, he always managed to get up there first…I was five or six. That smell became a trigger."

"Was Mick home? Did you need him?"

"Yes, Mick was home, but I didn't need him. I didn't go into a panic attack. I simply acknowledged it and then replaced it with a more pleasant memory of the room, such as the mementos of old and new friends and family pictures. I placed my feet firmly on the floor, envisioning growing roots through the baseboard. The trigger faded. I walked to the window and opened it. A cool westerly breeze cleared the air in seconds. I smiled and reminded myself, *this is the moment. I am safe. The dark world is behind me.* Then, my eyes opened. The breeze felt colder. And I quickly scanned the room." Lilly took a deep breath, held it in for a few seconds and released. "You know, Mary Sue, there's still that quiet fear in me. It's not controlling me all the time, but it's there. Just waiting, I guess."

"Waiting for what?"

Lilly shrugged her shoulders. "I had a life sentence emotionally and physically from the abuse and he got away with everything. He lived a full and fancy life, but I will tell you this." Lilly looked directly into Mary Sue's eyes. "That horrible debilitating fear and shame is not going to get that far ahead of me ever again."

They sat quietly, wrapped in blankets, allowing the ocean wind and the warming sun to do what it was meant to do.

It has been said, 'time heals all wounds.' I do not agree. The wounds remain. In time, the mind, protecting its sanity, covers them with scar tissue and the pain lessens but it never goes away.

—Rose Kennedy

REFERENCES

Crime Reports

Rape is the most underreported crime; 63 percent of sexual assaults are not reported to police.[1]

Campus Sexual Assault

One in five women and one in sixteen men are sexually assaulted while in college[2] and more than 90 percent of them do not report the assault.[3]

Child Sexual Abuse

One in four girls and one in six boys will be sexually abused before they turn eighteen years old.[4]

325,000 children are at risk of becoming victims of commercial child sexual exploitation each year and the average age at which girls first become victims of prostitution is twelve to fourteen years old. For boys, it is eleven to thirteen years old

---

1. Rennison, C. A. (2002). Rape and sexual assault: Reporting to police and medical attention, 1992-2000 [NCJ 194530]. Retrieved from the U.S. Department of Justice, Office of Justice Programs, Bureau of Justice Statistics: http://bjs.ojp. usdoj.gov/content/pub/pdf/rsarp00.pdf.
2. Krebs, C. P., Lindquist, C., Warner, T., Fisher, B., & Martin, S. (2007). The campus sexual assault (CSA) study: Final report. Retrieved from the National Criminal Justice Reference Service: http://www.nc- jrs.gov/pdffiles1/nij/grants/221153.pdfhttp://www.ncjrs.gov/pdffiles1/nij/grants/221153.pdf.
3. Fisher, B., Cullen, F., & Turner, M. (2000). The sexual victimization of college women (NCJ 182369). Retrieved from the National Criminal Justice Reference Service: https://www.ncjrs.gov/pdffiles1/ nij/182369.pdf (d) Delisi, M., Kosloski, A., Sween, M., Hachmeister, E., Moore, M., & Drury, A. (2010). Murder by numbers: Monetary costs imposed by a sample of homicide.
4. Finkelhor, D., Hotaling, G., Lewis, I. A., & Smith, C. (1990). Sexual abuse in a national survey of adult men and women: Prevalence, characteristics and risk factors. Child Abuse & Neglect 14, 19-28. doi:10.1016/0145-2134(90)90077-7.

CPSIA information can be obtained
at www.ICGtesting.com
Printed in the USA
LVHW041335200423
744756LV00001B/25